T0304466

MONEY FOR COUPLES

No more stress. No more fights.
Just a 10-step plan to create your
Rich Life together.

Ramit Sethi

WORKMAN PUBLISHING | NEW YORK

Workman
Workman Publishing
Hachette Book Group, Inc.
1290 Avenue of the Americas
New York, NY 10104
workman.com

Workman is an imprint of Workman Publishing, a division of Hachette Book Group, Inc. The Workman name and logo are registered trademarks of Hachette Book Group, Inc.

Design by Maggie Byrd
Cover design by Suet Chong
Cover photo by Menelik Puryear

The publisher is not responsible for websites (or their content) that are not owned by the publisher.

Workman books may be purchased in bulk for business, educational, or promotional use. For information, please contact your local bookseller or the Hachette Book Group Special Markets Department at special.markets@hbgusa.com.

Library of Congress Cataloging-in-Publication Data

Names: Sethi, Ramit, author.
Title: Money for couples : no more stress, no more fights, just a 10-step plan to create your rich life together / Ramit Sethi.
Description: New York : Workman Publishing, [2024] | Includes index.
Identifiers: LCCN 2024034764 (print) | LCCN 2024034765 (ebook) | ISBN 9781523523689 (paperback) | ISBN 9781523523702 (epub)
Subjects: LCSH: Couples--Finance, Personal.
Classification: LCC HG179 .S47 2024 (print) | LCC HG179 (ebook) | DDC 332.024—dc23/eng/20240830
LC record available at https://lccn.loc.gov/2024034764
LC ebook record available at https://lccn.loc.gov/2024034765

First Edition December 2024

Printed in the United States of America (VER) on responsibly sourced paper.

10 9 8 7 6 5 4 3 2

Author's note: To protect privacy, some names have been changed.

*To every couple
who wants to live
a Rich Life together*

Also by Ramit Sethi

I Will Teach You to Be Rich
I Will Teach You to Be Rich: The Journal

Contents

Part 2:

INSTANT MONEY ANSWERS IF YOU'RE . . .

WHAT IF TALKING ABOUT MONEY FELT GOOD?

L et's pretend that I just knocked on your front door. It's me, anthropologist Ramit Sethi, here with my clipboard to observe you and your partner talking about money for the next month. What will I see in your behavior? What will I notice in your body language? And what will I hear you say?

Tell me if any of these phrases sound familiar:

- *"I can't believe you spent that much!"*

- *"I just want a plan! That's all I'm asking for."*

- *"It feels like we'll never have enough."*

Or perhaps I wouldn't notice anything, because maybe you don't talk about money at all.

In millions of homes around the world, we're having the same fights about money. One partner feels anxious, the other buries their head in the sand to avoid talking about it. One agonizes over the budget, the other spends on whatever they want. We avoid discussing finances, we tiptoe around difficult conversations, and in the process, we allow money to drive a wedge between us.

I've seen this with people all across the country as I've gone inside their homes to talk about money on my Netflix show, *How to Get Rich*. I've also experienced this in my own relationship: My wife, Cassandra, and I have had really tough conversations about money. We've avoided the topic, we've disagreed, we've even seen a therapist to help us get on the same page about a prenuptial agreement.

At every step of the way, I wondered: *How is everyone else handling money in their relationship?*

That's what you'll learn in this book: a way to truly connect over money, even if you and your partner see it totally differently. Money doesn't have to be a source of stress, guilt, and shame. It can instead be a source of joy, connection, and possibility. I believe this because I've seen it in my own marriage now, after a lot of work—and in the lives of millions of people who've used my material.

To make that transformation, we're going to start by changing the way you *talk* about money, which will change the way you *behave* with money, which will ultimately change the way you *feel* about money.

There are lots of misconceptions about money in relationships. We've all heard the pop-culture idea that "money is the number-one reason for divorce," but a 2009 study by Lauren M. Papp, E. Mark Cummings, and Marcie C. Goeke-Morey showed that couples don't even broach the subject of money very much. According to actual time diaries kept in relationships, the top sources of fights are kids, chores, and communication. That's because we don't talk about money until it blows up. And when money causes problems, it's bad:

> "Spouses rated [money-related] conflicts as much more intense and significant than other conflict topics. . . . Husbands and wives reported that they and their partners expressed more depressive behavior expressions (i.e., physical distress, withdrawal, sadness, and fear) during conflicts about money relative to other topics. Husbands expressed more angry behaviors (i.e., verbal and nonverbal hostility, defensiveness, pursuit, personal insult, physical aggression, threat,

and anger) during conflicts about money compared to other issues . . . and wives reported greater depressive behavior."

In other words, we start by bottling up our money disagreements. Those disagreements fester into fights and, worse, a long-term lack of connection. I'll show you how to flip that dynamic on its head and use money to build connection toward a life you *both* want.

Once you and your partner know how to talk about money, everything changes: You'll create a vision together so you can row in the same direction. You'll have a simple financial system that you both deeply understand. And you'll both know why you're saving,

I Want to Hear Your Story

Before we go further, I want you to know that I talk about money in a different way from what you're used to. I won't be lecturing you about $5 coffees or telling you to cut everything down to the bone so you can use your money "someday" when you're 92 years old. I'll be showing you how to live a Rich Life today and an even richer life tomorrow—together.

Another thing I do differently: I'm going to give you my email address because I want to hear from you—and I read every message. Yes, really! I'm active on social media, but you can email me at relationship-checkin@iwillteachyoutoberich.com, subject: "New book reader." Tell me . . .

1. What's an example in the last 30–60 days where you and your partner weren't on the same page with money? What happened?

2. If you and your partner could get on the same page with money, what would that look and feel like?

While I wish I could reply to every message I get, I can't anymore—but I try as much as possible.

investing, and even spending. Those persistent arguments will disappear, and you can focus on using money to live your Rich Life together.

What is a Rich Life? It's not necessarily about buying fancy cars and houses (although if you want to, great! I'll show you how). It's an expression of your ideal life in which your money, relationships, and leisure time work beautifully. Everyone's version of a "Rich Life" is different and unique.

A Rich Life can be traveling for two months every year.

A Rich Life can be buying a beautiful cashmere coat.

A Rich Life can be shopping at the grocery store without worrying about prices.

And a Rich Life can be having the time to pick up your children from school every afternoon.

Your Rich Life is uniquely yours. That's what my system is all about—helping you and your partner design your vision together and use your money to make it a reality.

This book gives you a 10-step program for building a shared vision around money, even if you and your partner see money completely differently. You'll learn specific techniques to get your partner involved, including exactly what to say. You'll even learn where things might go off-plan—and how to handle it. And when I come back to your front door with my anthropologist's clipboard a couple of months from now, I'm going to see something amazing: two people working together as a team.

Why Do We Talk about Money Only When Something Goes Wrong?

Most of us discuss money only when something goes awry. That's how we begin to associate "talking about money" with fighting. Think about it: When was the last time you had a conversation about money and enjoyed it?

When I gently ask couples if they have a standing meeting to talk over their finances every month, they stare at me like I'm speaking Klingon: "What? Why would we set up an *agenda* just to talk to each other? That's . . . weird."

Weird?

Is it a little weird to have an agenda to talk about money with your partner? Yeah, okay, maybe at first. Do I care? No!

I swear, most Americans would rather stick hot needles in their eyes than feel "awkward" for a single millisecond. Here's what's really going on: We associate talking about money with feeling bad—so why would we ever want to talk about it *more*?

You know what I think is worse than weird? Going 40 years fighting about money, dancing around money, or avoiding talking about money altogether, and never implementing a system to make decisions about money!

Talking about money shouldn't have to be weird. It's a skill you can learn, and when you get good at it, you'll actually start to *like* doing so. I'm asking you to trust that you'll build the skills to become very good at it.

Real Couples, Real Numbers

When my wife and I really started talking about money, right around when we got engaged, I looked online for guidance. The most common advice was "Sit down and have the conversation."

What conversation?

Literally, I wanted someone to give me the words. Tell me exactly what to say. Tell me what to avoid. Tell me how to start the conversation, how she's likely to react, and what to do if we start fighting.

Give me the system!!

But there wasn't one. So I created it.

I started with the *Money for Couples* podcast, where I work with real couples on their biggest money disagreements. Some have six figures of debt. Others have millions of dollars and still worry

8 Things I've Learned on My Podcast

1. Fifty percent of couples I've spoken to don't know their income. (That's not a typo.) Ninety percent of couples don't know how much debt they're in. One hundred percent of couples with credit card debt have difficulty saying no to their children.

2. People who accumulate millions of dollars often struggle to spend it—even when their spouse is about to divorce them for being cheap.

3. The overwhelming majority of people who come on the podcast—people who describe their financial problems as a 9 or even a 10 out of 10 and go through extensive screening—have not read a single book on personal finance. It's shocking, but it's also human nature.

4. The lower earner is almost always obsessed with the c-word—*contribute*—because they wonder if their nonmonetary contributions are as valuable as money, which is much more easily measured in our culture. (The answer is yes!)

5. A shockingly high number of couples with credit card debt have very specific purchases, such as Apple Watches and iPads with cellular connections.

6. Men call themselves "the provider" and women are taught to keep a secret savings account "just in case."

7. Many couples argue about shopping at Target for years and years, but the fight is rarely actually about Target. It's about spending over 65 percent of your income on fixed costs, which we'll cover in Chapter 7.

8. When people get into financial trouble, it's almost always about two purchases: their housing and their trucks (excuse me, vehicles).

whether they'll have enough. What you quickly discover is that the way you feel about money is highly uncorrelated with the amount you have in the bank.

The couples I speak to share their income, their debt, where they spend money, and what they worry about. When describing what they learned about money from their parents, they often cry. It's riveting, especially because we've never seen how other couples actually talk about money.

These brave couples apply to be on my podcast because they need help and they know they're not going to be mocked or shamed. They need a new way to connect over money—to change the pattern of fighting into something positive—and a realistic system that simplifies their money so they can work toward a powerful vision together.

That's why I wrote this book. I wish I could speak to every couple who applies to be on my podcast, but with more than 1,000 people on our waiting list, it's impossible. This book will share the most valuable insights for you to build a healthy relationship with money.

Many of those couples from my podcast show up in these pages, sharing intimate stories and real numbers. I find immense comfort in hearing how other people grapple with money, talk about money, and bond over money. I know you will, too.

Are You the "Money Person" in Your Relationship?

In 90 percent of the couples I work with, one partner is "the money person." I get it—in any relationship, one person might empty the dishwasher, the other takes out the trash. One handles home repairs, the other deals with the laundry. It just makes sense that one person would handle money, right?

Wrong.

Unlike washing the dishes, money cannot be delegated to one person, because money cuts across everything: where you live, what you eat, what you do for fun, even *who you are*. Managing money is less like shopping for groceries and more like parenting. You rarely hear of just one of two partners "doing the parenting thing"—nor should there be one partner "handling the money."

This is foundational: *Both partners must be involved in the family finances*. When you internalize the importance of both partners having financial skin in the game, you'll start to understand why so many couples report the same fights:

- *"The minute I walk in the door, he asks how much I spent at Target."*

- *"She constantly looks at the credit card bill and says I spent too much going out with my friends."*

- *"He tells me to cut our grocery bills, but he has no idea how much I've already cut to the bone."*

If one person is the "money person," you'll never build a true team that works together on creating a Rich Life.

People will go decades arguing over petty expenses, never realizing that the *real* problem is that one person is in charge of money. It would be like thinking you hate cooking for 20 years, only to realize that you have a poorly lit kitchen with bad ventilation and rusty knives. Now that we know what's actually wrong, we can fix it and move on. What a relief!

Naturally, one person might have more of a knack for money. We see this in all important aspects of life—in parenting, in planning travel, in maintaining family relationships. But both partners have to care about money, because it affects every part of your lives. Both have to talk about finances regularly, build a system together, and evolve it over time. If you don't create a shared vision and make decisions as a team, it's easy to fixate on meaningless minutiae like spending on coffee or snacks, or issues I call $3 questions. We should spend more time asking $30,000 questions.

When you're stuck asking $3 questions, you're constantly playing defense and arguing about random transactions instead of

$3 Questions vs. $30,000 Questions

Where people try to save money:

» $3 coffee

Areas that actually matter:

» Setting up automatic investments (potential upside: $250,000)

» Minimizing investment fees ($50,000+)

» Creating a debt-payoff plan ($50,000)

Ask $30,000 questions, not $3 questions.

building a vision and using your money to live it. And even if you "win" by slashing spending money on small or random expenses, then what? Did you actually get anywhere? Do you know what to do with the $3 you saved? Do you even feel better? The answer is no.

Maybe I'm weird, but I have a personal policy against suffering through thousands of tedious, pointless arguments for the rest of my life. That's why *both* partners have to understand what the $30,000 questions are, and then agree to focus on them together.

Here's how it works for me. In my marriage, I handle our investments because I'm more knowledgeable about investing and my idea of a great Saturday night is reading *The Journal of Asset Management*. But crucially, Cassandra and I still *talk about* investments together: We discuss what percentage of our income we're investing, where that money is being invested, how much we expect to have in 20 years, and if we should contribute more or less this year. That's the level at which we're discussing our money—not how much we spent on coffee last week.

Money is my job, so from the beginning, it would have been easy for me to be the "money guy," but I insisted we both be involved for three reasons.

1. Eventually I'm going to die, and if I go first, I want Cassandra to feel confident knowing exactly what to do with our money. (There's an epidemic of women who are left unequipped to handle their finances when their partners pass away. They're easy targets for predatory financial sharks. I will never leave my wife in this situation, and I look forward to her laughing and hanging up on the worthless Goldman Sachs wealth advisors who might call her after I kick the bucket. I'll be watching with popcorn from heaven.)

2. I want us to both be good stewards of our money, so we discuss it and nurture it together, like a garden. Good stewardship means we spend it meaningfully, we donate to causes we care about, and we decide what will happen to it once we're gone.

Excuses, Excuses

"We don't need a book—we just need a budget."
Let me put this bluntly: A budget is not why you and your partner can't get on the same page about money. The issue goes much deeper. For the vast majority of people, a budget is a tactical solution to a psychological problem. We find these solutions appealing—even if they don't work!—because in our culture, we're taught that numbers are important and feelings are not. A budget won't save you, but learning how to connect over money just might.

"My partner will never do this with me."
Maybe that's the case. So what are your options? To give up? To do things the way you've always done them? If that hasn't worked, let's try another approach: mine. As former Netscape CEO Jim Barksdale said, "If we have data, let's look at data. If all we have are opinions, let's go with mine." Even if you read this book completely on your own, you can make enough progress to get 85 percent of the way to where you want to be.

3. Finally, it's a lot more fun to manage money together! When we talk about money, we get to plan our dream vacations together, think about where we want to spend more (or less) next year, and create a beautiful culture of money in our household.

It would have been a lot simpler in the short term for me to just handle the finances myself. But the payoff from building a shared understanding of money is so much greater than an "easy" approach. Every couple has money challenges, Cassandra and me included, and talking about money regularly and proactively has helped us deal with ours. When we got married, we had very different perspectives on money. As business owners, we have irregular income and expenses. But because we have consistent money conversations, we

"Our problems go a lot deeper than money."
You're right! But let's start with money, because with every day that goes by, you're losing a lot by not investing money together.

"Maybe this would work, if only . . .
    . . . we earned more."
    . . . we didn't live in such a high-cost-of-living area."
    . . . my partner wasn't so irresponsible."
    . . . the economy wasn't so terrible."
    . . . and so on (fill in the blank).
Yeah, probably. Life would be a lot easier for me if I were 6'3" with an Australian accent, but here we are. We play the hand we're dealt. You can simultaneously acknowledge the need for systemic change *and* focus on what you can control—and this book is about taking control of your money together.

"Talking about money is stressful and depressing."
That's why I'm here! It doesn't have to be, and it shouldn't be. My system is going to help change all that for you and your partner.

have a shared language, and we know how to use it, in good times and bad. We're true partners in our Rich Life, and this is what I want for you and your partner, too.

A New Way to Look at Money

This book will help you shift away from associating money with dread, fear, and resentment. Instead, you'll learn what to say and do to connect money with a sense of competence, joy, opportunity, purpose, and generosity. And yes—you and your partner can do this together, even if you don't see money exactly the same way.

Will it always be easy? No, of course not. Is your partner going to be as enthusiastic as you are? Maybe not. But I've worked with couples in all situations, and whether a couple has $800,000 in debt or millions of dollars, they need the same things: better communication and a system that sticks. I have a system that's worked for thousands of couples, and it will work for you.

In the following pages . . .

- *You'll learn exactly what to say when talking about money*, even if your partner resists these sorts of conversations.

- *You'll get the steps to create a joint vision of your Rich Life*—one that fits you as an individual and as a couple.

- *You'll learn how your past affects the way you feel about money*, and how to change your story to one that feels positive and future oriented.

- *You'll learn how to think beyond the month with your finances.* For many of us, managing our money feels like driving in the fog and being able to see only 50 feet ahead. You'll build a real vision months ahead—even years ahead. What a relief.

- *You'll discover how to work smoothly as a team*, making decisions together through the lens of your Rich Life.

- *You'll know how to advocate for yourself—without fighting—*when it comes to spending, saving, investing, and the way you both handle money.

- *You'll have an airtight money system* that needs only an hour a month of maintenance, including the exact accounts and a real plan.

- *You'll start to finally feel* good *about money.* Best of all, this is a feeling you'll share with your partner, because you did it together.

By opening this book, you've sent a signal to yourself—that money's important to you, that you're not going to apologize for caring about your finances, and that there's room for you and your partner to become closer via your money. You've also embraced the idea of getting some help. I'm going to give you everything I give the couples I work with—word-for-word scripts, tactics, probing questions, psychology examples, and more. At times I'm also going to push you, just like I push them.

I promise that as soon as you and your partner have one good money conversation, your whole outlook will change. You'll realize this is an entirely new approach to money. And by the end of this book, when you've built trust with your partner, when you've had several conversations where you both smile and feel *good* talking about money, you'll see that money is something you can take control of—together.

Now let's get started.

PART 1

10 Steps to a Rich Life— Together

YOUR FIRST POSITIVE CONVERSATION ABOUT MONEY

*Use these easy word-for-word
scripts and keep it light*

"Can you think of a time in the last 30 days when the two of you weren't on the same page with money?"

This is the question I ask couples when they come on my podcast. It seems innocent enough, a softball, something to help guests open up to me with a funny story and maybe a laugh. But the question is no accident. It's the highly calculated result of testing over two dozen different questions to find this specific one.

I've discovered that when most of us talk about the role of money in our relationships, we suddenly get vague and generic:

- *"I'm a saver. They're a spender."*

- *"I just wish they would make a plan."*

- *"We just can't seem to agree about money."*

Those might be technically true, but they don't get to the heart of what's really going on. For that, we need to get into real specifics with real details. We need to get more real, not more vague!

So, when I asked a recent couple about a time they disagreed about money in the last month, they both took a deep breath and proceeded to talk for the next 12 minutes. They assigned blame, they preemptively defended their own behavior, and they revealed how anxious money made them.

I loved it. But finally, I had to interrupt.

I asked, "Have either of you ever felt good about money?"

"No," they both said.

What a breathtaking moment. When I cut in, they were busy arguing over the price of a $15 lunch, which was a tiny symptom of what was actually going on in their relationship: *They both feel bad about money.* All their disagreements stem from that. But if I'd simply asked them, "What's the problem with money in your relationship?" they would have said, "We're just not on the same page."

Details matter. The words you choose are like an X-ray of how you feel about money. We avoid money, we fight about money, we worry about money, but the truth is revealed in the everyday words we use.

That's why we're going to focus on *how* we talk. I want you to see what it's like to have a great conversation about money, where you're both smiling and you both feel connected.

Redefining "The Money Conversation"

Let's start by understanding how most of us think about "The Money Conversation."

Notice that small but telling word: *the*. We believe that we need to have "the" conversation about money to get on the same page—as if a single chat is going to change everything in our lives! Would we have merely one conversation about parenting? Or taking care of our elderly parents? Of course not. We understand that important topics deserve our ongoing attention.

So reframe your money conversations:

"We get the privilege of having lots of conversations about how we want to use money to create our Rich Lives. And we get to talk about it together for the rest of our lives."

What a relief! You don't have to have the perfect conversation. You get many opportunities to talk about money. You're not in a rush, and nobody expects you to magically know what to say the first time around. You're bringing together two different ways of seeing money, two different family histories, two different visions of what your life will look like.

Talking about money is a skill, and you're about to start building that skill together. Like the first time you rode without training wheels, it's likely you'll "fall off the bike" at times. Acknowledge that it's not easy, own it, even have fun with it. You can say this: "Look, I'm nervous about this. Sometimes I might say the wrong thing. But I'm excited about getting better at this with you." Lead with your vulnerabilities, which make it easier for your partner to open up about theirs.

Before you sit down, I recommend you outline the conversation—don't wing it. If you had an important upcoming meeting at work, I bet you wouldn't just spitball it. Eighty percent of the work is done before you ever set foot in the room, so I always visualize my important conversations in advance, anticipating where things might go wrong and planning for it. Consider that if you were an Olympic bobsledder, you'd visualize every curve before your big race. Similarly, take this conversation seriously—it may not be "the" talk, but it does help set the foundation for the rest of your financial lives.

Here's how to create a great outline: First, get clear on what you want out of the conversation by taking a couple of minutes and jotting down everything on your mind, which might look a little like the following list.

- What is this $16.39 charge at the gas station last week?

- Did you fill out the forms for your health insurance?

- Will we have enough to retire?

- What is this credit card that I found stuffed in a drawer?

- How can I get you to talk about money with me?

- The kids' school has another field trip, and I don't know where the money should come from.

- What's a Roth IRA?

Now zoom out: Save all those questions you wrote down—you'll get to them eventually. Your first money conversation is not about *most* of those things. In fact, if you jump straight into asking about a

Reframing the Language We Use Around Money

The words we use to talk about money are extremely revealing. For example, you could say, "We *have* to talk about money today [sigh]," or you could say, "We *get* to talk about money today [high five]." Imagine the impact of speaking about money positively over decades together. How would that shape your perception?

You can change the way you look at money from dread to opportunity, and quickly. It starts by intentionally choosing different language—even if the conversation is only inside your head. For example . . .

Instead of: "We can't afford it."
Use this: "We can't afford it yet, but we're building a plan to save for it."

Instead of: "I would never pay for this."
Use this: "In the past, I would never have paid for this, but I'm starting to understand why some people would."

charge on last week's credit card bill, you'll be stuck asking $3 questions forever.

Take that list, look at your questions, and circle the one thing that matters more than all the other ones combined. In the list above, there is only one real topic to tackle for your first money conversation: "How can I get you to talk about money with me?" Solve that, and the rest follow.

Here are examples of "good" questions for this first meeting:

- What would it look like if we both felt good about money? How often would we talk about it? What would we do more of? Less of?

- What's one thing I can do to help you feel more comfortable talking about money? (And vice versa.)

- What kind of financial values do we want to teach our kids?

Instead of: "That's for rich people, not for people like us."

Use this: "I didn't grow up doing that, but if we want to, we can plan for it." (Unless it's something outrageously expensive like buying a private jet, in which case try this: "That's a nice plane, but I'd rather take a family vacation together.")

Instead of: "Must be nice to spend that much. We can barely afford . . ."

Use this: "We choose what's important for our Rich Life, and other people choose what's important for them."

The language we use becomes our identity. What kind of language have you been using?

I used to jokingly call myself a "skinny Indian guy"—it became a self-fulfilling prophecy and something I believed was extremely hard to change. In reality, I just hadn't yet learned the skills of lifting weights and eating right. Looking back, I wish I had never said that about myself.

Your language shapes your reality. Choose your words carefully!

Now that you've carefully considered what you hope to talk about, you can make a clean, simple outline like this:

Our First Amazing Money Meeting

- Why this meeting is going to be awesome

- How I feel about money (How about you?)

- How I want to feel about money (How do you want to feel about it?)

- Next steps (Let's talk more next week.)

Let's break down each part of this outline for your chat—excuse me, your "First Amazing Money Meeting."

THE CONVERSATION ITSELF (15–20 MINUTES)

Why this meeting is going to be awesome. Tell your partner why you're so excited to talk about money. Mention that you're reading this book and how it's going to feel great to build something together. Make sure your energy is high.

> "I've been reading this book on couples and money, and it's giving me so many ideas for how we can talk about money together. The author writes about how all these couples manage their finances and how we can save money and spend money on the stuff we love."

How I feel about money. Most of us never actually describe our own feelings about money. Think of it: When was the last time you said, "I feel scared" or "I feel worried"? When was the last time your partner shared their feelings? I recommend you lead with vulnerability here by sharing first, then ask your partner how they feel about money—*and listen.* Ask clarifying questions, even if the responses aren't what you're expecting. Remember, this is an opportunity to describe your feelings, not to make accusations. (Our therapist gave us the Wheel of Emotions, which was very helpful. Search for it online to use it!)

> "I feel confused by our money. Like, I just don't understand that spreadsheet that we use. I wish I did, but it doesn't make sense for the way I think."

> "I feel worried. I know you've said everything is going to be okay, but I get anxious when I look in our checking account and it's running low."

> "Sometimes I feel resentful about money because I manage our monthly bills and our grocery shopping and I would really love some help. I think I feel alone."

How I want to feel about money. Paint a powerful vision that goes beyond "not worrying" about money. Avoid focusing on what you don't want to feel like and describe what emotions you *do* want to feel.

> "I want to feel knowledgeable about money. I want to feel confident. I want to feel like I have a partner, like you have my back and I have yours."

> "I want to feel good about money so we can make a plan for the things we'd like to do with our money. I know we've talked about taking a trip to Iceland, about having a weekly date night . . . That's what I want us to both feel good about."

> "What about you?"

Next steps. Keep it short! Better to have a brief, positive conversation than a long, exhausting, negative one. My philosophy: Declare victory and go home! You have lots of time to talk about money together. For the first meeting, your goal should be to feel good—and then end on a high note.

"This makes me so happy. I think we should wrap it up today, but I just want to tell you how much I love you and how good it feels to be able to talk about this. Can we talk more next week? I would love to start making a plan with our money. Maybe Saturday afternoon?"

Adapt the scripts above for your own situation. As you can see, the first conversation is short, honest, and upbeat. And bear in mind: Nobody taught us this. Most of us get more guidance on sex than talking about money! So give yourselves some room to laugh if things feel a little uncomfortable.

Tips to make your first money conversation go smoothly

- Reframe the meeting for yourself. What if this were fun? What if it were easy? What would your body language communicate? What would your face convey? Then do that.

- Show your partner some grace. You've been reading this book and thinking about the money talk. Your partner most likely has not. Your approach, no matter how gentle, will catch them off guard. Be sensitive.

- Expect to hear some phrases that may trigger you ("I'm just not good with money"). When I hear people talk about money, they frequently use certain phrases on autopilot. Chances are, they won't even remember saying them tomorrow. Understand that people behave in peculiar ways when they feel stressed or surprised. Listen, then ask another way. If you get stuck, move on.

- When you talk about how you want to feel about money, focus on what you *do* want—not what you *don't* want ("I don't want to feel worried" becomes "I want to feel confident"). This is important because it's easy to get mired in the negatives, but creating a vision is about what you *do* want.

- Keep in mind that your job is not to answer every question your partner throws at you, or to "check off" every item on the agenda. Stay focused on your North Star: to have a money conversation where you both feel good.

- At the end, give your partner a hug and say, "I love you." Then don't talk about money for the rest of the day!

What *not* to do

- The same thing you've always done. Same topics, same phrases, same tone, same location, same, same, same. If you want to make a change, then change.

- Bring up the subject in bed, right when one of you finishes work, or when you're distracted, hungry, or tired.

- Treat the conversation as an obligation. (*Sigh.* "Okay, I know you don't like talking about money, but . . .") Reframe: "Talking about money is a gift! We get to do this together! And this will be a marathon, not a sprint, so let's have fun along the way."

Where and When to Meet

Think about where you'll have your conversation and when you're going to talk. Ideally it'll be in the morning in a calm place with no distractions such as children running around. (Easy for me to say, I know—but this is important. Find a way.) Try to set aside a block of quiet time where you're both present and engaged. If it needs to happen a few days in the future, that's fine.

- Ask a leading question to which you really know the answer—that is, set a verbal trap. ("What do you think we should do to cut our spending? Okay, and what about that hobby of yours? I keep telling you, you need to stop . . .")

- Feel the need to solve every problem in one conversation. You have plenty of time.

GOOD OPENING LINES

- If you know your partner will be excited to talk about money: *"I want to try something new. I want to use the exercises in this book I'm reading so we can start to plan our Rich Lives together."*

Talking about Money When You're Dating

If you're dating to find a long-term partner, there's nothing wrong with wanting to know how your date thinks about money. If you end up together, your finances will be a core foundation of your life, affecting where you live, how you spend your leisure time, what opportunities your children have—just about everything. Of course, you don't want to be a weirdo, pulling out a 67-page folder of financial questions on the second date. When the time is right, ask genuine questions and listen closely: People reveal almost everything.

Here are some questions you could pose.

"What did your family do for fun when you were growing up?"
Your date might say they went skiing in Aspen or, if they were like my family, they went to the public library and $1 movie theater. Either way, this tells you a lot about their upbringing and their likely views on money.

- If you have a contentious history around money: *"I'm wondering, would you be open to talking about money? I want us both to be able to feel good about it. How about Wednesday night?"*

- If you're both new to talking about money: *"I was feeling confused about money, so I bought this book and I want to get your input. Can I ask you a few questions?"*

It's okay if you get an odd reaction when you say you want to have a money talk. Most people are caught off guard when money comes up, especially because they've been conditioned by a lifetime of negative money conversations, so their reactions are often abrupt or even angry. They instinctively feel like they're going to get in

"How much should we tip?" Sometimes you can ask. Other times you can simply observe what they do. Does your date tip poorly? Do they offer to split costs? Are they generous, proactive, and considerate? These qualities show up early.

"How do you picture your future?" If you've developed a crystal-clear vision of your life, you might want to simply share it and gauge their reaction. In the West, this can seem shockingly forward and is usually best held until later in the dating process, but in other cultures, this is discussed on day one. For example, my parents got married seven days after they met, so they had to be immediately direct with what they were looking for.

"Can we talk about how to pay for this trip we're taking next month?" A first trip is a perfect opportunity to talk about money. It's relatively low stakes, both of you want to impress each other with how easygoing you are, and you likely have different views on who should pay and what's worth it. Great! Just one suggestion: Come with an idea of what *you* want. Otherwise, it's too easy to ask your partner what they want and let them dictate the terms of the discussion.

trouble. Imagine how you would have reacted if previously—before you began your journey of financial self-improvement—someone had told you they wanted to "talk about money." You probably wouldn't have wanted to hear it, either!

Once you understand that your partner may be hesitant or resist this conversation, you'll be able to give them space to say whatever comes into their mind, then gently redirect them to your main goal.

Here are some examples:

Partner: "Uhh . . . okay." (The subtext: "This is weird.")
You: "Okay, awesome. I'm reading this book, and I want to get your thoughts on how we can . . ."

Partner: *Sigh.* "Another one of these?"
You: *Smile.* "I know we haven't talked about money in a positive way before, and I want to change that so we can both feel good about it."

Partner: "Haven't we already tried this?"
You: "Yeah, we have. I think I approached it the wrong way. I want us both to feel good when we talk about money. Would you be open to trying again?"

Partner: "Fine, I'll do whatever you want" (while mentally checking out).
You: "Okay, great—thanks. Is this a good time or should we do it later this week?"

Partner: "Why do you always need to talk about money?!"
You: "I love you. It's really important to me that we find a way to talk about this together. Would you be willing to trust me and try this together?"

TABOO WORDS YOU MUST AVOID

When it comes to money, certain words and phrases instantly cause people to become defensive. Many of us fall into the trap of saying at least one of them, which almost always derails the conversation. By not bringing up any of the following, you'll give yourself a massive advantage at having a successful first money conversation.

- *"Budget."* Everyone hates budgets, including me. Just don't say it.

- *"Credit card bill."* If you have credit card debt and you bring this up in the first conversation, it will suck any positive energy right out of the room. You have time to talk about it later.

- *"We need to get serious."* If you were going to try playing pickleball for the first time and the coach said, "You really need to get serious," how would you feel? Your goal is fun and connectedness, not lecturing.

- *"You always . . ."* and *"You never."* If someone says you "always" do something bad, the natural reaction is to argue back, so using this phrase will trap you. Quick trick: If you get stuck, focus on the "we," not the "you."

- *"I just want to . . ."* This use of *just* is interesting because it's so common and so casual—but the problem is that *just* minimizes your goal. Resist that urge to shrink the importance of money. Your vision is to build a Rich Life, not to "just" stop fighting or "just" agree on how much to spend at Target. Although it might seem easier to focus on a small topic, people tend to react better to a larger vision: *I don't want to stop overspending at the grocery store; I want to live a Rich Life.* This conversation is the beginning of a new way of treating money with the respect it deserves.

WHAT TO DO IF YOU START FIGHTING

It's going to happen. At some point, you and your partner will argue about money. That's normal! My wife and I still disagree about money. The point is to anticipate and plan for it, so when it happens, you know exactly what to do. Here's a list of handy phrases you can use when you have a disagreement.

That First Money Conversation When You're Moving in Together

Moving in is another perfect time to talk about money, because you're both making a change that will affect your finances in a big way. Begin the conversation confidently: Money is a normal topic to discuss when you're cohabitating. Treat it accordingly and avoid apologizing for bringing up the subject ("Ugh . . . um . . . I guess we should talk about splitting the rent?"). The goal is to simply open the topic of money and gently shift your identity to a couple that talks about it—as all people in healthy relationships do.

Start with one of these:

"I've been thinking about finances. Can we talk about it? I'd love for us to get on the same page about money."

"Honestly, I'm not super comfortable talking about money. But I think this is a great chance for us to do it."

"It's important to me that we talk about money together. I want to start the conversation so this becomes something that's normal for us."

Be open and listen as much as you talk. Don't start with a hidden agenda—like a plan to get your partner to admit they spend too much on video games. And remember, you're not going to cover everything in one conversation.

Within three conversations, you want to determine . . .

» the mechanics of how you're going to handle shared costs (rent, utilities, groceries, eating out).

» your financial numbers (income, debt, how you both choose to spend your discretionary money).

» whether there are any red flags you want to address immediately or over time.

» when to reconvene and talk about money again.

- *"Can we take a break?"* It's okay to regroup for a minute, go get a glass of water, and even peek at your notes to get back on track.

- *"Can you help me understand what you mean? I don't think I'm getting it—and I really want to."* Vulnerability is connective. Use it more often!

- *"I'm feeling overwhelmed right now. Can we pick this back up tomorrow?"* If the conversation is veering off in a way you can't manage, it's time for a longer pause. Express empathy and wrap things up for now. It's not your job to meet every challenge your partner raises. Your job is to begin working toward positive communication around money. Sometimes that requires ending the conversation early.

Conflict is inevitable, but you can certainly disagree about money without fighting. On my Netflix show, I spoke to a young couple, Christian and Millie. Christian revealed that he'd lost $80,000 on a single investment. I can understand being upset! But to their credit, they didn't fight—even when they disagreed, they talked through their issues and reminded each other that they were a team.

Looking Ahead to the Next Conversation

Let's assume you had a short, positive first conversation.

In Chapter 3, you're going to begin designing your Rich Life vision together. Between now and then, you can continue building your connection around money. When you schedule your next meeting, ask your partner to add a topic to the agenda. This signals that discussing money is a team activity—not just you leading and them following—and it gives them time to contribute so they're part of the process.

When you're thinking about the agenda, play with big and small topics. The big ones are lifestyle questions and Rich Life dreams. The small topics are questions like how to handle a specific issue, such as who will take the car in for service or whether to switch banks for your checking account.

In advance of the meeting, jot down something you've noticed and appreciated about your partner since the first meeting. This doesn't have to be related to money. Here are a few examples my wife and I recently shared with each other:

- "Thanks for taking the lead in planning Christmas with our parents. It was really cool to see everyone playing those games together. I never would have thought of those activities, so I really love seeing you create these memories with all of us."

- "When I had that [medical issue] last month, it meant a lot that you took a day off work and drove me there and took care of me. I really felt loved, so thank you."

- "I've noticed you've been asking if I need anything, and how I'm doing, more often. It makes me feel cared for."

Topics for Future Money Conversations

» How much income and debt you both have (if you don't already know)

» Setting up a will, if you don't already have one (you should)

» Who should be the guardians for your kids if you become incapacitated or die (fun topics for a Saturday night!)

» What role you'd like to play in helping family members, including taking care of elderly parents

» What kind of lifestyle do you envision in 1 year? 5 years? 10 years?

Think up a few, then choose one. This will be the first thing you say at meeting #2; you're going to build a new habit of starting off money conversations with a compliment, which totally changes the dynamic. Later, when you implement Monthly Money Meetings in Chapter 10, you'll use this practice, and soon it will become second nature.

Chapter 1 Checklist

❑ Prep for your first money conversation. What is the key question you want to address? How can you start the conversation in a way that will make your partner feel safe and engaged? How will you react if it doesn't go the way you planned? Make a simple agenda and share it.

❑ Have your first money conversation. Keep it short, positive, and future focused! Remember, you don't have to cover everything in one talk.

❑ Schedule your second conversation. Keep the momentum going. Ask your partner to add at least one item to this meeting's agenda, and lead with something you appreciate about them in your next money conversation.

UNDERSTANDING YOUR MONEY PSYCHOLOGY

Uncover your invisible scripts, hidden memories, and the four Money Types

Sara was telling her husband, Charlie, about an amazing bachelorette party at the beach she'd just returned from—a "20 out of 10," as she put it. "I'm not a beach person and Charlie really loves the beach," she told me. She was excited to share the idea of the two of them going to the ocean together. But Charlie's instant answer was no: "We can't afford that. We can't do that."

Charlie explained, "What I imagined is us renting a house that was 90 percent empty, and us just paying for something that would be unused. I don't know. It's beautiful. It's beachfront, has a pool, and I thought, *Sure, that sounds nice, but I'm not going to enjoy paying for a house that's almost empty.* So I said, 'We can't afford that.'"

"I felt like someone had popped me like a balloon," Sara told me. "What do you mean we can't afford that? I felt like I couldn't even dream with him without getting shot down."

Could they afford it? Unquestionably yes. They earn $282,000 plus bonuses—and they live in Mexico City! I discovered the truth only when I asked Charlie about his childhood. He grew up middle class surrounded by much wealthier classmates. Eventually, his mom went back to work and made more money than his dad—which led to his dad being resentful about being the lower earner. His parents have been fighting about money for 40 years, and now those fights have bled into Charlie and Sara's marriage.

So when Sara suggested a beach vacation, Charlie's emphatic response—"No!"—was not really about the beach house or even their finances. It was about his money psychology.

The way Charlie feels about money is way out of sync with their actual financial status. This disconnect—having money but always worrying about spending it—is common. And you can always trace it to how someone grew up.

Invisible Scripts about Money

Childhood money experiences create deep grooves. They shape who we are and can affect us for decades, often our whole lives. We like to imagine that we make money decisions based on budgets and cold, hard logic, but the truth is we're often just repeating what we were exposed to—whether that's a scarcity mentality, a sense of ease and abundance, or fear and confusion around money.

Our relationship with money plays out in big and small ways. Here's a simple example: As we push our shopping cart down the grocery store aisle, we want to believe that we're making a careful cost-benefit calculation when we stop in the snack aisle. In reality, our parents taught us that love meant eating Ritz crackers as an after-school treat. Forty years later, we mindlessly reach for the Ritz crackers, never realizing that our behavior has been shaped by our invisible scripts. These are the beliefs we hold so deeply that we don't even realize we have them.

If you constantly worry about money, you almost certainly have invisible scripts. For example, one of the most common invisible scripts is "investing feels like gambling." Some scripts are positive, some are negative (sadly, most fall under this category), and some are appropriate for specific times in your life.

The good news is you can acknowledge where you came from and decide where you want to go. When it comes to the invisible scripts you inherited from your parents, it's important to remember that your parents did the best they could, but I doubt they read books on money like you're doing at this very moment. They probably didn't understand all the intricacies of investing and money psychology. But you're learning that now, which means you have the opportunity to rewrite your story.

The first step is admitting that generational habits are very real. If your parents didn't talk about money, it's likely you don't talk about money. If your parents were always worried about money, you probably are, too.

I make it a point to ask couples what money messages they remember hearing as children. Here are some of the most common answers. Do any resonate with you? (Mark any that you grew up with.)

- ❑ *"You can't afford it."*

    - ❑ "That's too expensive."

    - ❑ "I would *never* pay that much. What a waste."

    - ❑ "Don't get too big for your britches."

- ❑ *"A man is not a financial plan."*

    - ❑ "Keep a little money set aside, just in case."

    - ❑ "You might as well stop working since all your income is going to childcare." (Moms' wages are often the first to go without truly considering the effects on women's careers later on.)

    - ❑ "You need to save your money." (Young women are often told to save, but rarely taught to invest.)

❑ *"You will never have a lot of money."*

    ❑ "Being in debt is just part of living."

    ❑ "You come from a long line of teachers and farmers. Don't expect to earn much money."

    ❑ "We don't need money to be happy."

❑ *"Be a man."*

    ❑ "Men should provide for their family."

    ❑ "Your job is to be the rock. Men don't worry about emotions."

    ❑ "Why would you stay at home? Dads work."

❑ *"Keep up with other people."*

    ❑ "Did you hear? John bought a new house. . . ."

    ❑ "How can they afford a third vacation this year?!"

    ❑ "You don't rent when you have three kids."

❑ *"Investing is for rich people, not for you."*

    ❑ "We keep our money in the bank."

    ❑ "The stock market is just gambling for the wealthy."

    ❑ "I'd rather buy gold or silver. Something I can touch with my own two hands."

❑ *"Things will work themselves out."*

    ❑ "Stop worrying. Things always turn out fine for us."

    ❑ "I'm more of a 'go with the flow' kind of person."

    ❑ "You're so obsessed with money—can't you relax?"

❑ *"Rich people are shallow."*

    ❑ "Must be nice . . ."

    ❑ "More money, more problems."

    ❑ "Of course *they* can afford to spend $500 on a meal."

Pivotal Money Moments in Your Life

Many of our money beliefs are formed at very specific moments in our lives. What's conveyed at these pivotal times—like holidays, birthdays, and graduations—often sticks with you forever. This list will help you uncover money moments that you may have forgotten but still continue to affect you today.

When it comes to money, what do you remember about . . .

» holidays with your family?

» birthdays?

» allowances?

» graduations?

» what you wore to school?

» back-to-school shopping?

» how your parents talked about money when bills were due?

» your first job?

» your first love?

» applying to college?

Now choose one positive memory and one negative one. Let's dig into these memories.

» What happened?

» How did that shape your view of money?

» How does that lesson show up in your life today?

This shouldn't take a lot of time. Usually, the first thing that pops into your head reveals a lot about your relationship with money.

Of the invisible scripts you checked, pick one and go deeper:

- Where did this script come from? Get specific. Where were you sitting when you first heard it? How many times did you hear it?

- How has this script affected you and your relationship?

- How can you rewrite it so that it's something that serves you today?

What Are Your Invisible Scripts Costing You?

Michelle and Dan from episode #56 of my podcast are in their early thirties, and from the outside, they look like they're in a great place financially. They have a high household income, and they've already saved $200,000. The problem is, nearly all that money is sitting in a low-interest savings account, with only $25,000 invested.

Michelle and Dan are Worriers (see page 39). Because Dan works in the volatile oil and gas industry, he's understandably anxious about their finances—especially because he's lost his job three times in the last six years. As a result, he and Michelle behave very conservatively with their money, keeping most of it in a savings account rather than investing it. But what does being "conservative" cost them?

I'm not talking in metaphors. I mean it *literally*: How much money are they losing because of their beliefs about money?

The real answer is $4.6 million. Let me show you the math:

- If they change nothing and keep their $25,000 invested for 32 years, they'll have $217,881.

- If they also invest the $200,000 that's sitting in savings, they'll have $1.9 million.

- And if they *also* invest 10 percent of their gross incomes— even assuming they do not grow their income at all over the next 30 years!—they'll have over $4.6 million.

If you compare what they're currently doing with what they could be doing, the results are stark: They're losing over $4 million by being scared of money! Most of us spend our time feeling guilty about buying a $5 coffee, but we're in fact losing hundreds of thousands or *millions* of dollars by not focusing on what really matters long term.

Ironically, while Michelle saves and saves because of a vague fear of losing money through investments, by not investing she actually *is* losing over $140,000 *per year* for the next 32 years!

She describes what makes her nervous: "I don't feel like I'm savvy with money. I don't understand it. I'm just afraid of losing it."

I tell Michelle that by keeping her money in savings, she's losing money *right now.* She lost money in the hour we talked! She hears me, but the message doesn't really connect. Numbers are just an abstraction, blocked by a lifetime of worrying about money.

Like a lot of people, Michelle has an all-or-nothing view of investing. Here's what that sounds like:

- "Either I invest it all or keep it safe in a savings account."

- "Investing feels like gambling, and I don't want to lose all my money."

- "What if I don't have access to my money for an emergency?"

If Michelle understood the fundamentals of personal finance and compound interest, she wouldn't be asking these questions. But of course, few of us do. My philosophy is that it's okay not to know everything about money—but it's not okay to let a lack of knowledge cost you millions of dollars.

I suggest the possibility of a middle ground. What if they don't have to invest every penny they have? Michelle and Dan could start by taking 50 percent from their savings to put into investments. Or even 20 percent. Like in all parts of life, to make a big change, we have to start small.

Oh, and for anyone who feels that investing is gambling: Investing in the stock market is not gambling. There are ways to limit your risk. To put it bluntly, if you're afraid of losing money and you keep all or most of your money in a savings account, then you're not addressing your fears—you're letting your fears keep you small and ensuring that you *actually will run out of money*. To become confident with money, you have to become competent. And that involves identifying—and questioning—your invisible scripts and beliefs around money. Otherwise, they might end up costing you $4.6 million.

How much are your beliefs costing you?

Now let's confront other common money beliefs.

Money belief: "It's impossible to know what's going to happen in the future."

People use this belief to justify throwing their hands up and doing nothing with money. In reality, we can look at the past 100 years of data, through recessions, wars, and technological breakthroughs, and have a fairly good idea that saving and investing will work in your favor. Saying, "We just don't know what will happen" sounds logical, but it's not a valid reason to avoid taking control of your money—it's almost always fear being dressed up as caution.

Money belief: "We can't give up this house/car/summer camp."

Be very careful about sizable expenses like a bigger house, luxury car, or kids' activities, because once you begin spending, it's very hard to stop. I've had countless conversations with couples who are losing money every month, and when I ask what they'd like to cut, they are paralyzed with indecision. "Well, we can't cut Nikky's swim lessons. And we need two cars . . ."

It's almost never the small purchases that are the problem—although that's where most people mistakenly focus their efforts. I'm actually not troubled by people spending money on organic grapes or shelling out an extra $50 at Target. But once you commit to something becoming a part of your fixed costs (and your identity), it's almost impossible to cut back. My personal philosophy: Choose the areas that are important to me, then be sure that when I *start* spending, I have enough money to never go back. For example, I love nice hotels. I didn't begin booking them until I knew I would never have to cut back on that expense. We're mindful of committing to major purchases—for instance, my wife and I rent our home by choice—knowing that once we buy a house, we're not going back.

Release the Pressure Valve Around Money

When I ask couples if they follow an agenda when talking about money, they look at me like I'm crazy. An agenda? Like at work? That's *weird*. But think of what that reaction implies: that we usually talk about money only reactively, when there's an issue. Repeat that over months and years and we come to associate "money" with "problems." Money becomes a source of stress—even an enemy to be avoided.

Ironically, when I ask the very same couples about a disagreement they've had around money, they'll literally talk to me for hours. Money is on our mind—it's something we agonize over, worry about, dream about—but deep down, many of us hate it. Isn't it bizarre that we claim to value money, but then we actively try to avoid it?

What if we took a different approach with money? We could create systems so we didn't have to track every little expense. We could look at our important numbers before they became problems and handle problems before they became fights.

To achieve that, consider using a technique to "release the pressure valve." In your house, if you have a pipe that's going to burst, you slowly release the pressure valve. But with money, we let the pressure build up. We ruminate about money, worry about it, but rarely talk about it in a healthy way . . . until there's a big fight.

So let's build the habit of releasing the pressure around money. Start by doing a quick money check-in on Sunday evenings: "How are you feeling about money for the week?" Or: "How can we both feel good about money this week?"

This three-minute habit might seem small, but by talking about money regularly, you're slowly releasing the pressure in your relationship. You're lowering the stakes and teaching yourselves that money can be something you discuss when there isn't a pressing problem.

Money belief: "I can't make more money."

As someone who's landed multiple jobs, negotiated my salary, and hired many people, I believe that if you're adding value to your organization and you understand what it takes to be a top performer, there's likely room to increase your salary. (And if you want to make more but your boss won't increase your salary, I recommend looking at other jobs.)

It's true that there are some situations in which it's genuinely difficult to increase your income. For example, if you work in certain sectors—education, government, nonprofit—it's unlikely that you can negotiate your salary. But I know of a *lot* of teachers who have used my material to start a side business. They've become tutors, they've created online programs, or they've switched jobs, and they are now making much more than they used to.

I cover all of these techniques on my website and in my programs. The most important thing is realizing that if others have increased their income, there's no reason you can't, too.

You *Can* Change Generational Money Dysfunction

I worked with a young couple, Sarah and Kevin from podcast episode #80, who had a large income . . . and a lot of debt. They dug themselves out by selling their house and starting over. But six months later, they were back in over $50,000 of debt, thoroughly mystified. Sarah used the Innocent Doe routine on me (see page 112), saying, "I have no idea what we spent the money on!" Then we crunched the numbers. Within two minutes, she told me about multiple vacations, an expensive business coach, and a "nonnegotiable" $55,000 a year on private school tuition for their kids.

With $300,000 of income, they didn't realize that they absolutely could not afford this. Turns out the pattern of overspending stemmed from Sarah's childhood. Like a lot of people, Sarah was crystal clear on her mother's similar behavior but clueless about her own. On our Zoom call, she was positive and upbeat (hanging on the wall behind her were framed affirmations, like "This year is going to be different"). But when we looked at their finances, she was totally disengaged. When I told her, "You need to run the numbers," she said, "I'm not good at that." But to escape generational money dysfunction, you have to *get* good at that.

Fortunately, there's no question you can get good at managing money, just like you became good at driving and speaking English. Money is no different! You have to believe that money management is a skill that you can learn—and you have to see the importance of spending time and attention on it.

I've met couples who, in one generation, went from being poor to paying off debt, saving, and even becoming millionaires. But to truly become skilled with money, they had to make it and *simultaneously* tackle the psychology part of it to shed their limiting beliefs. If they hadn't worked on improving their money psychology, they would have unconsciously passed on the very same attitudes and behaviors that they grew up with.

The 4 Money Types

There's a common saying in the personal finance world: "Personal finance is personal." The implication is that we're all so different, so unique, that one-size-fits-all advice does not apply. I don't love this saying, which gives people an inflated sense of individuality and encourages an endless search for bespoke advice.

I prefer a different saying:

Most of us are mostly the same.

That is, most of us want to be able to spend on the things we love and know that we have enough. Most of us want money to be less of a source of stress in our relationship. And most of us have a core financial identity—a Money Type—that helps explain the way we behave with money. This is great news! If we can understand ourselves, we can understand how to change.

Your Money Type cuts across income levels and age. If you understand your type, you're one step closer to breaking the patterns that are getting in your way.

Are these Money Types reductive? Sure. Are many of us a mix of types? Yup. Can we change our Money Type over time, with the influence of a partner or the help of this very book? Absolutely.

But you can learn a lot—and quickly identify things you'd like to change—by understanding your Money Type right now.

THE AVOIDER

Rebecca and Joe from episode #57 have two little kids and a third on the way. Joe handles the family finances on his own, just like his dad did (red flag #1). They're overspending on rent (red flag #2), and they both feel frustrated by money. Rebecca ignores money issues (red flag #3), but gets stressed out, then sends panicked texts.

Joe explains: "Usually, I'll get a text during the day about how insufferable our current living situation is, because we can't just open a door and let our children run outside." Rebecca admits these messages are pointless and damaging: "I'll send him texts like, 'This is miserable. I can't do this.'"

Joe is ready to work on their finances together, but Rebecca won't come to the table. She doesn't look at bank balances or credit card bills. She won't even look at a printout of a worksheet. When she and Joe are scheduled to talk to me, she nearly sabotages the session.

Early in our meeting, I ask, "How much money do you think you have?" Rebecca's answer: "I honestly don't know. I have no idea. I would literally be making up a number." Later, I spend two hours trying to get Rebecca to enter a single number into a spreadsheet while she avoids, stalls, and distracts. One single number!

Rebecca is a classic Avoider. Of the four Money Types, Avoider is the most common.

The Avoider uses a variety of conscious and unconscious strategies to deflect and procrastinate when it comes to money.

Sometimes they know exactly what they're doing. Other times, they're genuinely oblivious to the motivation behind their tactics. Deep down, they're afraid of confronting the reality of their situation. That fear may come from ignorance ("I should already know about money"); from a sense that it's too late ("I'm 50 and I haven't even started saving"); from embarrassment ("I don't want to look stupid in front of my partner/kids/friends"); or from a general sense that if they find out the truth, it just might be as bad as they imagine.

Common behaviors: Dodging conversations; not opening mail; refusing to look at online accounts or automatic payments; ignoring parking tickets; playing innocent; reframing avoidance as a virtue ("money just isn't important to me"). Also: overspending.

Favorite phrases:
- "You're so much better at money. I'm not good at math."
- "Fine, we can talk about our bills, but first, why did *you* spend so much last weekend? I thought I told you . . ."
- "Ugh, not this again. Let's talk about it next week. I'm tired from work."

What you're losing by being an Avoider: By refusing to deal with money, you're simply kicking the can down the road, where the problems become worse. If you don't confront reality and make decisions today, you'll end up with your back against the wall tomorrow, forced to make difficult financial decisions with few good options.

What it's like being married to an Avoider: Avoiders can drive their partners crazy. Sometimes they behave like sulky children, giving one-word answers or sabotaging conversations with petty fights. ("Why are you so obsessed with money?" "Don't you trust me?" "Can't we just relax for once?") These are all strategies—both conscious and unconscious—to avoid getting real about money. Notably, I find that partners of Avoiders have often entered into a dynamic where they "rescue" Avoiders, cementing each other's roles.

How to reach an Avoider: The best way is to show them what their beliefs are costing them, including how their avoidance is hurting their family and what they're missing out on.

For a great example of this, let's go back to Rebecca. During our session, I refused to rescue her by giving her the answers. I waited patiently until she finally got honest with me, explaining exactly what she was doing by not looking at her accounts. It was basically the Avoider's credo: "When you [face reality], sometimes you see where you need to shift. But if you're not looking, then you can just keep doing what you're doing." Bingo. If you're buying the things you want and you aren't facing any real consequences, why would you want to talk about money?

That's when I helped her understand the costs of her avoidance. Here's what she said: "Because I'm avoiding [money], I actually don't realize what we *can* have. I *think* I'm getting more by hiding from it, but I'm actually getting less." This is one of the key lessons for an Avoider: By avoiding the pain and embarrassment of dealing with money, they're also missing out on what their money could do for them.

My advice for the Avoider

- Ask yourself, *What do I get out of being an Avoider?* (Please avoid saying, "I don't know." You get something out of avoiding or you wouldn't do it.) The most common response is "I get to ignore my money so I don't feel bad." Then ask yourself, *What if I keep denying? What if I could become good with money? Would I tell my children to avoid something important because it makes them feel bad?*

- Play out the future: In 10 years, if you continue avoiding, where will you be? (Don't avoid this question!) Get specific: What will your living situation be? How will you choose vacations? How might your children experience money after watching your habits day by day?

- What effect are you having on the people around you now? Especially your spouse and children. Avoiders rarely think about the collateral damage they're causing. I want you to think about it deeply.

- Consider this phrase: "We don't need a crisis to take control."

My advice for partners of Avoiders

- Avoiders need specific expectations, skin in the game, and clear boundaries. For example, if your partner is an Avoider, it wouldn't work to say, "I want you to help out with our finances!" Much better: "We've agreed to spend less than $700 per month on groceries. I'd like you to be in charge of that number and to update us every two weeks."

- Start off with gradual ownership. Work together to give the Avoider a couple of things to manage, but paint the picture of the kind of partnership you have in mind. For example, they might begin by tracking two categories in your Conscious Spending Plan (coming later in the book on page 123), but eventually they'll be in charge of planning the financial side of vacations and managing insurance.

- Finally, establish boundaries. This is a difficult topic to talk about, but boundaries are important for everyone involved. For example, if your partner forgot to pick up your kids from school, I'm sure there would be swift consequences—from the school and from you—including setting crystal-clear expectations going forward. With money, it's important to outline what continued avoiding will mean: Maybe your family won't be able to go on vacation this holiday or eat out on the weekend. On the other hand, if your partner upholds their end of the agreement, also lay out what positive things will happen for your relationship. Set clear boundaries, then stick to what you said.

THE OPTIMIZER

Optimizers are maniacally focused on their numbers. They love rules and beating the system. They track everything and are usually quite skilled when it comes to day-to-day money management. But they live almost entirely for the future. They don't know how to use money to live a Rich Life now. (I have a soft spot for Optimizers because I am one. Left alone, I would have a 32-part spreadsheet tracking my spending, favorite hotels and restaurants, daily blood pressure, favorite coffee beans, amount of sunlight every day, number of compliments I gave my wife, hobbies, number of friends I've texted in the last seven days, and then run a weekly report and monthly program to optimize every number. Come to think of it . . . this sounds like heaven to me.)

Common behaviors: Maintaining 13 spreadsheets; reading 34 different FIRE forums (that's "Financial Independence + Retiring Early," for those in the know); running yet another Monte Carlo analysis; engaging in online debates about the pitfalls of the 4 percent rule; and spending more time opening credit cards for free points than actually traveling.

Favorite phrases:
- "What if I don't account for all the variables?"
- "Have you read this new strategy for a backdoor Roth?"
- "I paid for my flight to NYC with points. Yeah! It only involved signing up for 26 new credit cards and tracking every bonus award for 18 months!"

What you're losing by being an Optimizer: Optimizers are boring. Ask an Optimizer what their hobbies are, and they'll say, "Well, I like to check my spreadsheet." They don't think it's a problem that they can't spend money to have fun. They have a target net worth they're working toward, but when they attain it decades from now, they'll realize they weren't chasing a number at all—they were chasing a feeling. They surround themselves with others who chase the same small, dim dreams. What they don't comprehend is that a Rich Life is bigger than a single number—and you can't wait to start living it until some day in the future. By then, it's too late.

What it's like being married to an Optimizer: Because Optimizers focus relentlessly on numbers, they often become unbearably cheap. They cleverly frame this as a virtue: *I'm not like those superficial people. I don't need a glass of fancy wine. I'm perfectly happy with water.* Their austerity becomes their identity. Their partner feels judged, because everything the partner enjoys or buys or wants will elicit the same tense question: "How much does that cost?"

Optimizers (including me) often struggle to connect to their feelings. If you ask about feelings, they'll often give you a cerebral answer about what they *think* but not what they feel. For many Optimizers, it's been years since they described a single emotion around money.

The logic of an Optimizer: Here's a real-life example from episode #77. Tommy is 60. He's run his own business for more than 30 years, loves his work, and plans to keep going. His wife, Caroline, is getting ready to retire from a stressful job. Together, they have amassed more than $6 million. Caroline is excited to spend on things they both love, like travel. But Tommy just can't do it. Like a true Optimizer, he keeps putting off any significant spending until tomorrow, saying they "need to save up" for their next trip. His thinking:

- Even with a net worth of $6 million, Tommy keeps very little available in savings, because he wants to maximize earnings on every dollar . . . hence the need to "save up" for a trip.

- As a business owner, Tommy looks at vacation time as money lost, so it's hard to find enjoyment in the prospect of a long trip.

- Tommy is locked in the hustling mindset of a young entrepreneur . . . even though he's been in business for 30 years!

It's easy to roll your eyes, but many Optimizers will end up in exactly this situation—with lots of money and an inability to spend it meaningfully because they cannot turn off the "optimization" lens through which they view the world. Tommy did an excellent job saving money, but he now sees spending as "losing" (and saving, of course, as "winning," even though he doesn't need to save another cent for his entire life). I encouraged Tommy to reframe "spending" to "building memories" and to reframe "cutting back on work" to "turning the page to the next chapter of his life." He and Caroline have earned the right to focus more on meaning than on money.

Sidenote: In our podcast interview, Tommy promised to book a big trip to Italy for fall. But before we ended our call, he'd delayed the trip to the following year. What did I tell you about Optimizers?

My advice for the Optimizer

- Accept that you love to optimize. That's never going to change, and that's okay! I never tell anyone to stop feeling a certain way. Instead, my approach is to add a new layer to the way you engage with money. Just as you can develop a taste for new foods, you can develop a taste for spending money meaningfully. Hang out with people who are a little more spontaneous. Money behavior is contagious. If you love to optimize, fine—but now that you're already great at optimization, spend more of your time spending money on things you love.

- Look at the last month. What was meaningful? Chances are, it's people, experiences, even things. Not your boring spreadsheet.

- Take 5 percent of your net income every month and spend it on something fun and nonessential for yourself. You *must* spend this money every month, and you must spend it on yourself—not on anybody else. I know, I know—your brain is screaming, "Ramit, that 5 percent compounded would turn into $100,000!" There are times when I need to gently share a piece of advice called STHU: Shut the Hell Up and spend this money. This is how you learn the skill of spending.

My advice for partners of Optimizers

- Your partner is always going to love the numbers. That's a skill that should be appreciated and praised, because mastering the numbers is a key part of a Rich Life. When you compliment them on this skill, they'll love it.

- Develop the ability to gently redirect them to other areas of a Rich Life. Ask them to articulate how much is "enough." Then ask them why. Help them understand that a Rich Life is lived outside the spreadsheet by recalling your favorite times of the last 12 months (none of which were sitting in front of a computer). Ask what it would feel like to do more of those this year and enlist their help to plan for it. If you want help guiding these conversations or meeting people in similar situations, I recommend joining my Money Coaching program.

- Create specific times when you can talk about the numbers— which will "scratch their optimization itch"—but also be clear about other times when you want to talk about financial topics other than the numbers, like dreaming about your Rich Life.

THE WORRIER

For the Worrier, money conversations are almost always negative. They worry about running out of money. They worry about how much they spent over the weekend. After a while, they worry about why they worry so much!

Sometimes, Worriers have a real reason to be concerned: They might genuinely be in a bad situation. Often, they learned to worry through family history, such as a parent losing a job. So their feelings about money are understandable; they're trying to be responsible and fend off trouble. But even when Worriers have more than enough money—even millions of dollars—they rarely stop worrying. The way they feel about money is highly uncorrelated to the amount in the bank, and Worriers seem to find a sense of control in stressing out over money.

Common behaviors: Lying awake at night playing out worst-case scenarios; catastrophizing over small expenses; digging up old issues; logging in to accounts daily (they don't automate their bills so they have to sign in to pay each one).

Favorite phrases:
- "What if . . . we both lose our jobs?"
   . . . the market never bounces back?"
   . . . our home loses value?"
   . . . the sky falls?!"

What you're losing by being a Worrier: Because Worriers tend to spend more time thinking about what can go wrong than what can go right, they're playing life on defense. Each time a Worrier gives in to worry, they deepen the grooves. The worries are often insatiable black holes because they're based on feelings, not a number—or anything fixable! Worriers live a smaller life than they have to, focusing only on what can go wrong.

What it's like to be married to a Worrier: Often, it's a bummer. Every time money comes up, the conversation centers on the Worrier's fears. No teamwork, no dreaming—just one partner trying to reassure the other. Even for couples who have a lot of money, these conversations are exhausting.

Inside the mind of a Worrier: Amy's worldview is threaded through with worry. She and her husband, Andre, have legitimate concerns about their finances. But in episode #62, when I ask Andre to describe their money conversations, he says, "It's like . . . the storm is coming—better go get some water and batteries!" During our session, I ask Amy, "If we solved all your financial problems today and you were debt-free tomorrow, how would you feel?" Amy says, "To be honest, I have no idea. I've never been debt-free. I *think* I would feel a little bit lighter. But then I would probably be stressed out because I wouldn't know what to do next."

Amy's answer is revealing. She has likely worried about money every day for the last 20 years. Yet when I ask how she would feel if all her debt were gone, she has no idea. Worriers find it inconceivable to think of a life without worrying. They've rarely considered why they worry—or what it would be like to stop worrying—because they don't know any other way. And for some, worrying has become their identity.

My advice for Worriers

- Ask yourself, *What do I get out of worrying?* (Remember, you get something out of it or you wouldn't do it.) *Does it make me feel in control? Do I feel comforted when I worry? Do I associate "worrying" with "caring" or "being prepared"? Who would I be if I didn't worry as much?*

- Play out a worst-case scenario. Say you miss a credit card payment. What's the worst that can happen? A $50 late fee, some interest, and your credit score goes down for two months? In the grand scheme of life, it's irritating but not the end of the world. Now, what's the worst that can happen if you *keep worrying about money forever*? Your spouse stops talking to you about money, you drift apart, and then . . . divorce or death. Which one is more important to tackle?

- Think about how your worrying affects your partner: Do they even talk about their dreams anymore? What if this dynamic continues for the next 30 years? Also, what are your kids learning from watching you worry about money?

- What's an area of life where you feel confident, competent, and decisive? Worriers always have at least one area where they feel comfortable (it's often parenting or their job). Ask yourself, *What does it feel like when I'm in that role? Why don't I worry as much in these moments?* Now, apply that same feeling to money: *What would it feel like if I were as capable with money as I am in that other part of life?*

- Put a box around certain worries, like paying for groceries or the price of coffee. Make this process ceremonial. Say, "I'm not going to worry about these things anymore." Write them on a piece of paper and then burn the paper. (Start with small items, then grow your box over time to encompass larger items like eating out, vacations, and even retirement.)

My advice for partners of Worriers

- Good news! Worriers can change. The key is to understand that they will always worry, but you can help them add another dimension to their relationship with money: confidence, competence, curiosity—even excitement! Here's what won't work: telling them to stop worrying, showing them a bunch of numbers on a spreadsheet, or reassuring them that "it will be okay." My advice is to understand on a deep level what they're worried about. Sometimes, they do have a legitimate reason to be worried (and that reason might actually be you!). Other times, they're worrying because that's the only way they know how to relate to money. Often, Worriers can't even articulate why they're worried, but with time and patience, they can come to express what they're feeling and why—which is the first step toward change.
- Once you both know why they worry, you can ask them what would make them feel better and figure out small steps to get there. (Note: Everyone thinks they'll stop worrying at some point in the future—usually when they have $50,000 or $100,000 more—but that never happens.) Worriers change when they have skin in the game (for example, they manage part of the family finances), when they're educated about money, and when their finances are extremely simple so they can understand them.

THE DREAMER

Dreamers use magical thinking when it comes to money. Something is always "coming soon" that will pan out and change their financial situation. You'll often see Dreamers falling for get-rich-quick schemes—time-shares, crypto, multi-level marketing, and dubious passive-income businesses. Dreamers can be optimistic and motivating: *If you just stick with me, this one's going to hit, and we're going to be able to pay off all that debt.* But by avoiding reality, they're forcing someone else to carry their weight. They constantly reiterate that "it will all work out," and they disdain people who follow traditional paths like a nine-to-five job. They might use pejorative phrases to describe other people—even those who are more financially stable!—by saying they're "trading time for money."

The key to Dreamers' magical thinking is that they're insulated from reality. (On my Netflix show, for instance, Frank and Nathalie were Dreamers, always seeking the next deal, and it was challenging to explain to them that most wealth is created by managing costs and slow, automatic investing.) Dreamers face no real consequences, which allows them to continue their beliefs—even as they fail to make consistent income. They are often with a partner who's responsible and handles the finances, which enables the Dreamer to continue being completely unrealistic. Not surprisingly, I've seen many Dreamer/Worrier couples.

Common behaviors: Carrying a balance on credit cards; borrowing from family and friends; secret spending; investing in get-rich-quick schemes; reading Robert Kiyosaki and Grant Cardone.

Favorite phrases:
- "It's going to be fine! It always is."
- "The universe will provide."
- "I just know I can't work a nine-to-five."
- "I just need to [insert highly complicated set of actions, each contingent on the other, that must all happen sequentially,

which the person has never successfully completed] and then we'll be good."
- "Why don't you trust me?"

What you're losing by being a Dreamer: Short term, it's actually great! Why bother paying attention to all this stuff if you don't have to? But long term, being a Dreamer can devastate a relationship. A Dreamer can exist only because someone else is carrying the load. If they had a radical change in life circumstances—like divorce or a layoff—they wouldn't be able to continue their usual pattern, and their house of cards would collapse.

What it's like being married to a Dreamer: It's incredibly stressful, because Dreamers aren't functioning as financial teammates. The non-Dreamer must become the voice of reality and therefore comes off as negative and nagging. Partners of Dreamers often describe themselves as parenting a child. It's frustrating, it's unromantic, and it's infantilizing for the Dreamer.

Inside the mind of a Dreamer: David's complicated relationship with money began in childhood, when his mom was "always worried about money, money, money." By the time he was 17, he told me on episode #82, "I just was like, 'F*ck money, man. I'm not even gonna care about this at all.'" David, now 45, chose to ignore money, believing it would all work out in the end. He continually paid the minimum on his credit card debt, having no idea that a 26 percent interest rate would essentially keep him in debt forever. His wife, Melody, 39, wrote, "What do you do if your partner is self-employed but overwhelmed and not booking work, over $20K in credit card debt, and not open to money talk 'until he's out of debt,' but has no plan for when that will be because 'we have time' and he's 'happy with where he's at' and you pay for everything?"

My advice for Dreamers

- I have no advice, because you're not reading this book.

My advice for partners of Dreamers

- In my experience, Dreamers change only if their partner radically alters their approach. Dreamers need a true wake-up call. I recommend you carefully illustrate—in a format they understand—where the current financial trajectory will take you as a couple. Make them understand how this affects *them*, their day-to-day life, and your relationship. Then spell out your expectations and the boundaries you're setting. For example, rather than having yet another conversation where you ask them why they do the things they do and desperately try to understand their perspective . . . don't. Instead, decide what you need from them, tell them, and be crystal clear about what will happen if they do (or don't) deliver.

- Only you can decide how far you want to go. But let me put it this way: If you left town for six months, a Dreamer would figure it out . . . or they would crash. If you truly want your Dreamer partner to change, you must make it clear that you won't be picking up the slack anymore. If they're forced to fend for themselves, most Dreamers will do what needs to be done.

- One last thing: This is extremely difficult and very advanced. Conversations like these involve understanding yourself, setting boundaries, and navigating a complicated dynamic. I highly recommend talking to a therapist to help guide your conversation.

Building a Healthy Relationship with Money

We frequently hear about having a healthy relationship with food, but rarely do we discuss cultivating a healthy relationship with money. If anything, we're told that money is a series of dry numbers and ratios that nobody wants to learn about. But I believe a healthy relationship with money involves having an exciting vision, being flexible enough to accommodate life's changes, and talking about money regularly.

In the next chapter, you'll learn how to create that exciting vision with your partner. This is a skill that none of us is taught but is incredibly powerful. Later in the book, you'll learn how your plan can accommodate life's changes. Over time, you'll discover that you're building a healthier relationship together, which feels *good*.

You can work on this individually for now. It may take time to get your partner fully on board, which is completely normal. That's what this whole book is about! If you feel scared, lost, or confused, take a step back and remind yourself that you deserve a Rich Life with your partner. Trust the process as we continue this journey together.

Chapter 2 Checklist

❑ Look over the invisible scripts on page 23 and choose the ones that resonate for you. Then answer the questions on page 26.

❑ Talk with your partner about money beliefs from childhood. Review the examples starting on page 28. Listen as much as you talk!

❑ Do you see yourself in any of the four Money Types? Do you see your partner? What does understanding these Money Types tell you about how you approach money in your relationship?

❑ What's one change you want to make in your money behavior after reading this chapter? What action can you take this week to launch that change?

DESIGNING YOUR RICH LIFE VISION— TOGETHER

*How to get on the same page with money
(even if you see it differently)*

When I ask people, "What's your Rich Life?" about 95 percent of them give me the same answer: "I want to be able to do what I want when I want."

Deep down, I want to say, *Oh no, not this answer again.* But in my head, I hear myself saying, *Be professional, Ramit,* so I reply, "Wow, that's interesting. Out of curiosity, what *do* you want?"

One hundred percent of the time, I get a blank stare back.

That's because most people have never been asked this question. We've never thought about what our Rich Life would be. We've only been taught to pay bills and feel bad about money!

I'm inviting you to think about your Rich Life right now. Why do you work so hard? What do you get to *do* with your money? What's the point of it all?

This is a different muscle from worrying about paying your credit card bill every month or whether you'll have enough to help your kids with college. It's also different from spending on whatever random item you see at the store. This is taking a deep breath and thinking about how you really want to spend your money—in beautifully personal, important, meaningful ways. It's like the difference between picking a color to paint the walls and designing the plans for a new house.

Bring your partner along and let's have some fun. This chapter is all about getting specific about how you want to use your money, and by the end of it, you're going to have an incredibly crisp vision of your shared Rich Life.

The Rich Life Vision Process

As kids, we used to dream about money. *One day, I'll be able to buy all the candy I want! One day, I'll buy a super-fast sports car! One day, I'll go shopping without even looking at the price!*

But as adults, we lose that ability to dream with our money. Decades later, we find ourselves approaching life as a series of transactional decisions: *Should I take the bus or a cab? How are we going to pay for back-to-school supplies? Can we afford that vacation? Ugh.*

These questions are exhausting, and worse, there's no joy, no fun, no adventure. It's just one decision after another—each one forcing us to play small. When you're deciding on the 100th financial transaction of the month, do you actually have any idea how it will affect your finances? Of course not!

The process of designing a Rich Life vision lets you zoom out and dream together about the big things: Where do we want to live? How and where do we want to travel? Are kids part of our Rich Life? If so, how do we want to raise them? Your vision will be personal and inspiring, and in some cases, extravagant. And it's the crucial first step in transforming your relationship around money.

There are just two rules.

Rule #1: Be specific, vivid, and personal.

Avoid vague phrases like "We want to travel!" Instead, lean into vivid specifics: "We want to go to Tuscany and sip Chianti while watching the sun set over the olive groves." Then get even more specific: Exactly when do you want to go? How long will you stay? What seats will you have on the plane? What will you be wearing and eating? Hotel or Airbnb? What do you *not* want to see? (Personally, I'm fine skipping most monuments.) What will you do on your first day? Talk through it, from breakfast to bedtime.

In fact, what would elevate this trip from "nice" to *magical*? Spend a lot of time on this one. If you do this right, your answers should be different from any other couple's, because they represent your unique relationship.

Rule #2: Live a Rich Life today and a richer life tomorrow.

Here is a key fear for people as they start thinking about making a plan for their money: "So I have to wait until I'm 65 before I can have any fun?" No! I don't believe in waiting until "someday" to start living your Rich Life. As you brainstorm what's meaningful to you, focus on the future, of course—but also consider how to elevate your daily life starting today. What could you do to infuse your world with things that make you irrationally happy? Many people find that buying back their time gives them joy. Others want their house to smell good, or to have a new pair of sheets, or to get a fresh bouquet of flowers delivered every week. As you design your vision, remember to include large, bucket-list items and everyday things that make you happy.

There's a financial component to this, of course, but in my experience, when couples work through the nuts and bolts that we'll cover later in the book, they often realize that with a few key changes, they'll have more money than they thought. Because most people have never run the numbers, this leaves them stunned. If all you've known with money is anxiety and worry, it can be hard to dream. That's exactly why you're reading this chapter right now.

So trust the process. You're about to learn a new way of talking and thinking about money. Let's do it.

4 Steps to Your Rich Life Vision

The good news is you can create a solid vision in four steps.

The even better news is that creating this vision will bring you and your partner closer together.

I know creating a "vision of money" can seem silly. "Why are we talking about a 'Rich Life vision' when we really just need to pay our credit card bill?" It's tempting to stay down in the weeds as if the weeds will save you. But you've been in the weeds for a long time. Maybe it's time to try another approach.

So here's what I want you to do: Take $100 and put it toward your first Rich Life vision conversation. Use the money any way you want—but decide together. It could be for a babysitter, it could be for drinks at your favorite brewery, or it could be for Sunday brunch after the gym. Pick a fun setting. The perfect time to talk about your Rich Life vision is when you're both relaxed and happy—and not in your normal day-to-day environment.

Using the following activities, you're going to ask each other questions and get into vivid detail. If you like to eat out, I want you to compile your list of dream restaurants. If health and wellness are important to you, are you hiring a personal trainer twice a week? Taking a 30-minute walk with your son every afternoon? Describe exactly what your Rich Life looks like for you both.

Treat this with an open mind, even if you think you know exactly what your partner is going to say. One of the most beautiful moments in a long-term relationship is discovering you still have things to learn about your partner. Support each other here—don't criticize, negate, negotiate, or minimize. Get genuinely curious. Joke around. Tease each other playfully. If you're having fun, you're doing it right.

ACTIVITY #1: RICH LIFE FILL-IN-THE-BLANKS

Your Rich Life vision is all about going beyond generalities into the detailed specifics. That's what this exercise is for. Whether you're working on this solo or with your partner, this is a great way to start. Ask yourself or each other these questions. Grab a pen and fill in the blanks.

I wish we could spend more money on _____

_____.

[foods, things for the house, kids' activities, travel, convenience, wellness . . . Be specific!]

My dream vacation is _____.

If I could hire a coach for anything, it would be for _____

_____.

I'd like to buy _____ for _____.

                          [what]   *[person]*

If I had \$100 to improve my life, I would get _____.

If I had \$1,000 to improve my life, I would get _____.

I'd like us to live in _____ in _____.

                              [where]   *[what type of home]*

Wouldn't it be cool if we did _____ together?

I just don't care that much about _____.

I feel irrationally happy when I'm doing _____

                                                [what activity]

with _____.

                                    [what person]

Keep going!

In my Rich Life, I would wake up at _____.

I would shop for food at _____ and clothes at _____.

I would spend more time with _____.

I would exercise _____.
[how, where, and when]

I would have _____ for a weekday lunch.

Our home would smell of _____ when we step inside.

If we had a magic wand, I would _____ with our money.
[change/spend more on/spend less on]

Dreaming like this might not come naturally at first. Your mind might wander. You might even find yourselves itching to finish this so you can get back to fixing your money problems. Please remember that money should feel good, and going through these exercises is one of the first steps to take together. Stick with it!

ACTIVITY #2:
WHAT MAKES YOU IRRATIONALLY HAPPY?

I really, really love appetizers. When I was a kid, we couldn't afford them, so today, ordering anything I want at a restaurant feels like an incredible splurge. A simple $12 appetizer shouldn't make me this happy, but because of my childhood experience, I feel truly rich when I'm able to order anything on the menu. We all have something that makes us irrationally happy like this. In this activity, I want you to identify yours, which you'll use in your Rich Life vision.

Real Couples on What Makes Them Irrationally Happy

I asked my readers how they use money to feel happier. Here are some of my favorite responses:

» "Outsourcing our laundry to a wash-and-fold service. Best decision EVER."

» "Giving a 50 percent tip to the guy who cuts our lawn."

» "Going to live sports with my kids."

» "Paying a local rancher to stock my freezer with beef."

» "Houseplants. Choosing each one and bringing it home is such a treat. Weekly ritual of watering them feels like a little hug."

» "New music. In the age of streaming it feels great to actually own an album that you can rinse and repeat until the wheels fall off."

» "Breakfast burrito and nitro cold brew every Friday. It's a way to congratulate myself at the end of every week."

» "Going to the spa monthly. It helps me feel taken care of. I'd rather spend monthly on a spa visit than on an expensive item. If I had my salary cut, I would get rid of some of my subscriptions and other expenses just so I could go to the spa once a month."

» "Buying fabric makes me irrationally happy, thinking of the clothes I'm going to make—whether or not actual making takes place."

» "Craft supplies for my daughter—it gives us experiences of creativity together."

» "A pedicure every five to six weeks. Necessary? No. But feeling that one part of my life is put together when I look at my toes makes it worth it."

Below are broad categories meant to prompt extremely specific responses. Sure, you like eating out, but give me details ("going to our favorite restaurant with our best friends once a month" or "ordering in from the Italian place on a Friday after work"). Use these categories as conversation-starters. If you get stuck, just add this question to the end of any category: "Like what?"

What makes you irrationally happy?

- Eating out
- Travel
- Health, fitness, wellness
- Your kids
- Family activities
- Home and furniture
- Clothing
- Car

- Live shows
- Time in nature
- Convenience
- Learning
- Gifts/generosity
- Luxury experiences
- Charity
- Self-improvement

Not every category will spark something in you. These are just reminders. Vary the scale. Items can be as small as adding guacamole to your Chipotle order or as big as custom-designing a house.

ACTIVITY #3: DESIGN A PERFECT DAY

Remember, a Rich Life is lived today *and* tomorrow. So zoom in on one day next week—it could be a weekend, weekday, whatever you want—and craft "the perfect day." Think about how you want to wake up, what you want to see in the kitchen, if you want to walk the dog in the afternoon, what you want to eat, what the weather is like, which companions you might spend time with, what you're wearing, how much you're spending, and how you feel. This exercise is especially helpful for people who love to plan for the future because it helps you live in the present.

The perfect day for yourself

Morning: _____

Afternoon: _____

Evening: _____

The perfect day for your partner

Morning: _____

Afternoon: _____

Evening: _____

The perfect day for the two of you as a couple

Morning: _____

Afternoon: _____

Evening: _____

What are you *not* doing as part of your perfect day? Check all the activities that apply.

- ❏ Laundry
- ❏ Cleaning
- ❏ Dishes
- ❏ Commuting
- ❏ Home maintenance
- ❏ Errands
- ❏ Paying bills
- ❏ Reading Ramit's newsletter at iwt.com
- ❏ *Add your own.*

ACTIVITY #4:
ZOOM OUT AND WRITE YOUR 10-YEAR BUCKET LIST

One of my favorite ways to design your Rich Life is the 10-Year Bucket List—with a twist. You're going to create a fun list, and *then you're going to make one of the items happen.* Let's do it right now.

Ask yourselves, "What do we want to do in the next 10 years that would make the next decade incredibly meaningful and rich?" Dream big. Think "once-in-a-lifetime trip" or "special car" or "incredible annual family reunion." If you've written "Nice dinner out" on your list, you're thinking too small.

Some of your ideas might be for you alone. When I sat down with my wife, Cassandra, to do this exercise, one of my items was "Write a book in a beautiful hotel" (which is the very book you're reading right now—I wrote part of it at my favorite hotel in Kyoto). Other ideas will be for the two of you together. I like the 10-year time frame because it's long enough to think of meaningful items but short enough that you can get started now. Here's how to do it.

Sit together and write separately on individual pieces of paper (10 minutes). Jot down five items on your 10-Year Bucket List. Then take turns sharing your ideas, one at a time. When I did this exercise with Cassandra, we got curious about each other's answers: "You want to learn Spanish? Would you want to learn it online? Or are you thinking of going to Mexico City for a language immersion class?" Have fun with this. Tease or joke around with each other. "Skydiving? That sounds fun, but you might have to do that one on your own. I'll meet you at the bottom with a drink!" Keep the tone playful. You might even discover something you never knew about your partner's dreams: *Wow! I had no idea they wanted to do that.*

Pick one response that's meaningful to you both (10 minutes). The idea should be exciting and inspiring. It should feel big—maybe even uncomfortably big—but also achievable. In our case, Cassandra and I both got excited about having a 10-year wedding anniversary abroad. We love any excuse to celebrate with our friends and family, and because we knew we had years to plan it, we could do something really spectacular. Go back and forth and share ideas. Just remember that the point of this activity is to connect with each other.

Schedule it (3 minutes). Start by choosing *when* you want to do the activity. Be specific, down to the month and year. If you're thinking of taking a vacation with kids, for example, you probably know it's going to be during a school break. If you're not sure when, use your best judgment—but pick a month and year.

Estimate the cost (10 minutes). We're looking for rough calculations: If the item you're working with is a trip, for instance, jot down the major expenses (airfare, hotel, food, shopping), then add 30 percent to account for taxes and unexpected costs. You can Google the airfare if you want to, but don't get too hung up.

We had a funny experience when we tried to calculate the cost for our tenth wedding anniversary. On separate pieces of paper, we spent a few minutes coming up with a number. Separately, we jotted down how many people we wanted to invite and a very unscientific guess on how much it would cost for the event space, the planner, food, clothes, and travel for our family. Then we showed each other our numbers . . . which were wildly different. Mine was about three times larger than hers. We looked at each other with wide eyes. (What can I say? I like nice things and I want to spend a lot of money on moments in our relationship that we'll never forget.)

My suggestion here: If you've got two disparate numbers, go with the larger one. Why? Because it lets you dream bigger, and you can always get more precise with your plans later.

Build the system to ensure your Bucket List item happens—guaranteed (10 minutes). You know *what* you want to do, you know *when* it's going to happen, and you know *how much* it costs. Now let's make it happen.

Take the total cost and divide it by the number of months until the event. For example:

What: Family Vacation to Argentina
When: Five years from now (60 months)
Cost: $10,000
Amount to save each month: $167 ($10,000/60)

If your monthly number looks too high, don't worry—you have options. In the example above, you could stretch out the timeline by a year, which would mean you'd have to save only $139 per month. You could also cut back on other areas of your expenses. Or you could simply shrink the scope of your idea from $10,000 to $8,000, which would mean you'd have to save $133 per month.

In our case, we were seven years out from the event—or 84 months—so we divided our estimate by 84 and then set up an automatic monthly transfer to a savings account called "10-Year Wedding Anniversary."

What Our Rich Life Trip to Japan Looked Like

A few years ago, Cassandra and I wanted to visit Japan. I love coffee, she loves cosmetics, and we both love design, so we spent a lot of time planning the trip beforehand. Our custom itinerary was full of the things we enjoy—with lots of leisure time built in. (One of our rules when we travel is one big event every two days. The rest of the time, we can wander, eat, relax, or just do nothing.) In Tokyo, we hired a guide for a coffee tour, then hit a couple of special Japanese cosmetics stores that Cassandra had pinned. In Kyoto, we hired a guide who took us to the beautiful home of two architects who taught us about Japanese architecture. We made reservations at a few restaurants but otherwise ate at random places we stumbled upon. At the end of the vacation, we took a special cruise on a floating ryokan for a few quiet days to relax and plan our year ahead. This trip might sound boring or weird to you. That's okay! For us, it was just perfect. I want you to think about your own Rich Life experiences this way— super-specific, vivid, and full of pure joy for *you.*

Here are sample numbers:
What: 10-Year Wedding Anniversary
When: Seven years from now (84 months)
Cost: $25,000
Amount to save each month: about $300 ($25,000/84)

What I love about this is that you're taking real steps to make your Rich Life happen. It's simply a matter of time now: Because of the system you built, where you're automatically saving money in an account, you know that every single month you're getting closer to making your dream a reality.

Give yourselves a high five! You've gone from *We don't even know what our Rich Life is* to having a list of really important things that would make the next 10 years truly meaningful. And every month, when you talk about your finances, you can check in on this goal and see your progress.

If you enjoyed this exercise, get a copy of *I Will Teach You to Be Rich: The Journal*, where both of you can go into even more detail about your Rich Life vision and then compare your responses.

Getting Past the Obstacles

I get a lot of pushback on the idea of having these Rich Life conversations, which can seem contrived or simplistic, especially if your partner isn't on board. Here are the objections I hear most often, along with my responses.

Obstacle: "We're too stressed out right now. We need to fix our finances first. Then we can dream."

Of course, a Rich Life vision is easier if you have lots of money. But a Rich Life isn't necessarily about luxury. I'm very fortunate that I was raised by immigrant parents who were frugal by necessity. That taught me I didn't *need* lots of things. I can't remember ever going on a plane all together, because we couldn't afford it. Our vacations were road trips in our minivan from Northern California to Southern California, where we stayed with family.

I share this because in my early twenties, my Rich Life vision was being able to order appetizers (remember I told you how much I love them?). That's all! Then it expanded to being able to take a taxi on a hot summer day instead of the sweltering subway. Next it was being able to buy a round of drinks for my friends when we were out. As my financial abilities grew, so did my vision.

Your vision is important because you need a reason for working beyond mere survival. You might not be able to afford the dream vacation today, but by writing down specific details, you give yourself a North Star to work toward—a reason you're working so hard.

Obstacle: "This is overkill. We're simple people. All we want is to pay our debts and not worry about money all the time."

I want more for you than just not worrying. And frankly, being debt-free is not that powerful a vision! I've noticed that people in debt are often afraid of dreaming about their Rich Life because if they put it down on paper and *don't* achieve it, they feel like a failure. I want to encourage you to put that fear aside and build confidence in knowing you can follow through, even if it takes time. Designing a Rich Life vision is the first step in getting away from the distracting $3 questions and into the $30,000 questions that can truly change your life (your savings rate, your asset allocation, your debt-payoff date).

Obstacle: "Our Rich Life is to make sure our kids have everything we didn't."

I don't love this reasoning. A Rich Life is not simply abandoning your own dreams and giving everything you have to your kids. More importantly, this type of thinking is lazy. Quite candidly, it's lazy to give no effort to your own Rich Life and what your partner wants. Trust me, they have very specific things they'd love to do, if only you connected with them in a way that was safe, nonjudgmental, and aspirational. Finally, your kids don't want to see their parents living a joyless life where you model being a financial martyr by sacrificing all your individual desires. I told my parents that I want them to spend every last cent they have. They gave my siblings and me a Rich Life through their love, values, and a good work ethic. Their money is theirs to enjoy. (As I write this, they're on a trip to Mexico City. Seeing my parents enjoying their lives and spending their money makes me so happy!)

Obstacle: "What's the point of writing down a vision? We need tactics, not dreams."

Yeah, it's true—you do need tactics. And we'll get to them. But for now, trust the process. Trust that we will get to talking about your savings rate (Chapter 7), how to pay off your debt (page 231), and how to teach your children about money (page 255). Right now, the most important thing is for you two to get on the same page—building a foundation together—which will make the rest of your conversations much easier. If tactics alone were going to change things, you would have found them already.

What a Rich Life *Isn't*

Most of us dream too small, so I've spent a lot of time in this chapter encouraging you to think bigger. But some people misconstrue my advice as "You can buy anything at any time if it's part of your Rich Life." *No.*

For example, when I point out that some guy who earns $60,000 per year and drives six miles on flat, paved roads to his job shouldn't be buying a $90,000 truck, I always get comments like "Maybe that's just part of his Rich Life!" Let's get one thing straight: You can't just point at something you want, spin around three times chanting,

"Rich Life, Rich Life, Rich Life!" and then buy it with my blessing. That's not how it works.

Your Rich Life has to be something you can afford. It might take years to save for it, but you must be able to afford it, either now or after setting a realistic savings goal. I know you understand

Permission to Dream—Granted!

I was struck by something that Alyssa—who, with her husband, Ilan, was on the very first episode of my podcast— said: "I never felt comfortable to *want* in my life."

That's a pretty deep insight—and it's a sentiment I've heard from a lot of people. Alyssa explained that growing up middle class, she had everything she needed, "so I never thought I needed more. I never imagined having an extravagant life. I always imagined just having basic stuff. And for me, basic means a decent car and a decent home, like a 1,500-square-foot house."

Alyssa lost her job, then started selling baked goods on Facebook. Now she and Ilan have a baking business that provides enough income to support them both and continues to grow. But when I prompted Alyssa to dream big, she was stuck.

Turns out Alyssa grew up with an alcoholic father: "His needs were always the most important in the family, and we had to kind of work around what he wanted. *I grew up accepting what came to me.* I think that's what it really comes down to."

This is a common way of thinking and a common roadblock to dreaming up a Rich Life. It can take time and a gentle push to give yourself permission to dream beyond your current circumstances or lifestyle. After careful consideration, Alyssa told me, "I started thinking, *Maybe I can want that. I'm allowed to want.*"

intuitively what I mean, because if your friend said, "My Rich Life is buying a private jet," you'd roll your eyes.

Your Rich Life is *not* . . .

- something you buy but cannot actually afford (see page 155).

- something that's so big, you can never reasonably achieve it even with years of saving, thereby setting yourself up to never actually feel accomplished (such as in episode #25 of my podcast, where a doorman told me he wanted to be a billionaire).

- something you unconsciously spend considerable time and money on, doing it because everyone else does it, without ever examining whether *you* want it.

Be honest in choosing your Rich Life. Don't set yourself up for failure. I want you to dream in that sweet spot where things are aspirational but achievable. And if it's truly part of your Rich Life but you can't afford it today, add a savings goal and put money aside until you can. That's how you land on a vision that continues to inspire you.

"My Partner and I Don't See Eye to Eye on Our Rich Life Vision. Are We Doomed?"

No! You don't have to agree on everything when it comes to money. In fact, you and your partner will *always* have major differences in your approach to your finances—and that's okay. Once you realize that, it's immensely freeing, because now you can sort through what you *do* agree on.

Yes, you should agree on big things, like where to live. But even if one of you wants to have a ski chalet someday, and the other wants a farm, that's fine. Write it down. At some point, you'll say, "Let's talk about the numbers and what that lifestyle will look like." It's possible you could figure out a way to have both. You might rent the chalet for a week or two ... or you may change your mind when you learn what it really means to take care of sheep.

Here's a good example: I worked with a couple, Lauren and Alex, on episode #23 of my podcast. Lauren was was extremely focused on owning a beach house as quickly as possible. She was anxious about it and resented the cost of maintaining their current home, which required lots of repairs—every dollar spent today felt like a dollar she couldn't put toward her beach house. "[Money] feels like water just going through my hands, and I feel like time is running out," she said.

I was curious about this beach house. Where did her dream come from? Why a beach house in particular? Lauren told me that the house was about creating memories with family more than owning property. She admitted she was anxious about her parents getting old before she had the chance to host this family time that she imagined so vividly. But as I gently pushed, she acknowledged that she didn't need to *buy* a second home to do that. She could rent a house for beach weekends and live her dream right away—now!—instead of 15 years in the future.

Lauren resisted this idea for most of our conversation. I wasn't surprised. Often, we operate on scripts that were created decades ago, and we don't challenge or investigate them. But if we ask a few questions, we might discover creative and realistic ways to achieve our goals.

Your Rich Life might take an unpredictable path. By going through the process in this chapter and asking what you each *really* want, you can design a vision that fits you both and brings you closer together.

●　●　●

Chapter 3 Checklist

❑ Do the four Rich Life vision activities (pages 51 to 59) with your partner (or on your own).

❑ Zoom in on the "perfect day" exercise from page 54. Select one activity from your list that you can do within the week, even if it's not in the location of your perfect day.

❑ Make sure you completed the planning exercise in the 10-Year Bucket List—you've selected an activity, scheduled it, estimated the cost, and started automatically saving for it.

❑ Find a special place to post your 10-Year Bucket List so you can see it every day. It could be on your phone's background, your fridge, even a sticky note on your laptop. If you look at it and get excited, you're on the right path.

MONEY DIALS

*How to spend more—a lot more!—
on the things you love and less on
the things you don't*

In the last chapter, you sketched out your shared vision of a Rich Life. Fantastic! But if I asked you and your partner to take your Rich Life vision and turn it into a plan, would you know what to do? Most people wouldn't—yet. That's because developing a powerful vision is a first step, but the next is connecting that vision to your actual spending.

In this chapter, I'm going to give you a new way of looking at your spending. Nope, not the same old restrictive advice that tells you to track your expenses down to the penny, then cut back on everything. Instead, here's my approach:

I believe you should spend extravagantly on the things you love, as long as you cut costs mercilessly on the things you don't.

What do you and your partner love to spend money on? I don't mean what you "like" to spend money on. I mean *love*. Have you ever really thought about it? If you had $25,000 right now (assume, for the moment, that you were debt-free), what would you do with it? Your answer is what I call a "Yes" Money Dial.

Now if I asked you what areas of spending you don't care about as much and are willing to cut—maybe it's clothing or international travel or fancy restaurants—that would be a "Less" Money Dial. I call them Money Dials because you can "turn the dial" up or down just like turning a radio knob to adjust the volume. Knowing your Dials helps transform your spending, because once you identify them, you can spend lavishly on the things you love, as long as you cut costs ruthlessly on the things you don't.

Let's start with your Yes Dials—I want you to begin by knowing where you can spend more. Every one of us has at least one Yes Dial, and we all intuitively know what it is.

Here are the most common Yes Dials, in order:

1. Eating out/food

2. Travel

3. Health and wellness

After those three, there are many more, including convenience, relationships, and self-improvement. Conversely, there are things we spend money on that we don't care about as much—for some, it could be technology or self-care or home improvements.

This idea that it's okay to spend money on things you love is radically different from most of the money advice we've heard, which always focuses on restriction. *No more cappuccinos! No more vacations! No, no, no.* It makes us feel bad, it makes us play small, and it's judgmental by definition. What's the point of cutting back on the things we love until 60 years in the future when we're too old to enjoy them, anyway?

Money is meant to be spent in a meaningful way. We're going to use this approach to identify what you love spending money on. Once you're crystal clear, we'll talk about adjusting your spending to match your vision. Bear in mind that in relationships, sometimes you have the same Money Dials as your partner, and sometimes they're different. Either way is okay.

Together with your partner, circle on the next page all the categories where you love to spend money.

- Eating out/food
- Travel
- Health, wellness, and fitness
- Your kids (Get specific: Is it kids' activities, kids' clothes, or childcare?)
- Family activities
- Live shows
- Convenience
- Home improvement
- Gifts
- Personal relationships (for example, time and experiences with loved ones)
- Luxury experiences
- Charitable donations
- Status items
- Self-improvement (for example, self-development and coaching)
- *Add your own.*

Now put a big star next to the Yes Dial that you love most. Ask your partner to do the same, and don't worry if you have different Yes Dials. (My wife and I do, and many other couples do, too.)

Your "Yes" Dials Are Specific, Vivid, and Joyful

When you identify your positive Money Dials, it's obvious what you love, but it also becomes easy to see what you *don't* care about—and is therefore easy to cut back on—because you have a clear, vivid reason to do so. The reward is right there in front of you: If you cut back on *this*, you can spend more on *that*.

Recently, I asked members of my online community to share examples of spending money that made them truly happy. I received a range of interesting answers.

Here are some of the things they listed:

- *"I did a staycation with my partner."*

- *"I took a surfing lesson."*

- *"I bought my mom a phone for her birthday."*

- *"I got some old vinyl albums."*

- *"I bought a ring for my partner."*

With each of these answers, I pressed for details. People love to talk about their Yes Dials, but because our money culture is based around restriction, we're never really asked to elaborate on what we love spending money on. It feels uncomfortable, like we're bragging. Talking about it, however, reveals our interests and values. I find it fascinating and inspiring; when you get really vivid about what you love, you clarify your Rich Life priorities.

One guy said, "I've always been a collector. Currently I collect high-end military miniatures." Now, that's unusual! I love hearing about different ways people find joy in spending their money. Another person told me she loves paying for a housecleaner and a nanny. I asked her why. She said, "Having a nanny is expensive, but I *love* not having to worry when the kids have a day off at school or when they're sick. We used to stress out about it so much. Now, if they're sick, we can still go to work and know they have a person they love taking wonderful care of them. It's also such a luxury to come back to a clean house. It's worth it to take simpler vacations than we otherwise might."

Relaxation, relief, luxury—these are not words you typically hear in conversations about personal finance, but that's exactly what we're digging for. When you connect your money with the positive emotions in your life, you can proactively use it to design your Rich Life and live it. And the more you clarify what your Rich Life involves, the easier it is to slash spending in areas that *don't* fit.

Spending More on Family

"We live in Minnesota and have been nervously watching
the weather predictions to figure out how they will affect our
Thursday flight to Ohio to visit family for Christmas. Finally,
last night, we realized that we would be so mad if our flight
was canceled and our kids missed the first chance we've
had to have Christmas with their grandparents since 2018.
We have the money. Why are we even spending one second
worrying about this? So we changed our tickets to leave today
instead of Thursday. The change in price was nearly $1,000,
but we were happy to pay. (And their grandparents are
absolutely over the moon.)"   —*Siobhan*

Some people struggle to identify their Yes Dials—"Is it convenience or experiences or relationships? What if it's all of them?" If
this is you, try this trick: Open the photos on your phone and scroll
through them. They are often the best clues to what you've enjoyed.
If you see 340 photos of a single piece of sushi taken from different
angles, your Yes Dial is food.

Quadruple It: A Money Dials Exercise

At an event in Washington, DC, I was talking to a guy named Bill,
whose Yes Dial was eating out. I asked him, "What would happen if
you quadrupled your spending on restaurants? What would it look
and feel like?" He said, "I'd probably have to go on a diet because I'd
be eating out four times a week!"

Ha ha. This is a typical response, one of those G-rated jokes that
people make at professional functions to get a tiny chuckle in polite
conversation. But his answer was, in fact, quite revealing.

Most of us think about money in a linear way: "Spend four times more? I'd do it four times more often!" We automatically think "more spending" equals "more quantity." It's a simple, even childlike, view on the world.

I pushed back on Bill. "Where would you go?"

He thought about it for a second. "I actually keep a list of every Michelin-starred restaurant in the city."

"And who would you take with you?"

He took a long pause. "My family." The room was completely silent. When I asked why, Bill struggled for the words. Finally, his voice cracked: "I'd take them because they could never afford to eat at a place like that."

Bill just moved from a linear understanding of money to a multi-dimensional perspective, in which he's using his money to eat at higher-quality restaurants and generously treating the people he loves.

There's a lot of power in thinking about money this way. Sure, you can do more (quantity). But you can also increase the quality, the experience, and the number of people you bring with you.

Now it's your turn. Pick one of your Yes Dials and imagine turning it way up—quadrupling your spending—multidimensionally. What would it look and feel like? If fitness is your thing, your initial answer might be that you'd take four times as many yoga classes. Go deeper: Instead, it could be getting a private instructor, or even booking that dream yoga retreat—and perhaps treating a friend so they could join you. Challenge yourself to think expansively, not just linearly.

Turning up the dial on travel could mean that you . . .
   . . . stay at nicer hotels.
   . . . go away for longer periods of time.
   . . . add specific experiences, like a safari or a river cruise.
   . . . invite friends and pay for family to come along.

Turning up the dial on learning an instrument could mean that you . . .
   . . . purchase new music for inspiration.
   . . . buy a new instrument.
   . . . attend in-person individual classes.
   . . . go to a weeklong music camp to be around other players.

Spending More on Fitness

"For the past month, I've had a private trainer. . . . He built a program for me, we have biweekly meetings, and I check in via text after every workout. This has been the most consistent I have been with exercise ever. I never realized how important it is to have a support system for fitness. Feeling strong, and grateful for a healthy lifestyle!"

—*Jared*

Same applies for basketball, improv, writing a memoir—anything you love and want to get better at.

Turning up the dial on clothes could mean that you . . .
    . . . shop at higher-end stores.
    . . . subscribe to a virtual styling service.
    . . . rent designer clothes for special occasions.
    . . . hire a personal stylist to introduce you to new labels, cleanse your closet, and refine your look.
    . . . go on a fashion shopping trip with friends.
    . . . take your mom to Paris for a fashion show.

When you think about the different dimensions of money, consider this: At the beginning levels of personal finance, people are almost always preoccupied with "What." *What can I buy? What can I afford? What can I get for my money?*

In my experience, as people become savvier with money, they start to explore more than quantity: They pursue experiences and memories and feelings. Instead of asking "What," they often ask "Who." *Who can I bring with me? Who can I surprise and delight? Who can I be generous with?*

My dream for you is to consider all these different dimensions as you design how you want to spend your money meaningfully.

Talking Money Dials
with Your Partner

One of my all-time favorite speeches is the one Stephen King gave at the 2003 National Book Awards ceremony. He recalled a time early in his career when he and his wife were living in a trailer, struggling to get by. Then he finally sold a book:

> "One of the few times during the early years of our marriage I saw my wife cry really hard was when I told her that a paperback publisher, New American Library, had paid a ton of money for the book she'd rescued from the trash. I could quit teaching; she could quit pushing crullers at Dunkin' Donuts . . . then she put her hands over her face and she wept. When she finally stopped, we went into the living room and sat on our old couch, which Tabby had rescued from a yard sale, and talked into the early hours of the morning about what we were going to do with the money. I've never had a more pleasant conversation. I have never had one that felt more surreal."

I remember the exact room I was in when I had my first real conversation about money with Cassandra. We talked about the kind of life we wanted to have, how often we wanted to travel, if we wanted children, how we wanted to take care of our parents. It was one of my favorite conversations because it was full of possibility.

Although pivotal events like a book deal or marriage can spark these conversations, you don't need anything that formal. Talking about Yes Dials is one of the most fun things you and your partner get to experience together, and you can do it anytime. Here's how to bring this up:

> "I'm reading this book about money psychology. The author talks about figuring out your Money Dials—the things you *love* to spend money on. I think my top one is _____, but I also love _____. What would you say yours is?"

[They answer.]

"Yes! That's what I thought it would be." (Or, "Wow! I'm surprised. I wouldn't have expected that!") "Okay, now, if you could *quadruple* your spending on it, what would you do?"

All I want is for you to get your partner to name *one* Yes Dial and give *one* example of what they'd spend more on. The idea is simply to open the door. Then move on! Sometimes money conversations can be long and detailed, but other times—like this one—they can be short and fun.

I include scripts like this because I want you to have every tool possible to build momentum in talking about money. If they don't feel like you, adapt them for your own style. As a rule, feel free to blame me if things get awkward. You can make me the bad cop, the weird guy, the author with the kooky ideas—whatever!

Later, you can bring up the topic again and pull from the list below. If your partner is into this, take turns asking each other these questions. They're juicy and revealing, and you can have some fun with it:

- Ten years ago, what was something you would have loved to spend money on (but now you wouldn't)?

- What's something you'd love to spend money on now but feel embarrassed to admit?

- If we could spend $250 four times a year to create amazing memories, what would we do?

- What's something that would be easy for you to cut back on? What would be hard?

- What could you buy every week that would make you happy?

- What was our best vacation? What made it feel amazing?

- What do we want to do for an upcoming milestone (the next big birthday or anniversary)?

REAL COUPLES TRY THE MONEY DIALS TALK

Kim, a member of my online community, reports that the Money Dials concept had a huge impact on the way she and her husband communicate about money and priorities. It even resulted in a home purchase.

Kim wrote this note:

Our spending conversations used to go like this:
Me: "I'd really like to update the house—the furniture, lighting..."
Him: "They're fine. It would be a waste of money."
[Discussion over.]

After approaching it differently with the Money Dials concept, it went like this:
Me: "What's really important to you about where we live?"
Him: "I wish I were closer to mountain biking and skiing. That's why we moved here, and it's a bummer to have to drive 60 to 90 minutes for those things."

Flash forward, and we've actually bought a property 5 minutes from biking trails and 40 minutes closer to skiing. I also get my decorating updates, but to him, they're incidental and that's cool. Win-win.

My observation: It's common to get into a dynamic where one person asks the questions and the other shuts it down. That calls for a new approach. Kim did a great job drawing out her husband on his Money Dials through genuine curiosity. I'm sure there's still work to be done on his end to become more communicative about his vision of how he wants to spend money, but they're on the right track.

Rocco, another member of my community, had a different experience when he invited his partner to talk Money Dials:

"It didn't end well. We are quite opposite. She has a home from her previous marriage, and basically that's where her money goes—to the mortgage and maintenance. When I tried to discover her Money Dials, she refused to talk about it. She said she goes to zero every month and doesn't have spare money to reallocate . . . lots of guilt and scarcity feelings appeared, and I had to stop the conversation. I plan to write down *my* Money Dials and show them to her. I'll ask if she can do the same (maybe alone first) and then see if we can look at them together."

My observation: This must be frustrating for Rocco. When one partner is ready to make changes and the other isn't, it can unearth schisms that go far beyond money. I admire that Rocco stepped back and gave his partner room to process the discussion, along with developing a gentler approach moving forward. I have confidence in them both!

Spending More on Convenience

"I'm not much of a handyman, and I don't like doing handyman things. A little while ago I hired someone to come over and put up some shelves and assemble some furniture. Though I probably could have figured it out myself, I wouldn't have done as good a job, and it took pressure off me to do something I don't enjoy. Money well spent!"

—*Trevor*

• • •

Learning How to Spend Money Meaningfully

Do you feel guilty about spending money? Many of us do. In this country, we're caught between the puritanical finger-wagging of financial experts telling us what *not* to spend on and the rampant consumerism pushing SUVs and Bora Bora vacations into our social media feeds. What do we end up doing? We buy—the trip, the car, the house, the clothes— and then we feel guilty about it.

It's the worst of both worlds.

There is a better way. A healthy relationship with money means you replace that guilt with the joy of spending on the things you love. *Spending money meaningfully is a skill.* And talking about Money Dials as a couple will help you get clear about what really matters to you.

Your first step is listening to my personal plea: Please stop agonizing over tiny expenses while ignoring what really matters in your spending. Here's a phrase I've heard from couples thousands of times: "We try to cut back, but nothing seems to change." When I look through their numbers, it's almost always the same pattern. They're trying to cut back a little bit on everything: 5 percent on groceries, 5 percent on gas, 5 percent on eating out, car washes, trips, cable, everything!

This is ineffective and, worse, it's a miserable way to live. This would be like a chef saying, "Something doesn't taste right. Let me cut back on every single ingredient in this dish." No!

The right approach is to look at your big areas of spending and surgically focus there. What are you and your partner willing to cut back on? Not just 5 percent, but a number that gives you the freedom and cash to spend *more* on the things that matter to you?

Your "Less" Dials List

Okay, *now* we can talk about the areas you want to cut back on.

Notice that this is where most money conversations start. But first, we've spent tons of time getting specific and vivid about where you want to spend *more*. Now, with your vision of what spending extravagantly would look and feel like, we're ready to cut costs mercilessly on your Less Dials, the things you don't care about. And remember: We're going to make big changes here.

Go back to your results of the Rich Life exercises you did in the previous chapter. What's *not* on your 10-Year Bucket List or in your perfect day? For example, there might not be a single mention of anything involving eating out four times a week, but if you look at your spending, you'll realize you're eating out a lot. If that's the case, this is a prime area to cut back on. It's not part of your vision—that you both created!—so make a change, cut back, and redirect that money to something that is part of your Rich Life.

You might also discover, for instance, that even though your Rich Life never once mentions resort vacations, you've taken plenty of those, but what you really love is camping and being in nature. Reorient your travel to what truly matters to you. Another common misalignment: Many people are spending a lot on expensive vehicles when their Rich Life vision has no mention of vehicles at all. Cutting back on auto expenses is difficult; you may be locked into payments, and it might not make financial sense to sell. But going forward, think about spending less on your car—for example, holding it a long time without buying a new one—so you can spend more on other areas of life. (More on vehicles on page 246.)

Recognize that dialing back—even on things we don't care about that much—can be really hard. Once we get used to having something (a nice car, beauty treatments, even organic fruit), it's extremely difficult to imagine life without it. In many ways, eliminating certain spending can feel like eliminating a part of your identity.

But to live your Rich Life, you have to make trade-offs. That's what this step is about. And I promise that when you're spending money on your Yes Dials and feeling connected and happy together, you won't be thinking about the expenses you cut.

When you look at your own life for places to dial down your spending, here are three shortcuts:

1. *The biggest opportunities to cut back: housing and cars.* These are the two areas where we unknowingly overspend the most. They are the hardest to change, but if you discover that you're severely overspending, downsizing your housing and vehicles are the biggest levers.

2. *The easiest opportunity to cut back: eating out.* Most of us spend a lot more eating out than we realize. This is often the fastest change that can produce hundreds of extra dollars every month.

3. *Invisible costs add up.* Almost nobody carefully tracks their grocery spend, and usually almost every couple can save

Trade-Off: Car Payments for Convenience

"Growing up, my parents leased their cars and I didn't think anything of it, so I did, too. Of course, I now know better. *(Ramit's comment: Leasing is typically appropriate only if you're wealthy or a business owner who can credibly use the vehicle for business reasons.)* It took a while to figure out the best way to end the cycle. The cheapest way was to buy out the lease on our 2019 Honda CR-V in cash, and that's what we did. Excited to drive it into the ground for 8 to 10 more years and have no car payments. I take excellent care of my car, and it's like a game to me to see how many miles I can get. I have turned up Money Dials, including convenience, in the form of hiring a housekeeper and getting my hair washed and styled every week, à la my grandma." —*Min*

$100–$200 per month by shopping intentionally. Next, take a look at all the subscriptions you've accumulated: Are you actually watching, listening to, reading, and using all of them? Then there are the invisible costs around travel—such as transportation, tips, and taxes—that we rarely account for. Wherever you cut, be sure to redirect that money to something of value to you, such as one of your Yes Dials, paying off debt, saving, or investing.

Remember, your Rich Life is yours! For example, if you saw how much I spend on clothes or travel—it's a lot!—you would be shocked. But my Less Dials list makes it possible. I drive a 19-year-old Honda Accord. I keep my laptop and phone for years. My wife and I rent a small apartment. This strategy keeps our fixed costs low, which in turn allows us to splurge on travel, personal trainers, and convenience.

TALKING WITH YOUR PARTNER ABOUT LESS DIALS

Discussing Less Dials with your partner requires some finesse. Don't come in hot with a list of 18 things you "need" to cut back on. Don't weigh all expenses equally—the three biggest expenses matter more than 10 small ones. Go slow to go fast: Discuss how aggressive you have to be, ask their opinion, and make your decisions together, with the clear reward of being able to increase the volume on your mutual Yes Dials.

A few other tips:

- *Lead with vulnerability.* You might say something like, "Look, I don't know exactly what we should change. But I do know that right now, our finances aren't working. I'm stressed, we don't feel good, and I want us to build what feels good to both of us. I have an idea: Can I start by suggesting something I would cut out of my own spending? Then I'd love to hear what you think." There's power in admitting how you feel about your expenses and making the first move; ultimately it will bring you closer together.

- **Be genuinely curious.** For instance, ask questions like, "Why do you think we keep ordering delivery? I think it's because work has been so hard these days, and by Thursdays we're both tired." Dig deeper: *When* do you spend? What prompts that spending? Often, you'll both be surprised by why you're actually spending money. When you can untangle the psychology, the change is more likely to stick. Treat your spending like I would treat it on my podcast: I would be fascinated, I would be curious, and I'd want you to recalibrate your spending so it's going to the things you value.

- **Think more about the key numbers and less about each individual decision.** If your partner wants to spend $15 on something you disagree with, and you can still hit your numbers, I recommend you *agree enthusiastically*. Your goal is not to "win" each individual spending decision—in fact, you shouldn't be the spending police. Instead, your goal is to hit your numbers in a guilt-free way that you both feel good about.

Same Money Dials, Different Spending Habits

Even if you and your partner agree on your Yes and Less Money Dials, it can take some tweaking to get things running smoothly. Elise and David, for instance, agreed to cut housing costs so they could dial up spending on experiences, like travel or concerts. Elise: "We decided to keep our fixed expenses really low after a lot of debate about homeownership. No plans to save for a down payment; renting a two-bedroom apartment in a cheaper city; sharing a paid-off, used Honda Civic. Cutting costs was pretty easy to decide on together."

When You and Your Partner Don't Agree on Less Dials

The good news is you don't have to agree on all of your Money Dials! For example, my wife loves self-care. Me, not so much. But we make it work—our joint account pays for our personal training (valuable to both of us), while she pays for her personal self-care with her own money.

It's not always so easy, of course. We all have a finite amount of money, and we have to make choices. What happens when you're not aligned on your Less Dials? When one of you is ready to cut spending on ordering in or nights out, but the other isn't? When you're willing to stay in a cheap motel or cancel your gym membership, but your partner isn't? How do you make meaningful cuts together?

The answer is to recognize that you're working toward a bigger goal—your Rich Life vision—and there will be trade-offs. In Chapter 7, you'll create your Conscious Spending Plan, which will help you decide where you can compromise and where something is just not possible. And in Chapter 9, I'll show you how to set your accounts up so you both have individual money that you can use for anything you want.

But David found it hard to bring himself to *spend* money. "He admits he gets stuck on cost because he was praised so much for being frugal and 'good with money' by his rather cheap parents," Elise says. She explains how she and David found their way to a solution:

"I'm the main planner and purchaser. Usually, I'll be the one who plans a trip or researches things we need, like a new appliance, then present it to my husband. He *always* needs to think about it before pulling the trigger and sometimes says no without ever actually looking into market prices or asking me about the value. Last Christmas, he vetoed my desire to do a Great Barrier Reef tour while in Australia because it wasn't worth $700 per person to him. He booked with a cheaper company instead—and that company ended up canceling on us at the last minute (they had terrible reviews—he knew it was a risk). He didn't think about me and my priorities when he was feeling anxious. We now have a system where he gets *one week* to 'think about it' or look for a suitable alternative, and if I still want the more expensive option, we split the cost 50/50 up to his price, then I pay the rest from my personal savings."

Don't roll your eyes! I love their unique solution. Every couple has their own habits and rituals. I don't care how odd it sounds to other people if it's fair and it works. In this case, Elise and David learned that David needs time to think, but they set a deadline and a method of paying for experiences. This is an example of creating positive rules to help you use your money to live your Rich Life.

I suggest three specific guidelines for being decisive when you see money differently:

1. ***Determine who owns the decision.*** In relationships, it's really common that one person is in charge of travel expenses and the other is in charge of household expenses. Sometimes you need your partner's agreement, other times it's merely a courtesy, and occasionally you don't need to loop them in at all. Before you get into a long back-and-forth about whether something is worth it, ask yourself, *Who owns the decision? What level of involvement do I need here?*

2. ***Know your numbers.*** You can't make financial decisions based on feelings alone. If one of you is being indecisive, it's fair for the other partner to say, "Can you pull out the numbers and tell me how you're thinking about this?" This eliminates the doom loop of feeling bad but not knowing why, then dragging your feet and driving your partner crazy.

3. ***Elevate the conversation to your Rich Life vision.*** If you face a random financial decision, ask yourselves, *Does this fit into our Rich Lives?* If so, and you can afford it, then do it! You've already done the hard work of designing your vision in Chapter 3. Don't reinvent the wheel.

Learning to Think Bigger

When my wife and I were engaged, we went out to dinner with two married couples. They asked us what we were planning for a honeymoon. We were excited—we had planned to go on a weeklong safari. Then one of the couples mentioned that when they went on their honeymoon, they took six months off and traveled the world. *What?* Then the other couple said, "Oh, yeah, when we took our honeymoon, we traveled for a year. It was life changing."

Cassandra and I walked out of that restaurant looking at each other. *Did you hear that? Who are these people?* It would have been easy for us to leave it at that. But we'd been working on our money psychology together. So we asked the magical question: "What if?"

What if we took a long honeymoon? What would that look like? Is it even possible? Who does that? How could *we* do that?

Fast-forward a few months. We'd talked about that dinner conversation over and over and played the "What If We Did That?" game. We talked about all the reasons we couldn't do it, like our schedules and the cost—plus, it's just crazy!

Despite all the very good reasons *not* to do it, we found ourselves more and more excited about the idea. Finally, we decided to take a six-week honeymoon. And because one of our joint Yes Dials is relationships, we each independently came up with the idea of inviting our parents along for part of the trip. We told them to just show up at the airport and not worry about anything else. We got them seats together, and when they landed in Rome, we had transportation waiting to bring them to our hotel, where we had a week full of activities planned. We took them to a farmers market with a chef, chose vegetables, then cooked a five-course meal together. We visited a 100-year-old winery. I arranged a private tour of the Vatican for my mother-in-law, which was especially meaningful because she never thought she would have the chance to visit it. When they left,

It's Okay to Not Want to Travel!

I've noticed that when dreaming up their Rich Life, people hyperfixate on travel. People constantly talk about traveling (even if they haven't gone anywhere in the last five years). I even give a lot of travel-related examples in this book! It's just one of those things we naturally include as part of our Rich Life.

But is travel really part of yours? It's okay if it's not! This is why I push you to get really specific with your dreams. Don't just say "travel." Where do you want to go? For how long? What do you want to do there?

If you lack answers, or your answers are uninspiring, get honest with yourself. Maybe you just don't want to travel right now. Maybe later in life. Maybe never! The point is for you to create a vision of things that genuinely excite *you*.

For example, I don't really love meditation, but I constantly feel pressured to meditate as part of some mythical self-care routine. No thanks, guys. I think I'll just click Refresh on another 400 subreddits on personal finance, politics, and housing policy, just like I did yesterday.

On the flip side, before you dismiss traveling, consider that maybe you haven't ever traveled in a way that feels exciting to you. Are you still staying at budget hotels? Still feeling obligated to see the usual tourist stuff even though you don't care about it? Is there a way to craft a magical experience and try it once? Get honest with yourself, and if travel isn't one of your focuses right now, that's fine. There are plenty of other Yes Dials to choose from.

Cassandra and I continued on our honeymoon to Kenya, India, and Thailand.

Looking back, we remember this as one of our most memorable trips. We turned up our relationships Dial, decided to spend more on our honeymoon, and created meaningful memories that will be with all of us forever. That's what Money Dials can do.

The Joy of Being Intentional about Your Money—Together

Imagine you're on a raft floating down a river on a lovely, warm day. If the river goes left, we all go left. If it goes right, we all go right. I find that this lazy river attitude is how most people approach finances— passively, aimlessly, going with the flow. It's pleasant, sure, but it's mostly waiting for the river to carry us somewhere.

With your money, though, it's a lot more fun to pick up your paddles and row in the direction you *want* to go—especially when you do it together. Making decisions jointly will help you reach your goals faster—but just as important, you'll be having fun along the journey.

We all begin our relationships thinking of ourselves as a team, but life has a way of chiseling away at that togetherness, bit by bit. My wish is for you to reconnect on your shared vision, because in my experience, couples who treat money as a team realize they can live a much richer life than they ever imagined possible—as long as they're rowing together.

Your Rich Life matters. Take it seriously. Don't talk yourself out of it or minimize what you love. If anything, make it bigger. Yes, you like some weird stuff—embrace it! Your Yes Dials can be like a magic wand, helping you expand what means the most to you as a couple. When you define them together, it becomes much easier to cut back mercilessly on the things that don't matter. And that's when you're operating as true partners.

Chapter 4 Checklist

❑ Identify your Yes Dials. What do you want to spend more on? If you quadrupled your spending on one thing, what would it look and feel like?

❑ Talk to your partner about their Yes Dials. Did any of them surprise you? What are your shared Yes Dials? Make a plan to increase spending on those now and in the longer term.

❑ Identify your Less Dials. First, look back at your Rich Life vision. What's *not* on it? That will help you identify some Less Dials. Next, identify two major categories where you're willing to spend radically less. Now you have options for where to cut back and redirect that money to a Yes Dial.

❑ Take a concrete step toward bringing one of your dreams to life! Take a Yes Dial and create a plan to make it happen, whether it's saving for it or using money you've already set aside.

5

A QUICK
SNAPSHOT
OF YOUR
FINANCIAL LIFE

Discover your net worth in 30 minutes

I hate jigsaw puzzles. When my niece was five years old, she asked if I would do one with her. I told her I would rather calculate amortization rates for a 30-year mortgage. She ignored me and brought out the puzzle anyway, which meant I had to pretend to enjoy 20 minutes of torture until she finally gave up. Watching her pack that puzzle up and put it away was the best moment of my life.

For a lot of couples, this is how finances feel—like a stressful, chaotic 1,000-piece jigsaw puzzle. It's not clear where to start, and it's definitely not fun.

Good news: You don't need to assemble some giant puzzle to understand your finances. You just need four pieces.

The Only Numbers You Need to Calculate Your Net Worth

Assets (current value of car, home, property, business)	$
Investments (401(k), nonretirement—all investments)	$
Savings (bank savings account, emergency fund)	$
Debt (student loans, credit card debt, mortgage, car loans)	$

These four numbers will give you a "snapshot" of your finances, including how much you have and how much you owe. Together these represent your *net worth*, which is an incredibly helpful number to know. You might be worrying about day-to-day money but be much further ahead than you realized! Or you might be spending dangerously without knowing that your debt is too high.

The theme for this exercise is *speed*, not precision. No matter how complex your finances seem, you can do this quickly. I want you to get approximate numbers out on paper quickly—combined assets, combined investments, combined savings, combined debt—and not worry about being 100 percent accurate. Estimating within $10,000 is fine! You can always tweak the numbers later.

I've found that some people resist the "rough" aspect to this exercise. We're overwhelmed by money, but when we get the chance to simplify our finances, we cannot escape the need to overcomplicate things. That's because our brains are wired for precision, so when we see anything having to do with math or numbers, we transport ourselves back to eighth-grade algebra, where we have to get every single number absolutely correct. Stop it! *For this section, approximate is fine.*

Let's break down each piece of your net worth.

Assets. This is the current value of your car, house, and any other property or business you may have.

- How much would your house sell for if you listed it today? If you're not sure, open a real estate site like Zillow, plug in your address, and use that as the best guess. Don't factor in any debt yet (we'll do that later).

- Same with your car: The level of rigor I'm looking for here is Googling your car's make, model, and year and seeing how much other cars like it are selling for. Maybe drop it by $500 to account for that time you spilled cranberry juice on the passenger-side seat.

- If you own any special assets like jewelry or art, feel free to list them in this section, but since we're not in *The Great Gatsby*, I doubt this applies to most people.

- Do not include "future" assets, like an anticipated bonus or an expected inheritance (Aunt Margaret could live to be 110). Taking a conservative approach means you count only the money you actually have. You want to build your one-page financial document assuming the worst—not the best— because then any surprises you get will be positive ones.

- The entire "assets" section should take no more than five minutes. Approximate it and move on.

Investments. This includes your retirement accounts and any other investments you have, such as a health savings account (HSA), index funds or mutual funds, or even individual stocks. If it's an investment, it goes here.

- Yes, your retirement accounts, such as 401(k)s and Roth IRAs, do count! I'm saying it twice because this is one of the most common questions I get. Retirement accounts are investment accounts!

- Some people have stock options. Personally, I don't factor them in until they're actual cash in the bank, but it's up to you. (Again, I encourage you to be conservative in your estimates, which is why I wouldn't count them.) Restricted stock units are another category where you should do your best to estimate the value.

- Remember, don't get caught up in the minutiae. A few thousand dollars here or there makes no difference at this stage.

Savings. Separate from investments, this is the liquid savings money you could access tomorrow. This includes money in your bank savings accounts, your emergency fund, and any savings earmarked for specific future purchases (such as a down payment). This does *not* include money in retirement accounts.

- You can technically add your checking account to this category. It doesn't really matter, because most people don't keep much money in their checking account.

Debt. This includes credit card debt, student loans, car loans, your mortgage, and any personal loans.

- It's helpful to break these loans out by type (for example, student loan versus credit card debt) for a quick bird's-eye view of your debt categories. Like this: $56,000 total debt ($48,000 mortgage, $2,000 CC debt, $6,000 student loan).

STEP 1: Grab the low-hanging fruit.

Grab a piece of paper, divide it in four, label each quadrant (Assets, Investments, Savings, and Debt), and jot down the accounts you need to check for each section. You might be able to dispense with one of the sections off the top of your head. For instance, if you rent your apartment and don't own a car, your assets might be zero. Done with that section! If you have no credit card debt or student loans and know the amount of your mortgage, debt is easy to fill in. Get the low-hanging fruit first and keep moving forward.

STEP 2: Log in to all your accounts together . . . slowly.

I want you and your partner to do this together. Set aside some time, gather your logins, make two cups of tea. Don't treat this like a list of things to be checked off. Slow it down, take a minute to breathe, and

What Stops Us at This Step

"I don't know the password."
Surprising, but this is what prevents most couples from
creating their financial snapshot. Take your time, but I want
you to log in to these accounts. Reset your password if
you need to (and ideally use a password manager so you
eliminate this issue going forward). Be patient with yourself
and your partner.

**"It will take us forever to do this because I have an old 401(k)
at Fidelity and a new one at Schwab."**
When I have tasks that make me want to poke my eye out, I
like to break the process into two parts. Here's how I would
do this: First day, gather all the information about your
accounts, including the logins and passwords. Next day, log
in and write down the amounts. If I didn't chunk it like this,
I would go insane when I discovered I couldn't log in to three
consecutive accounts, and I would start cursing out Fidelity.

**"I don't know the exact value of the options that are part of
my compensation, because they haven't vested yet."**
We're not trying to run a DCF analysis on your RSUs, nerds.
A rough estimate is fine. If you find yourself calculating
anything more complicated than a sixth grader could do,
you've taken a wrong turn. Keep it simple!

reflect on what the accounts show. Ask each other questions: "What
do you think about that number?" "Are you surprised by it? I am!"

Create meaning out of the mundane. You might be dusting off
these accounts after years. You're probably looking at them together
for the first time. Be gentle with each other.

Worriers and Avoiders might notice themselves physically tens-
ing up, unconsciously trying to change the subject, or even sabotaging

this entire process. If you see your partner struggling, acknowledge it and encourage them. The reality is, being stressed is part of the process for just about everyone. I *want* you to feel some tension in these conversations—and then work through it—because you're building the skills to handle bigger and bigger numbers as a team.

If it becomes too much, remember that you don't have to get everything done in the first try. Take a break. Come back the next day. But come back together.

Here's what to say if your partner wants to bail: "Sure, let's wrap it up. I want us to feel good about this, and I appreciate talking about this today. Let's pick it up later this week."

There's a lot of meaning in taking care of your partner in this way. The goal is to get better at doing money *together*. Empathy goes a long way.

One last thing, and this is important. When I was younger, I would have tried to power through this step. Getting through the "to-dos" as efficiently as possible would have been a point of pride—"I got it right!" But that would have been a mistake. The point isn't to be efficient, it's to build a Rich Life together. Like building any kind of meaningful relationship, that takes time and compassion. I wish I could have taken off my "efficiency" hat and put on my "meaningfulness" hat. I hope you do that now.

STEP 3: Do the (easy) math.

Once you've got a total in each quadrant, it's easy to calculate your net worth. That's what this exercise is all about.

Add together assets, investments, and savings. Subtract debt. That's your net worth.

$$\begin{array}{r} \text{ASSETS} \\ + \ \text{INVESTMENTS} \\ + \ \text{SAVINGS} \\ - \ \text{DEBT} \\ \hline \end{array}$$

THE TOTAL IS YOUR NET WORTH.

If that's a positive number, great!

If it's a negative number, don't worry. Many couples have a negative net worth once they factor in their debt alone. The numbers don't mean you're good or bad people—they're just figures reflecting your finances today. We'll work through it.

Now celebrate your accomplishment and give yourselves a break from talking about money for a couple of days. You've done a lot.

What If My Partner Is Still Not Into Any of This?

A reader named Krystal who recently became highly motivated about finances has been struggling to get her husband on board. She wrote this note:

> "I've learned that it is incredibly hard to get your finances in order when you've been doing the same dysfunctional money things for many, many years—and when one partner (me) is fully on board, and the other isn't. . . . It's just taking him much longer to come around to the ideas while I'm ready to jump in and do them all, so I've had to just take the reins and drag him along for most of the changes."

Dragging someone along just doesn't work. Krystal has thought about and worked toward her Rich Life, but her partner hasn't, and not surprisingly, she's frustrated.

I'll bet if I were to time travel into the past and tell five-years-ago Krystal, "Hey, you need to pay off your credit card and automate your savings and aggressively increase your investments!" she would roll her eyes and ignore me. Now that she's trying to do the same thing to her husband, he's resisting.

Krystal is in a different place from him. She's focused on building emergency savings (which her husband thinks is unnecessary) and saving up for Rich Life goals, including a trip to Paris with her daughter in a couple of years, which she describes in vivid detail: "I want to visit the Louvre with her, see the Eiffel Tower, walk through fancy French shops, and drink strong French coffee while eating an authentic croissant at a sidewalk café." But her husband hasn't gone through the same journey she has.

The tough reality is that everyone needs to go through their own process to prioritize a Rich Life. Some partners may take a while. You can help a partner along by asking nonjudgmental questions that are focused on their interests—*not* on what they "need" to do. In this case, I'd recommend Krystal roll out these gentle questions over the course of several conversations with her husband:

- *"What do you think about where we are with our money?"*

- *"If you could change anything, what would it be?"*

- *"If we keep on this path, where do you think we'll be in a year? Where would you want to be?"*

Reality Check: Have You Asked for Help?

Sometimes we tell ourselves stories about how we're rowing the boat alone without having actually *asked* our partner to participate. We say . . .

» "My spouse will never want to work on finances with me."

» "It always falls on me."

» "I guess I'm the money person in the family."

Sometimes those stories are true, sometimes not. Ask yourself, *Have I asked for help in a clear, friendly way? Am I "forgetting" anything? If someone were looking in on my life, would they say the same thing?* Maybe your partner isn't quite as resistant as you think; maybe they are. Make sure the stories you tell yourself reflect reality.

Once you're on solid ground—with your partner realizing *they'd* like something to change, as well—you have permission to say, "Okay, what do you think we should do?"

If you use brute force in this process, you'll be dragging your partner along for the rest of your life. But once they get there on their own, and the two of you are both rowing in the same direction, you can quickly make up for lost time.

Now that you know your net worth, we're going to set the numbers aside and focus on your money dynamic for a bit. Then we'll come back to the numbers.

Chapter 5 Checklist

❏ Make a date with your partner for a login session. Access your accounts—bank, credit cards, retirement accounts, any other investment accounts, loans, everything. Jot down all the numbers.

❏ Add up your savings, assets, and investments, and subtract your debt—that's your net worth. Talk about what you discover. How does this number make you feel? How can you use it to take positive steps toward your Rich Life?

❏ If your partner is resistant, gently urge them to join you in the discovery process. Ask them, "What do you think about where we are with our money?"

6

CHANGING YOUR MONEY DYNAMIC

How to talk about money without fighting, getting stuck, or giving up

When I was a teenager, I attended a magic show with my mom (which, as I'm writing this, makes me realize just how uncool I was).

Damn, that magician was smooth. He would ask random audience members a question, then integrate their answers into the show without missing a beat. He was talking to the crowd, then bringing up a guest onstage, all while doing incredible sleight-of-hand illusions that none of us could explain. It genuinely felt like magic.

Now, decades later, I understand what was going on. On my podcast, my guests often feel that I can read their mind, especially when I predict the exact phrases they use with each other in private. To the person I'm talking to, it feels like magic. But in reality, I've seen it before—I've asked the same questions over and over with thousands of people, and now I can make predictions that seem unbelievable. They're not. They're simply patterns that most of us exhibit.

For example, when I ask, "What's your Rich Life?" the answer is virtually always the same: "I want to do *what* I want, *when* I want."

When I ask someone to elaborate on what they love spending on, their eyebrows go up, their eyes brighten, and they break into a smile—just about every time.

And when I ask why they have certain beliefs about money—like who should pay for dates—they're visibly startled. Their answers start with logic ("He earns more, so he should pay more . . ."), but if I push, they'll often say, "Well, that's just how I grew up."

That's honest. Our upbringing provides a powerful, unconscious model for how we think about money—and sets up certain expectations. We rarely realize the deep imprint this makes. It's unseen, unquestioned, and often sits dormant inside us—until decades later when we're arguing with a partner over a random expense that's suddenly become existential.

We've already explored your own money psychology in Chapter 2. Now we're going to explore your couples' money dynamic, which is the way that both of you relate to money together. In many relationships, the money dynamic is like an invisible third partner: There's your money psychology, your partner's money psychology, and the dynamic of how you both communicate about money.

A lot of this goes unnoticed, even for couples who've been together for decades. For example, if you have certain expectations about what type of house you should live in or how often to travel, it's no surprise that you fight about money. Most of us never share our expectations out loud! These unexpressed desires are part of a "secret wish list" your partner might know nothing about. Many of us expect our partner to do certain things when it comes to money, but we never say exactly what—because we may not even be aware of it ourselves.

Take a look at the phrases below. Do any of them sound familiar?

- *I want them to participate with our finances—even just once! It feels like I have to do everything around here.*

- *I want them to think long term before making another impulsive purchase.*

- *I want them to stop being so cheap!*

- *I want them to plan a vacation and not leave it to me like always.*

- *I want them to come up with a financial plan for our family. What are we doing? When are we going to retire? ANYTHING!*

Invisible Scripts about Love and Money

In Chapter 2 I talked about invisible scripts, the beliefs we hold so deeply that we don't even realize we have them. Now consider this: What invisible scripts around money do you have in your *relationship*? Does your partner follow the same invisible scripts? What would it take to rewrite those scripts?

Here are some of the most common invisible scripts about love and money that I hear from couples:

» "Talking about money is unromantic."

» "It's normal to fight about money. Money is stressful."

» "He just isn't a money person."

» "I make it; she spends it!"

» "I don't need much, but it seems like they're always spending on something. Like, do we really need another toy for the kids?"

» "Rich Life? We're just trying to pay our bills."

» "We'll probably have our debt until the day we die."

We almost never talk about our expectations candidly. How could we? We rarely even know what we want! And we don't sit around with a magnifying glass, analyzing our relationships and looking for systematic ways to improve: *Okay, we need a change. Let me examine what went wrong and try something else.*

Nope, it's much more common for us to sigh and say, "Ugh, this isn't working. Let's keep doing it for 25 more years!"

So we push uncomfortable feelings into behaviors like arguing about how much we're spending at the grocery store, which over the years become deep, rutted patterns. Changing our own patterns is hard enough, but changing a dynamic in an intimate relationship is even harder. Fighting is familiar, it's comforting, and after all, what else can we do? We've tried everything!

In this chapter, I'm going to show you strategies you can use right now to stop the fighting and build a healthy relationship with money.

3 Common Couples Dynamics and How to Change Them

Yes, you can change the dynamic of your relationship! If you've been trying unsuccessfully to get your partner to talk about money for years, you can change that. If money always feels "heavy," or you talk and talk and never get anywhere, you can change that, too.

Let's start by taking our relationship dynamic seriously. Most of us recognize that there's a part of our relationship that we want to improve, but when we get into the nuts and bolts of what it would take to change, we have a peculiar habit of minimizing the issue:

> **Couple:** Our money disagreements are a 10 out of 10. We've even talked about separating.
> **Ramit:** Can you tell me what you think is going on?
> **Couple:** Well . . . I mean, it's not actually that bad. We fight about money sometimes. I wouldn't even call it a fight . . . more like a disagreement. It's definitely not as bad as other people. . . . Really, I think we just need a budget.
> **Ramit:** *(Stares in disbelief)*

This situation—where a couple has a crushing, existential problem, but whenever they start to talk about making a change, they instantly downplay it—is so common that I call it the Money Minimization Paradox. We'd rather stick with a bad dynamic we know than try to switch to something potentially better but unfamiliar. In other words, "Better the devil you know than the devil you

Starter Scripts for Avoiding the Most Common Money Fights

Overspending

Instead of this: "Oh my God, did you really buy that? Where is the money going to come from??"

Say this: "I realize I've gotten into the pattern of lecturing you about why we need to save. I don't think it's working. Do you? [No.] Can we zoom out and decide what we want our money to do for us, together?" (See more on overspending on page 155.)

Dividing financial labor

Instead of this: "You never want to sit down and plan our vacation! This is why we end up wasting so much on plane tickets and having to stay in awful hotels."

Say this: "I made a list of the things I've been in charge of with our finances in the last two weeks—and the things you've been in charge of. This list isn't fair to me. I want to talk about redoing our responsibilities. Can you talk Tuesday or Thursday evening?"

Spoiling the kids

Instead of this: "You can't say no to the kids! You spoil them. They'll have no self-control, just like you."

Say this: "Let's make a list of the money values we want to teach our kids. Which ones are they already learning from us? Which ones do we want them to learn?"

Taking ownership of financial challenges

Instead of this: "You're sticking your head in the sand. Why do I always have to be the responsible one?"

Say this: "It feels lonely over here thinking about this on my own. I love you and I want a partner in this."

don't." The antidote to minimization is to set clear stakes on what will happen if you don't change: "We'll run out of money in eight months," or "We'll fight about money for the rest of our marriage," or "Our kids will pick up our money stress and feel the same as they get older." Determine specific, real stakes with no minimization. *Then* you're ready to make a change.

This book is about changing your approach to money from defense to offense, which requires recalibrating your communication dynamic. To live a Rich Life, you have to be honest—honest with yourselves and honest with the people around you.

To help you identify your dynamic, here are three common—and unhealthy—dynamics that I see all the time in my work with couples, along with my advice for changing them.

THE SITCOM DYNAMIC

We all know a couple who've been fighting for years, jabbing, bickering, bantering. Their schtick is fast-paced, dizzying, sometimes entertaining, but after a while, uncomfortable. At first, they finish each other's sentences and tell great stories. You can tell they're playing this game together, poking fun at each other, and it's quite likable in the beginning.

But if you look deeper, you see they're both playing a part. Often, these couples have not had a truly genuine conversation about money in decades. Let's look at an example.

Michelle and Eric (from podcast episode #58), who have been through some tough financial times, have been rerunning the same dialogue for the past 25 years. "We're like the Costanzas, George's parents on *Seinfeld*," Eric says, "bickering like two little kids, back and forth, back and forth."

Michelle grew up wealthy, and to this day, she expects her husband to provide for her. Eric makes $55,000 and feels like he can't give his wife the lifestyle she wants. This dynamic has been causing conflict for decades. And now in their fifties, they both feel that they've missed their time to invest and retire comfortably and that they might have to keep working until they die.

This manifests as angry-amusing banter, a perpetual bicker-fest that occasionally explodes. Speaking as someone who doesn't particularly enjoy this dynamic—and rarely sees it among my couple friends—I was shocked by some of the conversation. Here's a moment from our session:

> **Ramit:** Eric, when's the last time you remember talking about money with Michelle?
>
> **Eric:** It comes up occasionally, but it's very surface. We don't go deep. Every time I try to talk about it with Michelle, she just pushes me away. She's like, "I've got this. Stop messing everything up."
>
> **Michelle:** That is so not true. You've never said, "Let's sit down and do this." Or else you do it for like 30 seconds, and then it doesn't come up for three more years.
>
> **Eric** *(to me)*: So you see what I'm dealing with now.

Notice how performative this is. They set up the joke, and then they turn to me for a laugh. Eric "looks at the camera" and gives an eye-rolling comment. They're playing to the crowd. At a certain point, it's obvious they're not really talking to each other—they're both playing characters.

I ask Michelle and Eric if they like this dynamic.

"No!" they both say. "We want to change."

So why is it still going on, nearly three decades into their relationship? I ask a simple question: "What are you getting out of this dynamic?"

(The first answer to this question is always "I don't know" or "Nothing." So I gently push back: "You do know. Think about it." Then I wait. The next answer is always the truth.)

Eric answers: "I think we're just comfortable bickering. It makes me feel not as bad about what happened in the past . . . and like I'm right, for once."

There it is. The truth: *It feels good to be right.*

And what happened in the past? Bankruptcy, conflicting expectations about the kind of life they should be living, and years of avoiding sincere conversations. Instead of creating a shared vision of their life, they've retreated to opposite sides of the ring, fighting to be right and gradually becoming adversaries, not partners.

Worse, their bickering creates a false sense of accomplishment: Even though "winning" an interaction feels like success, it in fact keeps them stuck. By creating the *impression* that they're dealing with money, these fights have completely distracted Michelle and Eric from planning for their future—for decades! They've both adopted masks to avoid uncomfortable conversations about what they really expect and yearn for.

Bottom line: The Sitcom dynamic is a mask to cover genuine pain. It's a way to bury uncomfortable emotions—often a lack of control—and to feel like you're making progress when you're really not. You may win this argument, but you've lost the ultimate goal of being partners.

What to do: Ask yourself, *What do I get out of this dynamic with my partner? What am I avoiding by bickering? What emotions am I masking when we pick at each other over small things?*

I love the concept of masks because we all wear them at times, and we all intuitively understand that we can put masks on and take them off. Look at your relationship dynamic as a mask you can remove and examine. Once you see its shape and dimensions—for example, sarcastic, avoidant, or fear based—you might decide to "take off" that mask and replace it with another.

Remember, just because this is the way you've always talked about money doesn't mean it's the way you need to continue communicating. The important thing is to recognize the dynamic you've fallen into and decide it's not serving you. (Try: "I want to make a change. I think we can do better in our money conversations, and I have an idea.") Then talk about the kind of dynamic you'd like to create together.

THE CHASER/AVOIDER DYNAMIC

If you bought this book, it's likely you're a Chaser. And you've been running after your Avoider partner, trying to get them to talk about

Your Financial Role Models

Whom do you admire with money? I once interviewed a Navy SEAL who told me he'd created a "mental dojo" filled with mentors he'd turn to for advice. This was purely his own intentional creation—some of these mentors were alive, some were long gone. His mental dojo was simply a thought experiment for him to learn from the people he admired from afar.

Try it! For example, think of someone you respect with money: Would they buy a car if they had credit card debt? How would they handle a young child asking for an expensive toy? What words would they use when they wanted to talk about money with their spouse?

Interestingly, more than half of the couples I speak to are stumped by the question of whom they admire with money. When they have no positive role models for money, is it any surprise they struggle with it?

When looking for financial role models, think about your friends in relationships or your extended family. And if you can't find anybody there, think about characters in a TV show or a movie. (Sometimes, I use Captain Picard from *Star Trek* for leadership questions.) It could be whoever you want. Then ask yourself, *What would that person or couple do? How would I describe the way they think about money? If they were in my shoes, how would they approach a decision I'm facing?*

What you're doing with these questions is creating new "grooves" in the way you think about money. I also like this approach because sometimes it's easier to channel someone else than it is to get in touch with ourselves. What would this couple do if they were, say, considering buying a new SUV? Well, they probably would sit down, write out the total cost of ownership (see page 154), and talk about it: *Do you think we can afford this? No, I think we should probably wait a year and then talk about it again.* Try it.

money for your whole relationship. That's what this dynamic is all about: the pursuer and the pursued, like Wile E. Coyote and the Road Runner.

The Chaser is desperate for some sort of participation in their finances so it feels more like a team—but their partner won't even talk about money. The Chaser has tried everything—being nice, being stern, bringing up money stuff at a different time of day. Nothing works. And even if they do succeed, it's only momentary, with their Avoider partner giving a half-hearted effort before slipping back into their usual role of indifference.

The Chaser might even feel like they're the one at fault. *If only I could find the right way to approach this,* they might think, or *I know I get mad sometimes . . .* And that makes sense because the Chaser is often a huge bummer. They're anxious. They constantly worry. And their partner wants no part of this. (All of this, of course, is unfair, because the Chaser has generally been thrust into this role against their will.)

Here's an example: Lily and Sean, who make a combined $140,000 a year, are way overextended on their fixed costs. Lily takes on the stress and manages the money, solo. Sean describes the feeling when Lily brings up money: "I can feel myself disconnecting—it's like, *not this again,* and I'll just drift away and think about something else."

They describe their dynamic further:

Lily: I don't want to throw Sean under the bus, but if I try to talk about money or get him to partner with me on a decision, he glazes over and disassociates. So I've felt fairly alone—and then I feel a little bit of guilt because since I'm the one in charge, it's my fault we're here.

Sean: It's tough because she does have reign over the finances as far as paying the bills and everything. And when we talk about finances, it's always about an impossible decision that there's really no answer to, like what we can spend less on. But Lily's on top of it—she does such a good job.

Does Lily like this dynamic in which she has to chase Sean? No! Does anyone? Hell no! One of the tragedies here is that the Chaser is trapped in an escalating cycle of wanting more shared participation in the finances, not getting it, and then becoming increasingly aggressive, which drives the other partner away even more. This is well documented in the Pursuer/Distancer dynamic that therapists regularly see.

Please also notice what Sean is doing here: He's using a strategy to divert attention and accountability. Sometimes it's conscious, other times unconscious, but no matter what, it has the same effect: He can keep avoiding money. Lily desperately tries to toss him the ball of responsibility, and he tosses it right back. As you can see, the pursued partner becomes evasive, almost slippery.

To the Chaser, this can feel bewildering. They'll walk out of conversations saying things like, "I tried to talk to him about following our plan and now *I* have homework? What just happened?" Then the Chaser doubles down, which causes the Avoider to be even more avoidant. That dynamic is perpetuated for years. Grooves are created. Both sides come to resent each other, and money becomes a massive trigger for fights.

Over time, the Chaser will continue doing all the heavy lifting and eventually blow up at a tiny issue. This gives the Avoider a chance to react with indignation and conclude they were right all along: *See? You're always stressed out about money. It's not normal to get mad over $5 at McDonald's!* This strategy buys them another few months of passivity, which is all they want. Avoiders will do anything to keep from talking about money in the short term, but they're never conscious of the long-term effects of their actions.

Bottom line: The Chaser/Avoider dynamic is cocreated. On one side is usually a people pleaser. On the other is a partner who both consciously and unconsciously cultivates layers of incompetence. Couples with this dynamic have usually never had a candid conversation about money.

What to do: I'm reminded of a phrase, "When you're accustomed to privilege, equality feels like a burden." The Avoider is used to the privilege of having their finances maintained by someone else. So when you're recalibrating your money dynamics—even if it's

The Parent/Child Variation

The Chaser/Avoider dynamic has a few variations, the most common of which is the Parent/Child dynamic. I've observed this play out in a number of ways:

» I've seen a man beg his wife to take away his credit card.

» I've seen a woman involved in a multi-level marketing scheme losing $3,000 a month (month after month!) while her husband stoically keeps their lives going. He sees himself as "the provider," of course.

» I've seen a spouse who has never paid a single bill and actually takes pride in not knowing how to log in to any family accounts.

The Parent/Child money dynamic—where one partner begins to function as the responsible "parent" when it comes to finances—is absolutely toxic to relationships for two reasons:

1. Your partner is not a child, and you're not going to get them to act like an adult by treating them like a child. (If you find yourself in the role of a "nag," you may be embedded in this dynamic.) It's critical to redefine the relationship from Parent/Child to intimate partners with a shared Rich Life vision.

2. This dynamic is sexual kryptonite: The "parent" figure feels understandably repulsed as a result of taking on this authority role.

The good news is, this Parent/Child dynamic is fixable. When you treat an adult like an adult, tell them what you expect, and set clear boundaries, they often rise to your expectations. Also, consider enlisting the help of a therapist.

nowhere near 50/50—expect intense pushback. Here are your goals to keep it slow and methodical:

1. *Agree to make a change.* Don't minimize. Lay out the situation and agree you both need to improve it. This is not easy, because very often in this dynamic, the Avoider is supremely comfortable and actively resists change.

2. *Hand over a small amount of responsibility to the Avoider.* Tell your partner you'd like them to pick a time to meet and discuss money. That's all. Baby steps. Then tell them you'd like them to contribute three agenda items (such as how much you spent in the last month on groceries, how much they think is appropriate to set aside for an upcoming vacation, or even the balance in your joint checking account). Remember: Tell them, don't ask them. You're subtly recalibrating the relationship by setting expectations, rather than asking and putting the power in their hands.

3. *Plan for resistance.* The Avoider will use a number of techniques to derail the meeting: They'll get mad, they'll act disappointed, they'll demean themselves ("I guess I just can't do anything right"), or they'll change the subject to something *you* did wrong. No matter what, don't take the bait. Anticipate what they'll do and remind yourself to stay focused. Use this phrase: "I think we're a little in the weeds. Ramit would probably say we should refocus on the positive. Can we try that?" (I'm sorry you have to take on the burden, but this is the reality of the situation.)

Once you've set a time to talk about money, don't talk about it beforehand—save your thoughts for the meeting. It's possible they won't follow through on the things you laid out. Have a plan for that, too (because not preparing is *itself* another form of derailing the meeting). For instance, remind them what you both agreed to, then reschedule the meeting for the next day.

More advanced: Most Chasers accept the framework of needing to *persuade* their partner to deal with money. I hate this. You're used to imbalance, so you feel the onus is on you to convince *them* of their shared responsibility. Chaser, I have a proposal for you: What if you rejected that frame entirely and didn't put yourself in the subordinate position of having to convince someone? You could tell yourself, *I'm not going to convince them. Instead, I'm going to communicate my expectations and they can choose whether they want to meet them or not.* Here are the points you want to convey:

- This is what it's like to talk about money in a good relationship (see page 119).

- These are my expectations for our money responsibilities.

- This is what I need for us to be successful as a couple.

It takes real fortitude to say this with conviction, because it's essentially an ultimatum. It's saying, "Let's do this. If we don't, here's what I will have to do." In an intimate relationship, that's as serious as it gets. But I want to give you permission to be clear about what you're feeling and to communicate what you need to have a healthy relationship, because this *is* serious. If you need help working toward this, please seek out a therapist.

THE INNOCENT DOE/ENABLER DYNAMIC

I've heard it a million times. I'll ask a simple question, like "Which bank do you use?" And one partner will look up at me and laugh. "I have no idea!"

My antennae immediately go up. I ask another question: "Why do you think you can't stop spending money?"

"I just don't know!"

This is the Innocent Doe technique, an unconscious script that many people follow to try to get out of answering uncomfortable questions. People who use this technique effectively say, "Little old me? Why can't I stop spending money? I just don't know! I do everything right. Do you know? Because I don't know."

The round-eyed innocent approach has historically worked for this person. They slowly enmesh their partner, their parents, or anyone else around them in their problems, often without even being conscious of what they're doing. They've found that over time, their technique works to temporarily avoid taking responsibility.

(This is essentially what I used to do in my middle-school art class, which I was bad at—because I never practiced—so I threw up my hands and persuaded my teacher to "help" with my projects, which involved her basically doing them for me.)

And, of course, Innocent Does have loved ones who have enabled them, usually for years. Their partner likely indulges this dynamic by "helpfully" giving them the answers, handling the household finances, even logging in to all their accounts because their Innocent Doe partner just has no idea how to do it.

The dynamic is striking when you hear it (check out episode #24 of my podcast). I'll ask the Innocent Doe a simple question. Out of nowhere, their Enabler partner will jump in to help and start offering solutions: "Well, have you tried this? Oh, okay, I see that won't work because you don't have the login for our IRA. How about this? No? What about that, and this, and that?" Suddenly, the topic has shifted away from the Innocent Doe's problems to something totally separate.

I've seen the Innocent Doe routine too many times to let it fly. When I call it out, there's always a stunned silence from couples, who've never realized they're playing this dynamic on repeat.

I want to acknowledge that Innocent Does often have been raised with no guidance on money. So when they fall in love and join forces with their partner—moving in, paying bills, struggling through the costs of housing and cars and surprise expenses—they have few financial skills. Innocent Does often find themselves handing over responsibility of their finances to their partner.

The problem is, if you don't understand how money actually works, you're at a disadvantage for the rest of your life. You overspend because everything around you is structured to encourage it. You get into trouble because accruing mountains of credit card debt is normalized and you don't understand how 27 percent interest rates trap you. The Enabler tries to help, offering advice and excuses, but ends up perpetuating the dynamic. Eventually, despite the Enabler's best efforts, they start to struggle with money, with debt, with shrunken dreams. The more you worry, the more you blame each other. What a tragedy.

This is one of the reasons I love my job. I know that with a few key changes, you can take control of your money and work together with your partner to make changes—bigger changes than you ever thought possible. But you can't do that if one person keeps playing the role of the Innocent Doe.

Innocent Does are also vulnerable because, unaware of the basic rules of money, they're drawn to get-rich-quick schemes. They feel

What to Do If You Find Yourself Talking about Money . . . But Never Taking Action

One of the most frustrating patterns in a relationship is *indecisiveness*. You talk and talk about needing to change . . . but nothing actually happens. If you're reading this and nodding, you know exactly what it feels like.

When couples are in this pattern, they're unaware of the real danger they're facing. One couple I spoke to was two months away from running out of money but continued to avoid making even small financial decisions. When you spend years on different financial pages, your positions each become more rigid and your decision-making skills deteriorate.

Now let's talk about what to do. My first suggestion is to see a couples therapist, who can help you identify the origin of these patterns and make changes. Some couples do this, but others don't. Maybe one partner isn't willing to see a therapist, or they can't find time, or they think it's too expensive.

What's really going on here is a total lack of urgency. Like for the Avoider from page 32, so far there have been no serious consequences for avoiding real decisions. But deep down, you know something is very, very wrong.

they have no other options, especially as they get older and run out of time. You'll often find them buying whole-life insurance ("He told me it would be tax-free money!"), falling for multi-level marketing scams ("It's passive income!"), and stumbling into other quackery.

I spoke with one Innocent Doe, Katie, who worked hard to get out of her pattern:

"After our conversation I realized how much I have always hated being told 'you can't afford it.' It was even harder to tell myself I couldn't afford something when I knew I had a credit card in my pocket saying, 'Yes you can.' But I see now that

The real secret is this: Even though this seems like a couples dynamic, *you* have to make a change on your own. You're reading this book for a reason; you're ready to take action. If you and your partner were going to do it together, you would have already done it.

The best way to make this change is to set expectations and then tell your partner what you need, like the points on page 112.

It's intimidating because it's so straightforward. You're not asking why your partner feels a certain way. You're not rehashing things from the past. You've simply made a decision and you're moving forward. Indecisive couples find this absolutely terrifying. *What if my partner doesn't listen? What if they get mad? What if . . . ?*

If I could sit with you, I would gently ask, "When you think of your money, do you know something is wrong? Then it's time for *you* to make a change."

Start saving. Make a Conscious Spending Plan (see next chapter). See a therapist alone.

Maybe your partner will come along. Maybe not. The point is that if you absolutely, positively know you have to make a change, sometimes you have to do it without your partner.

being incompetent with money caused me to feel deep shame, and that I expected to fail before even starting. I realized I need to systematically rewire the way I think and feel about money, starting with educating myself and understanding the fundamentals."

Bottom line: The Innocent Doe employs a strategy using "I don't know!" as a way to avoid uncomfortable questions about money. It's okay not to know something. It's not okay for "not knowing" to become your identity. The Enabler props the Innocent Doe up, allowing the situation to continue indefinitely.

What to do: You can change the Innocent Doe/Enabler Dynamic. It's unlikely that you'll immediately go from A to Z, but you *can* go from A to B, and take steady steps after that.

If you're the Innocent Doe, make a conscious choice to learn about money and to take small actions like putting $50 per month in a savings account. This one little step leads to 10 more steps, which leads to 20 and beyond. If you're the Enabler, jot down the dynamics in your relationship so they're clear in your head, then sit down with your partner and tell them that you want to recalibrate your relationship around money. Tell them you'd like their help to take one small step (such as their taking over a single bill), and eventually you'd like to have their help on more.

When you can both make changes together, your identity will change from "Innocent Doe" and "Enabler" to a couple who can manage their money together.

When You're Just Not Hearing Each Other: Haunted by Money Ghosts

If you and your partner constantly argue about money, but it seems like you're talking past each other, you might have a ghost: a *money ghost.*

A money ghost is a belief one of you has brought to the relationship that perpetually sits between you. So every time you and your partner talk about a money issue, you're not actually talking about the issue; you're talking about the *ghost*. And dealing with it can be incredibly frustrating.

Some common money ghosts:

- "I have to save, save, save every penny I can." *(This person will often save an unreasonably large amount of money, then feel miserable about not having enough money for day-to-day spending.)*

- "All debt is bad, and I am a bad person if I have debt." *(Constantly feels miserable about being in debt—worrying, feeling hopeless—but rarely makes a plan to pay it off.)*

- "We need to buy a house as soon as possible." *(Has tunnel vision around buying a house, which shows up as comparing themselves with friends who are homeowners. Often feels that money spent on anything other than a house is a waste.)*

- "I need to have $5 million by the time I'm 40, or I'm a failure." *(Uses an arbitrary number to define success—usually an unrealistic one that was chosen in their early twenties.)*

- "My partner was in debt before, so I don't trust them. If they start to spend again, they'll go back into debt." *(Lives in the past and won't acknowledge that people can change.)*

- "We come from a family of people who are all bad with money." *(Tells themselves stories that are often not based in reality.)*

- "We're never going to have enough. We're going to run out of money." *(Worries about what can go wrong but doesn't make a plan for what will actually happen.)*

- "What's the point of trying? We're too far behind for it to make a difference." *(Throws their hands up and essentially admits that they have no control, so why bother?)*

- "We have no idea what we're doing." *(Tells themselves that they're simple people who can't understand this complicated money stuff.)*

Peter and Sheena had a ghost problem. Sheena managed to pay off $50,000 of her $70,000 debt and was on track to pay off the rest. But her ghost—*all debt is horrible and must be crushed as soon as possible*—made life unsustainable and stressful.

She decided that she and Peter would put 60 percent of their income toward debt. They'd stop eating out. Sheena turned down bachelorette parties and all other opportunities for fun that had a significant price tag. On one occassion, Peter wanted to talk about what they could do for their tenth anniversary, but Sheena couldn't bring herself to even dream for a few minutes. It was All Debt, All the Time.

This kind of behavior often gets rationalized as virtuous. *I like to save. I'm on a mission to pay off my debt. I'll put everything toward this goal!* But, we rarely realize that tackling a goal too aggressively can be ineffective, like a crash diet. In Sheena's case, 60 percent of their income left almost no money for her to do anything else.

Sheena's money ghost made her overlook other important parts of her relationship. Every time Peter wanted to talk about money, it felt like he wasn't talking to his wife—he was talking to her debt-averse ghost. You can tell you have a money ghost if you go beyond a healthy plan into irrationally focused, even manic behavior. Examples include fixating and crying over not yet owning a house, becoming angry about a $10 charge, or—like Sheena—paying off debt so aggressively that you feel totally depleted.

If you dig down and investigate what's behind your money ghosts, you can usually find the root. For Sheena, it was fear of repeating credit card habits that had left her family members in bad situations. The good news is, there is a solution: When you identify a money ghost, you shine a light on it, which lets you take control of the ghost instead of the ghost controlling you. When you feel your partner isn't hearing you and the ghost is blocking your communication, you can call it out.

Pick a name for the ghost. Get theatrical! What's the name of the one who always whispers that you'll run out of money and end up eating out of a dumpster? Worrying Wally? Now go deeper: Worrying Wally wears tattered clothing and smells bad—not the ideal person you want to take advice from.

This should feel over-the-top because it is. You're literally imagining someone covered in trash whispering that you'll always be in debt. It's ridiculous. That's exactly how you'll internalize the absurdity of letting a money ghost control your money.

You can even have fun at the ghost's expense. *Oh no! It sounds like Worrying Wally is back. Wally? You here? I thought you were on vacation!* (Make sure to smile. This is a joke, not a verbal evisceration, a lesson I have to remind myself about every day.) Then pick another ghost you actually want to listen to, like Generous Gina, who says, "You can pay off your debt and live a balanced life." You choose who you're going to listen to.

What a Healthy Conversation about Money Looks Like

Have you ever actually heard a healthy conversation about money? For most of us, the answer is no. Nobody teaches us how to talk about this. We barely know how to think about and treat our *own* money! How are we supposed to know how to talk to a partner with different expectations and experiences? Money is the last taboo that's hidden behind closed doors, and besides movie scenes, most of us have never really heard another couple work through money disagreements.

For the important things in my life, I like to study the best and adapt what I learn. I remember reading one of those "What I do in a weekend" articles about a professional model, a guy who looks effortlessly healthy and glowing. It's easy to say, "Must be nice to be genetically blessed" (and I'm sure he is), but in the article, he shared how he walked miles to meet his friends for brunch, then went on a hike, then spent a couple of hours at the gym. When I read that, I loved it, because it helped me understand that if I wanted to get healthier, there were specific behaviors I could change. It wasn't just up to my DNA. I had control!

Now, I'm not going to be a professional model (unless it's modeling how to create a floor rug using my thick arm hair). But I want to know what excellence looks like because I can adapt lessons from models and Olympic swimmers and Nobel Laureates to improve my life.

When it comes to money, I want you to see an example of excellence. Below, I've scripted out what a healthy, positive conversation looks like. Use this. Adapt it for your needs.

Here's a conversation about the cost of groceries:

"I think we could probably be a little more thoughtful about groceries. Right now we spend $900 a month. We could maybe get it down to $700."

"Well, I'm the one who does the shopping. I don't think $700 is realistic."

Notice the understandably defensive response. Also notice how the conversation seemingly dead-ends here.

"I hear you. And I appreciate how much time you put into picking healthy food for us. What's a number you think we could reasonably spend?"

Notice how the initiating partner recovered the conversation by expressing appreciation and saying, "I hear you," then asking—not telling—what number the other partner thinks is realistic. They also "tossed the ball" back to their partner to make this a dialogue, not a monologue.

"I could probably make $750 work."

"That sounds great! If we're doing $750, that means we have to eat out one less time each month. Would you be okay with that?"

Make sure to ask for agreement, not assume it.

"That works."
"Awesome!"
Take the win!

Now, let me play this out a little further. Let's say the person who does the grocery shopping has agreed to $750 a month, but one time ends up spending $850. When you get together for your Monthly Money Meeting (see page 196), here's how you might deal with this discrepancy:

"You know what, I want to mention something. We agreed on $750 this month for groceries, but I went over that."

"Oh, okay. What do you think happened?"

This response is not accusatory, like screaming, "HOW COULD YOU DO THAT?" It's even softened by saying, "What do you think happened?" which is gentler than "What happened?" All of these subtle techniques invite open discussion.

"Well, one, we had that dinner party. Two, the baby skipped her nap, so she was screaming in the cart, and I wasn't paying attention to what I was tossing in there. But I think I can get us back to an average of $750 a month. It just means that for the next three months, I'm going to be a little bit stricter about what I get at the store."

I like this example because it hits on a lot of things:

- Empowering one partner to decide how to spend in a certain category

- That partner truly owning that spending category

- If things go off-plan (and they will), one partner using gentle language to understand what happened, and the other proposing a fix to get back on track

This could have been a fight, but instead it's a constructive conversation. Even better, both partners tackled a problem *together*.

Besides, in the grand scheme, an extra $100 isn't much. But building a bond between you two is extremely valuable.

And always, no matter what a money conversation is about, end with "I love you." You can never express too much appreciation to your partner, and if you associate money with a big, warm hug every time you talk about it, you'll quickly find that you both start to feel good.

More ways to conclude with loving appreciation and gratitude:

- *You're amazing.*

- *I'm so happy we get to work through this together, even when it's really hard.*

- *I couldn't do this alone.*

- *I feel so thankful to be able to talk about this with you.*

Chapter 6 Checklist

- ❑ Review the invisible scripts about love and money on page 101. Where do you recognize yourself and your partner?

- ❑ When you read about the couples dynamics, which one closely mirrors your own? Jot down a list of what you'd like to change in your couples dynamic.

- ❑ Identify one financial mentor—someone you'd want to emulate if you needed to make a big money decision. (They don't even need to know they're your mentor.)

- ❑ Identify your own money ghost, then name it, tease it, and gain back control.

7

CREATING YOUR CONSCIOUS SPENDING PLAN

Match your actual numbers to your Rich Life

By the end of this chapter, you're going to have a one-page plan that incorporates your Money Dials and Rich Life vision into your actual numbers so every dollar is going toward the kind of life you want to build together.

It's called a Conscious Spending Plan (CSP), and it will instantly show how you stack up on your spending, saving, and investing. This plan is simple enough that you can focus on four numbers—just four!—and still spend on eating out, concerts, or special activities for your children while also investing your money. Your plan will also give you a little wiggle room so when you have an unexpected expense, you'll be able to handle it.

Even better: No need to track the price of tomatoes or other random $3 expenses.

But I'm going to ask for one thing: You'll have to zoom out and look at your numbers in a different way.

We're usually so focused on day-to-day expenses that taking a longer-term perspective can feel weird. If I asked you to predict how much you would spend on groceries this year, imagine most people's first reactions: "Oh my god, I have no idea."

Don't worry—I'm not going to ask you to estimate how much you'll spend on grapes six years from now. But I am going to show you how to think about big money questions and then build them into a plan so you can actually achieve your goals. Questions like:

- *Do we want to live in a big house in Texas?*

- *Do we want to both work when we have kids?*

- *Do we want to spend Sundays with family?*

- *When do we want to retire—50, 65, 80?*

It's less about finding exact answers to these questions and more about forging the connection that comes from talking about them. Talking about money *regularly* makes it easier to talk about money *forever*. That way, when something goes off-plan—which is inevitable—you can stay calm, not get flooded with frustration, and focus on handling it together.

We'll use the Conscious Spending Plan to determine where you want your money to go (see the template on pages 288–289). Couples tell me this is the hardest part of the program. Candidly, it *is* hard, because now we're getting into specific numbers. My perspective: Everything valuable is hard, and I see this as an opportunity to create your Rich Life from a blank page. Let's do it together.

You Don't Need a Budget

In my experience, fewer than 1 percent of people ever stick to a budget longer than two months. Why? In a nutshell, budgets are overwhelming and ineffective, and they feel bad. Consider what it takes to merely create a budget: You have to tally your spending from the last several months (nobody knows these numbers). Then you have to create an arcane spreadsheet, with hundreds of rows tracking every dime, including how much you spent on baking soda in February.

And after all that work . . . you're just staring at a bunch of numbers. Do you know what to do next? Of course not. All you know is you've "been bad." To top it off, you have to keep tracking all your spending in this gargantuan spreadsheet *for the rest of your life.*

And for what? Sure, you might prevent yourself from overspending on Saran Wrap, but what do you actually get from the onerous tracking and restriction and finger-pointing for the next 40 years?

The answer is nothing.

You don't need a budget. Real money management is focused on designing a Rich Life and using your money to live it. Tracking tiny expenses is pointless if it's not tied to a bigger vision, which almost all budgets miss.

Imagine a CSP like a beautifully organized living room. When you set yours up correctly, your money management will feel *calm.* You'll build in room for the things you love—whether that means getting a couple of drinks when eating out, splurging on self-care, or creating a special weekly outing with your family—all while cutting back where you need to.

What Is a Conscious Spending Plan?

A budget looks backward. A Conscious Spending Plan looks forward.

Your CSP lets you decide *where you want your money to go.* If you want to have a weekly date night, or renovate the kitchen, or pay off your debt in six years instead of eight, you can build that in.

Here are the four numbers you need to master to make this work:

Fixed costs: ideally 50–60 percent of take-home pay (meaning after-tax money)
- *Includes your rent or mortgage, car payment, debt payments, groceries—anything that you must pay each month.*

Short-term savings: ideally 5–10 percent of take-home pay
- *Money you may need in the next 1–5 years, including an emergency fund, down payment for a house or car, vacation fund.*

Long-term investments: ideally at least 10 percent of take-home pay
- *Where the real wealth is created. Includes all investments: 401(k), IRA, and so on. This is long-term money you won't need for at least 10 years.*

Guilt-free spending: ideally 20–35 percent of take-home pay
- *The things you love spending on: eating out, travel, massage, beauty products, children's activities—it's your call.*

The philosophy here is simple: If you hit these four numbers each month, you have a very good chance of living a Rich Life.

It's that simple. No need to track 200 numbers every month. No need to argue about an unexpected $50 at Target. Just a beautiful system that lets you look forward—saving, investing, and spending on the things that matter to you—no matter what your income is.

Here's an example of how it works: John and Joan sit down once a month to review their numbers. They know their fixed costs, savings, investments, and guilt-free spending numbers, so their Monthly Money Meeting is straightforward.

They love eating out, so in their guilt-free spending, they have built in room to go to restaurants twice a week. Last week, however, they splurged on a big dinner out with family, and they've exceeded their number. No biggie—they both agree to skip eating out next week to get back on track.

They wrap up with a few questions to tackle next time they talk. Calm, cool, and methodical.

Before we start building your CSP, there's an important concept I want you to internalize. To live a Rich Life, you have to elevate yourself to a higher level of planning. For most people, this means anticipating your expenses one year out. As you become savvier with money, you'll start planning at the 5-year, 10-year, and even 30-year level. This may make you uncomfortable at first because we're so used to operating on a day-to-day basis. But you can't live a Rich Life if you're looking only a few days ahead.

Creating Your Conscious Spending Plan

You and your partner can make your CSP in three conversations. The first is quick and involves zero research. (I've also created a template for you on page 288, or search online for "Ramit Sethi CSP.")

CONVERSATION #1: GETTING A ROUGH DRAFT DOWN IN 60 MINUTES

Your first conversation involves estimating your monthly income and spending—no need to use anything but your head and a blank page. It will get you the outline of your CSP, like a pencil sketch you will color in later. The theme for today is *fast and easy*—you'll have plenty of opportunities to fine-tune things later.

Start by jotting down your gross and net income—that's what you make before and after taxes—as well as any other money you earn or receive. Divide by 12 to get the monthly income numbers.

For example, if your gross income is $75,000, and your net income is $63,000, write down...

Gross monthly income: $6,250

Net monthly income: $5,250

Then write down your four types of monthly costs. You may know some of these numbers off the top of your head, like your rent or car payment. Others you'll have to estimate. That's okay, but estimate high. (Here's why: If I'm training for a competition, I want to train harder now so the real thing feels easier. In the CSP, I want you to "train harder" by rounding *up* on expenses, because I'd rather you end up with an extra $2,000 at the end of the year than accidentally *owing* $2,000.)

Your Fixed Costs

Let's start with fixed costs, which are the expenses you must pay every month. Here's a simple way to think of fixed costs: Even if one of you lost your job, these are the things you would still be paying. Some of the numbers might vary month to month—like groceries— but just use an average and round up. This should be fast and easy— 20 minutes max—so work as a team, take your best guesses, and don't worry about accuracy. Give each other a high five at the end of the round.

Use these categories for now (you can add or edit them later):

- Housing (mortgage, utilities, insurance, and all other costs; if some of them are annual, divide by 12 to get the monthly cost)

- Car (loan payment, insurance, gas, maintenance, parking tickets)

- Medical (health insurance, prescriptions, and other regular medical costs)

- Debt (monthly payments for credit card debt, student loans, or any other debt except mortgage, which is already covered under housing)

- Cell phones and internet

- Groceries

- Essential clothing

- Donations

- Children's expenses (include items like diapers, clothing, and school supplies)

- Household (for example, drugstore and cleaning supplies)

- Pet (include food, annual care, and other bills)

- Miscellaneous

Monthly fixed costs (add up all of the above)............... $_____

Your Savings

This is what you currently put toward savings goals, such as an emergency fund or down payment on a house, every single month. If the number varies, pick an average and this time, *round down*. If it's zero—honestly, for most people it is—just put zero.

Monthly savings contributions...................................... $_____

Your Investments

These are regular contributions to your 401(k), 403(b), IRA, HSA, and any other investment accounts. (Note: I include a short discussion of pre- and post-tax investments on page 289.)

Monthly investment contributions............................... $_____

Nice job! We're almost done. The final category is my favorite.

Your Guilt-Free Spending

Think about the things you spend money on for fun. I call this category guilt-free spending because once you've finished this book and made a few changes, you'll be able to do the things you love without feeling guilty. When you're considering things like travel that happen sporadically, guesstimate an annual total, then divide by 12.

I've included some categories to help you ballpark your monthly spending on the items below. Remember, if you don't have the numbers in your head, just guess, but estimate high. You might be alarmed at how high the numbers are—especially if you round up. Most people are. That's good!

- Eating out/ordering in (include restaurant meals with friends and anniversary meals)

- Nonessential clothing (include discretionary purchases, accessories, even dry cleaning)

- Health/fitness (gym, sports, classes)

- Self-care (facials, massage, beard trims, nails, blowouts, haircuts and treatments, waxing)

- Subscriptions (Netflix, Amazon Prime, apps, games, all of it)

- Travel (add up the cost of annual trips, then divide by 12)

- Gifts (birthdays, holidays, etc.)

- Hobbies

- Home decoration and improvement (include home renovation here)

- Housecleaning

- *Add your own.*

Monthly guilt-free spending (add up all of the above)................ $_____

As a final step, take the total amount from each category and divide each one by your take-home pay to benchmark all your spending. For example: fixed costs of $3,000/take-home pay of $5,000 = 60% (this is a solid ratio to be at). The CSP makes it easy to see what's going on. Once it's all on paper, you can make decisions and redirect your spending.

BREAK TIME

Okay, it's time to sit back and relax for a second. You've got numbers on the page! That's an accomplishment.

In the coming pages, we're going to refine those numbers. Then I'm going to show you how to adjust them so you can pay off debt faster, save and invest more, and spend more on the things you love. You're going to get in control of where your money is going. Before we get to that, I want you to check in about how you're feeling right now. Are you shocked to see where your money is going? Excited to get some clarity? Freaking out? Hopeful? All of those are normal.

Each time you refine and revise your CSP, it'll become lighter, easier, and clearer. The more you work on your plan, the more you'll understand it and the more control you'll have. Soon, this CSP will be transformed from a list of numbers to a North Star for your Rich Life. We'll get there together.

But for now, I want you to step away, give each other a hug, and set this project aside. Don't even talk about money for the rest of the day! Go do something you both enjoy—and celebrate this huge accomplishment.

CONVERSATION #2: DIGGING FOR DETAILS

Now that you have a rough draft of your CSP, let's go back and make sure you got all those numbers right. To do this, you're going to go beyond your estimates and look at your actual spending. This is like taking a black-and-white drawing and filling in the colors.

I've included a simple CSP template on page 288. But I recommend you download the digital version (search "Ramit Sethi CSP"), which is even easier to use and does several of the calculations for you. One request: Please don't start from an old budget. Begin with a clean slate.

For this analysis, I recommend you choose both a "regular" month and an irregular month (like a holiday or big travel month) and average them. This 2-month view will let you see how your spending fluctuates. Then you're going to slot each expense into your categories (fixed costs, savings, investments, and guilt-free spending) and account for any surprise expenses.

By doing this, you're swapping in your estimated numbers from Conversation #1 with *real numbers*, which will make your CSP much more accurate.

Assembling your numbers the fast and easy way: Log in to your credit card website, which will let you pull all these transactions based on any month. They'll even categorize the spending for you! (If you use more than one card, do this for each of them.) This will let you determine how much you spent for gas last month, groceries, eating out, subscriptions—everything on your list. But here's where it gets tricky: Most couples don't pay for everything with credit cards. They pay cash for certain things, write checks for others, use financial apps like Venmo for paying friends back, and use different bank accounts for different expenses, which is why you might need to go one step further.

Assembling your numbers the more advanced way: If you want completely accurate numbers, create your own spreadsheet and analyze every expense for those months. Your credit card website will let you download your transactions, which you can then open up in any spreadsheet and recategorize using the categories on page 128 (pet care, groceries, and so on). Then review your bank transactions and do your best to estimate cash expenditures.

Looking at your real numbers will give you a crystal-clear picture of where your money is going—and where you can slash radically so you can spend more on the things you love. Below, I'll show you how to account for things like extra holiday expenses. And don't forget, you can always come back and refine your CSP later.

This process will likely take you a few hours. I recommend blocking off a couple of back-to-back, two-hour blocks, perhaps on a weekend. You can dig into the numbers, take a break, then pick back up and, ideally, finish the next day. If you still have unknowns, write them down and come back another day soon with a fresh mind.

Add your upcoming "one-time" expenses

One of the key factors in living a Rich Life is making a plan *before you need to.* That's exactly what you'll do right now with a 12-month view: setting yourself up so you're not surprised by "one-time" or irregular expenses.

Here's how you do it: Identify the expenses and the amount, divide by 12, then put that amount into the appropriate category in your Conscious Spending Plan and calculate the percentage of take-home pay. For example, if you know you're going to send your child to summer camp for $5,000, that's about $415/month ($5,000/12 months), which goes into your fixed costs under "Summer Camp."

Here are some common irregular expenses:

- Property tax

- Tuition (school, camp) or other education fees

- Car (repairs, maintenance, registration, purchase of a new car)

- Home (repairs, maintenance, upgrades, furniture)

- Tech purchases (phone, computer)

- Pet expenses (non-annual vet bills, toys, boarding)

- Holiday expenses (transportation, gifts)

- Vacation expenses (transportation, accommodation, food, drink, tips, taxes)

- Celebrations (anniversaries, birthdays, weddings)

- Entertainment (concerts, theater)

- Medical (dental, doctor's appointments, medication, treatment)

- Classes/lessons (such as programs from iwt.com/products)

- Food (eating out)

- Hobby/leisure costs

- Last-minute travel emergencies

- Life insurance premiums

It's easy to skip this exercise, thinking that these costs are impossible to predict. Resist that urge! The truth is, you can make decent estimates, and I want you to follow my 85 percent principle: Getting 85 percent of the way there is better than not planning at all.

Ballpark it. For example . . .

- *In June, we have that trip for my cousin's wedding* (airfare, hotel, rental car, transportation to and from the airport, plus 25 percent for taxes and miscellaneous costs).

- *We're probably going to need to replace the air conditioner in the living room. That's going to be $3,000, so we should put $250/month aside for that.*

- *The holidays will be big, because my whole family is coming in* (number of people you're buying gifts for times average amount you're likely to spend, plus food and drinks).

Your numbers are getting more accurate at this point. Now that you've factored in your averaged 2-month review and your 12-month estimates of upcoming expenses, let's finish it off: Add 15 percent to your fixed costs for anything you may have forgotten, and your CSP is done.

Many people find that their hearts are pounding as they fill out the real numbers for the first time. It's hard enough just to gather these figures; it's even harder to categorize them. But the most difficult thing may be grappling with our emotions, because the way we spend our money represents our choices, our priorities, our mistakes, even our identities. Most of us never take the time to lay our finances out like this.

That's the reason I broke this process of getting your numbers into multiple steps: For most people, analyzing their actual spending is incredibly intimidating. They believe they need to account for every cent before they can move forward, so they give up before they even start. What's more, they're scared of what they're going to find. I wanted Conversation #1, where you jotted down your estimates, to be a fast first step, setting you up for the more detailed work in Conversation #2.

Doing the work is hard—and the results often are, too. Most people's jaws are on the floor when they realize how much they're spending. If you're shocked, that's okay. When you factor in *everything*, the numbers can be overwhelming. It's scary to see that you're

CREATING YOUR CONSCIOUS SPENDING PLAN

spending more than you thought—and maybe also to discover that you're spending more than you have. The good news is that you've decided to shine a light on it.

My philosophy: It's better to know than not to know! Now that you're aware of where your money is going, you can adapt your spending to match up with your shared Rich Life vision . . . which is exactly what we're going to do in Conversation #3.

CONVERSATION #3: REALIGNING YOUR SPENDING TO MATCH YOUR RICH LIFE VISION

So far, you've jotted down what you think you're spending. Then you refined those numbers by digging into your actual spending, including planning for "unexpected" expenses. Now we get to realign your numbers to correspond with your Rich Life vision.

But before we get into the nitty-gritty of adjusting your spending, let's zoom out and look at exactly how you can use money to live your Rich Life. This will help you remember why you need to make some cuts. Let's do it right now!

Pick something you love. Maybe it's a new furniture set for your backyard or a weekend trip. For this example, let's go with the furniture. Talk with your partner about your vision for the patio set. Where will you put it? How many people do you want to accommodate? Will the furniture be upholstered? Do some online research and get a sense of what the set you envision will cost. Be sure to include taxes, delivery, and any ancillary costs like furniture covers for the rain. Divide by 12 to get the monthly amount you need to put away, then write that number down in the savings section of your CSP. For instance:

> "The patio set will cost us $1,200. We're going for the all-weather couches and a couple of tables. If we add $350 for an umbrella and $250 for price increases, taxes, and delivery, that's $1,800. If we want the furniture in a year, we'll have to save $150/month ($1,800/12). That seems like too much, so let's buy it in 18 months instead: $100/month. We can do that."

It's now an official savings item in your CSP! And in Chapter 9, you'll set up automatic savings so your money will be automatically going to your new furniture fund. (Of course, feel free to replace the example and numbers with something you want to buy or do.)

Now it's time to make some changes in your Conscious Spending Plan. You get to redirect your money to the things you care about, and use your Less Dials list in Chapter 4 to cut spending on the things that aren't part of your Rich Life.

The 3 Questions I Always Get about the CSP

1. "We know we need to cut back on eating out. Can we skip the CSP and just start there?"

No! Many of us *think* we know where we're overspending, but we don't understand the broader perspective on how our expenses compare with our savings, investments, and net worth. For example, many couples feel guilty about their takeout bill but never think about how much, if anything, they're automatically saving each month. The CSP will help you see the full picture and lay the groundwork for everything that follows, so trust the process.

2. "Isn't this just a budget?"

No. A budget is backward-looking, while your Conscious Spending Plan looks forward. More important, if you spend the rest of your life using a budget and you're successful, what do you get? Basically, you spent your life tracking random numbers. But if you're successful using the Conscious Spending Plan, which is a lot simpler, you will have lived your Rich Life, including eating out, traveling, buying things you love, and investing to build true wealth.

Tracking numbers is not the point. Living a Rich Life is. That's what your Conscious Spending Plan will help you do.

This is where you go from dreams to reality. As you move through this step, ask yourselves, *To live our Rich Life, what big change are we prepared to make?*

I'll help you make these changes. First, I want you to free up some cash every month. Working together, go line by line through your guilt-free spending and identify two categories where you can cut spending by 50 percent over a period of six months. Aim to cut 10 percent per month till you reach your goal.

3. "Can I fill out the CSP without my partner?"

You need to work through these numbers together so that when you start talking about making changes, you'll both understand what it will truly take. I understand that you may be busy, that one of you might not be as comfortable with the numbers, and that there will always be a reason to delay looking at them.
But you bought this book because you wanted to get on the same page. This is literally getting on the same page—so do it together.

If your partner is resistant . . .

» **Bring it up gently.** You could try saying, "Hey, I'm reading this book. . . . I'd really love for us to do this exercise together. Would you be down for that?"

» **Remember, this is a series of conversations.** It's not One Big Conversation. Keep things light, knowing that you'll have many more opportunities to talk about money.

» **Admit when you don't know the answer.** If you don't know the answer to something, raise your hand and say, "I have to be honest. . . . I don't know!" Make it theatrical. Be funny. Laugh together. If it's not critical at this very moment, jot it down and tackle it later. I'd rather you laugh and keep moving than get a precise number out to three decimal places.

Here's a fairly straightforward example:

Eating out: Current spending: $500/month
    Month 1: $450
    Month 2: $400
    Month 3: $450 (Sometimes you backslide!)
    Month 4: $375
    Month 5: $300
    Month 6: $250

Now let's tackle an example that's more complicated: irregular expenses like travel. Let's say you take four $1,200 trips every year, for a total of $4,800. How would you cut back? Well, you could reduce the number of times you travel, like this:

Traveling: Current spending: $400/month
    Month 1: $1,200
    Month 2: $0
    Month 3: $0
    Month 4: $0 (Instead of one $1,200 trip every three months, you decide to skip two, which cuts your annual spend by 50 percent.)
    Month 5: $0
    Month 6: $0

Or you could change the type of trip you take, such as making it shorter or staying in less expensive lodging:.
    Month 1: $600 (In this example, you cut the trip length in half.)
    Month 2: $0
    Month 3: $0
    Month 4: $600 (Here, you stayed at a cheaper hotel.)
    Month 5: $0
    Month 6: $0

As you can see, you have lots of options for *how* you cut your spending. The important thing is targeting the right number and creating your plan together.

Do this process with two separate expenses and you suddenly have *hundreds of dollars every month* to redirect to the things you really care about.

"We've Already Cut All We Can!" Is Rarely True

I know what it's like to feel like you're stuck. A few years ago, I was overwhelmed in my business. I had meetings every 30 minutes, I was pulled in 10 different directions, and I barely had time to eat lunch. I tried to cut back on meetings, but every time I tried to get out of one, some reason would come up that I needed to attend.

If someone had told me to "think long term" and make a plan, I would have stared at them blankly. I was just trying to get through the day.

Finally, after months of trying to play whack-a-mole with meetings, I canceled them all. I began with a blank calendar and asked myself, *What's important here?*

Marketing was important for my business, so I dedicated 25 percent of my time to marketing meetings. Products were important, so that was another 25 percent. Rather than cutting one tiny area after another, I just started fresh. And that made all the difference.

This is the same process you're doing with your CSP: starting over and matching your money with your priorities. This is much more effective than trying to cut one random expense after another. I've worked for hours with couples who were spending more money than they made, yet they had an excuse to keep every expense. I finally gave them a blank page and—like magic!—they suddenly changed all of their spending for the better.

For example, if you decide right up front that each month you're going to save 5–10 percent, invest 5–10 percent, and use 20–35 percent for guilt-free spending, you might suddenly realize . . .

- you don't really want to buy lunch four times a week anymore—you'd rather spend that money on two special dinners every month.

- you're going to have to cut the kids' swim lessons.

- there's no way around it—one of you will have to sell their car.

Remember, this is about recalibrating your spending so your money goes toward *your* Rich Life. I find that when couples work on their CSP, everyone agrees in theory that they want to spend extravagantly on the things they love and cut costs mercilessly on the things they don't. The problem is when I ask them to cut back mercilessly, they give me the same response. "There's nothing more we can cut. We've tried everything."

Reframe: You don't save and invest what's *left*. You save and invest *first*. This is what "pay yourself first" means, and once you pick savings and investment numbers (I recommend 5–10 percent each, minimum), the rest of your spending flows around that.

TALKING—NOT FIGHTING— ABOUT MAKING CUTS TO YOUR CSP

Let me tell you about a couple I worked with recently. Jennifer and Andrew had about $4,600 in credit card debt. When I went through their numbers, it turned out—to their shock—that they were spending about $600 per month on Grubhub, a food delivery service. That was money that could have been going toward killing off that debt. What was interesting about our conversation (episode #96 of my podcast) was how incredibly difficult it was to get this loving couple to talk directly about cutting down this expense.

Here we have a couple spending hundreds of dollars on takeout, which they admit is "really embarrassing," and yet they still struggled to talk about cutting back on it! That's because even an obvious expense like takeout isn't simple. It represents a splurge, a relief from the day-to-day responsibilities, and after a while, it's something you become accustomed to. The idea of cutting it out feels painful to contemplate.

I helped them discuss what Grubhub meant to them. Jennifer, who carried the domestic load by default—as many women do—wanted Andrew to *notice* when she was exhausted and needed help with food for the family. But until now, she hadn't been clear about what

Ramit's Financial Red Alerts

I've developed four simple questions that help you determine if your finances put you in extreme danger. I came up with these after speaking to couple after couple who would casually tell me about their $62,000 in credit card debt, two $70,000 trucks, and 78 percent of income going to fixed costs, while nonchalantly asking, "What do you think, Ramit?"

What do I think? I'm about to have a stroke! I can't breathe right now! How is my heart rate 195 and you're calmly sipping a lemonade?

If you're in danger, you need to know it—now. Ask yourselves these questions:

» On your Conscious Spending Plan, does your spending number exceed 100 percent?

» Do your fixed costs exceed 65 percent?

» Are you in credit card debt?

» Were you and your partner unable to get through Conversations #2 or #3?

If you answered yes to any of the above, this is a Ramit Red Alert, which means you need to make immediate changes. Tell your partner this is serious and you need to act swiftly. If you get pushback, blame it on me. Addressing these issues should be your top priority.

she needed. Even when I watched them talk, she would rush to offer solutions without letting Andrew figure out what to do.

I helped them have a constructive conversation where I asked her to "toss back the ball" of responsibility anytime Andrew tried to hand it to her. In the end, they freed up hundreds of dollars per month to put toward their credit card debt.

Andrew said, "The conversation made me accountable, and was probably one of the clearest we've had in a long time."

What do *you* want to say to your partner in plain English? What do they need to hear? You can say it clearly and still be nice. The best tools you have for talking with your partner about money are the CSP and your Rich Life vision. Talk about the documents rather than pointing fingers at each other. As you begin shifting things around, keep going back to this question: "To live our Rich Life, what big change are we prepared to make?"

Keep in mind that you're cutting back on certain things to fund others. In Jennifer and Andrew's case, they're not simply cutting back on Grubhub; they're becoming a couple that's debt-free. And they're building the skills to communicate clearly about what they want and need. Remember, a key part of cutting is deliberately redirecting that money to where you want it to go, because otherwise it just gets absorbed into your spending.

The CSP Commandments

Here are some dos and don'ts of recalibrating your spending:

Don't try to randomly cut back 5 percent on everything in all categories. It's depressing and it doesn't work.

Do choose two areas of discretionary spending and commit to cutting each by 50 percent over the course of six months, which will usually free up hundreds of dollars in cash every month that you can redirect toward your Rich Life.

Don't obsess about the "sacrifice" of what you're cutting.

Do start with the right mindset: You're not cutting things you love—you're *building the Rich Life you want.* This subtle shift puts you in control and gives you a *reason* for making these changes. If you view this process as simply eliminating all the things you love, you're doomed. Nobody wants to be restricted! I don't, you don't, your partner doesn't. Reframe your changes to focus on what you're building, not on what you're eliminating.

Don't point fingers and use language like "you always . . ." or "you never . . ."

Do talk about your vision, your numbers, and "our future." Use the pronoun *we* whenever you can. *("Looks like we're spending too much on X. . . . I really want us to be able to spend more on Y.")*

Don't cash out your retirement investments to pay off debt. A lot of couples see big numbers and panic, selling the only investments they have, which costs them dearly in the future. (The only exception is if you're in dire circumstances, but I would contact my lenders to ask for help, sell my house, and take on a second job before even considering cashing out investments.)

Do slow down before making dramatic changes. Explore all options, including calling your credit card or student loan company and asking for help. Many will work with you on a payment plan. Often, people in severe debt will do everything except the one thing that works: *Make a debt-payoff plan, set up automatic payments, and be patient.*

Don't call for a dramatic spending freeze if things look bad.

Do get real with yourselves: Are you genuinely going to change all your spending overnight? In my experience, sweeping proclamations almost never stick. I'm looking for real, sustainable changes that you're actually going to follow every single week. Better to save 5 percent consistently than to dream about suddenly saving 40 percent.

What to Do If Your Numbers Are Hopeless

It's easy to look away when you feel helpless. Some of us deny the truth ("It's not actually that bad!"). Others cuddle with their kids or spouse or take their dog for a walk.

I take comfort in the cutthroat world of business, where I find inspiration in dramatic cost-reduction techniques.

I'm serious. When companies have grown too much by overhiring or overexpanding, they are extremely good at recognizing it and making changes—fast. If they don't, they go bankrupt. Companies will "right-size" by cutting staff, downsizing office space, and redefining goals. You and I should be inspired by how swiftly companies move in order to survive.

Unfortunately, most of us don't do this with our own personal finances. We ignore the problem. We secretly hope it will fix itself. We come up with grandiose solutions ("We just need to earn more money!"). But what we really need to do is recognize reality and quickly make big changes, just like multibillion-dollar companies do.

Let me be clear what "big changes" mean: Selling your house and renting a small apartment is a big change. Selling your nice car and downgrading to an old, used car is a big change, as is pulling your children out of expensive after-school activities. These are unfathomable to most of us, and we'll try *everything except what actually needs to be done.* But if your numbers feel hopeless, this might be exactly what you need to do.

My philosophy: The changes are either going to come *from* you or *at* you. I prefer they come from you. No more avoiding the problem. Let's get aggressive!

Don't make vague promises about spending less.

Do get specific with the *big* areas you want to cut, even comically specific. For example, if you were to agree to cut down grocery costs, the conversation might go like this:

"Can we get groceries down from $800 to $600 next month?"

"I'll take that on. I think we can do it." *(Ideally one person takes ownership.)*

"Is there anything I can do to make it easier?" *(You're a team building your joint Rich Life. This is a great opportunity to work as teammates. If your partner doesn't volunteer this, tell them, "I would love it if you asked me how you could support me." They can't read your mind!)*

"I think if I just focus while I'm shopping, it won't be that difficult, but it's always chaos, with the kids in the cart asking for cookies. How about I shop on Sunday mornings, while the kids are home with you, so I can concentrate? That would really help." *(Notice how specific this is. Saving money on big items isn't just about "trying harder" or even setting an intention. It's about painstakingly peeling back the layers of logistics to discover why you're overspending and how you can cut back.)*

"Oh, that's no problem. I can do that."

"Thank you! This is going to be so great. I love that we're doing this together." *(Take every opportunity to celebrate and reconnect over your Rich Life.)*

Beautiful.

Your Emergency Fund

I love a healthy emergency fund. It's a financial moat that allows me the security of knowing that even if something goes wrong, my family and I will be okay. At the moment you need it most, you know it'll be there. Pay into it monthly and you'll slowly but surely fortify your financial position.

Emergency funds take a long time to fill up—often through years of slow, methodical contributions. That's fine! Add it as a line item under the savings section of your CSP. Then set up automatic transfers of 3 percent (or more) of your net income into a dedicated savings account (maybe call it "Break Only in Case of Emergency!"). The goal is to amass a sufficient amount to cover three to six months' worth of essential expenses—enough to keep the lights on, the fridge filled, your housing costs paid, and gas in the car, as well as any minimum payments toward debt. You can calculate that amount by tallying the fixed costs section of your CSP and multiplying by three or six—the number of months you've chosen.

Keep that money in a separate savings account and treat it as invisible. But when an emergency strikes, you'll be ready to take rapid action. If a parent falls ill across the country, get to the airport and pick a flight—any flight—without even looking at the cost. This is what you saved for.

I recommend you talk about what qualifies as an emergency so you have a clear list of agreements for when to tap your emergency fund. Here's what the fund is *not* for: covering expenses when your checking account is running low, major purchases you haven't saved up for (*"We should get that 75-inch TV now, while it's on sale, and we'll pay back the emergency fund next month"*), or to help fund a down payment for a house or car.

I hate knowing that one day my family might face an emergency, but I take comfort in knowing that we have our emergency fund, quietly waiting for the moment it's needed.

Always Ask Yourselves: "What Do We Get?"

There's just one more thing. I work long hours, sometimes weekends, and I take on a lot of risk. I always ask myself, *What do I get?*

You should ask yourselves the same question. Try it! Put your hand out, palm up—like you're about to receive money—and ask

The Joy of Guilt-Free Spending

Guilt-free spending is my favorite part of the Conscious Spending Plan because it's the area that brings the most joy, whether your version of joy is single-origin coffee pour-overs, a weekly massage, an afternoon of golf, salsa lessons, or eating out.

Your Conscious Spending Plan will tell you how much you have in guilt-free spending. (This is important because the amount in your bank account will ebb and flow, but your CSP will be there to guide you.) Let's say the plan tells you that you have $1,000 per month in guilt-free spending, and you and your partner decide to split that 50/50. What next?

» Each of you is in charge of $500 for yourselves.

» Every month when you meet to talk money (more on this in Chapter 10), you'll share how much of that you spent. This won't take long because you're just reporting on a number you own, so whether you spent $400 or $423 is beside the point. It's just an opportunity to confirm you're both on top of your guilt-free spending—*and* to share some joy. ("I had the best massage. We should go together next month!")

» If you exceed your guilt-free spending number, it's your responsibility to mention that and fix it.

» If you don't use your guilt-free spending, that's fine— you can roll it over. But don't make a habit of this. Just like certain companies insist employees take vacation days every year, I insist you use the money monthly. It's important for you to build the skills of spending money meaningfully.

yourselves, *What do we get? If we're making all of these changes to free up hundreds of dollars every month, what do we get out of it?*

You have to answer that question for yourselves, because it's specific to your situation. Maybe what you get is paying off crushing debt. (An extra $200 per month could save you over *two years of payments* on a $10,000 credit card balance.) Maybe it's taking your kids to visit their grandparents twice a year. You choose.

This is why it's so essential to make big changes to your expenses—I use the phrase "Cut costs mercilessly," and I mean it—so you can be intentional about where your money is going. When you have a crystal-clear vision of your Rich Life and you're constantly asking yourselves, *What do we get?*, you'll know that you're funding your vision for buying a sailboat or building a dream backyard garden—or whatever is important to you. This is deeply gratifying and powerfully motivating.

You work hard. You're going through this book together. *What do you get?*

•   •   •

Chapter 7 Checklist

☐ Over the course of three conversations, create your Conscious Spending Plan with your partner.

   1. The first conversation is light and breezy—just get your best guesses about your spending on paper, like an initial sketch.

   2. The second conversation lets you fill in the lines with details about actual spending, including expenses coming up in the next 12 months.

   3. The third conversation is where you and your partner commit to making big changes to recalibrate your spending to match your Rich Life vision.

☐ Take joint ownership of your CSP. Have Monthly Money Meetings (see page 196) to make adjustments and stay on track. Money is now a regular, positive part of your life!

☐ Open a dedicated savings account for your emergency fund and set up automatic transfers, even if it's only a small amount. Over time, you'll build your financial moat.

☐ Be sure to ask yourselves, *What do we get?* from recalibrating your spending. Be sure also to redirect the money you've saved toward something you care about—paying down debt, increasing savings and investments, or guilt-free spending.

8

MASTERING YOUR SPENDING

Tackle invisible spending, eliminate overspending, and buy back your time

There's a running joke among doctors: They're seeing a patient for a routine checkup and they ask how things are going. The patient nods and says, "Yup, everything's good!" They talk for a few more minutes, and as the appointment is wrapping up, the doctor begins to leave. She's halfway out the door when the patient suddenly says, "Oh yeah, one thing I forgot to mention, Doc . . . I've been bleeding from the back of my head for the last six days."

This happens on my podcast all the time. People will come on and earnestly say, "We just don't know where the money is going!" Then, three hours into our conversation, they'll casually drop a bombshell that blows my mind.

I remember a couple from Kansas named Austin and Annie. They were high earners in a low-cost-of-living area with a household income of $130,000. If they had been aligned with their money, Austin and Annie could have been in an amazing financial situation. But somehow their money was just slipping away.

At least that's how it seemed for an hour, while we talked about grocery bills, the cost of takeout, and other areas they disagreed about. Then Annie casually mentioned Austin's tools. "Tools? What tools?" It turned out that for his job, which he described as "turning wrenches," Austin was spending somewhere between $1,500 and $2,500 *per month* on tools.

"A year ago, I was $36,000 in debt strictly with tools," Austin said. "And the most I've ever bought a car for was $3,000. My toolbox itself cost more than any vehicle I've ever purchased."

As a guy who doesn't know the difference between a Phillips and a flathead, I wasn't even aware there were toolboxes that expensive. But I understand why Austin didn't bring it up earlier. When something is deeply woven into your identity—as Austin's tools are for him—your mind uses a variety of techniques to shield you from confronting the problem head-on. *Where is all our money going? No, it can't be my tools. I use them every day.*

That's why getting your numbers on paper is critical: It removes the narratives we create around our expenses and makes "invisible spending" black and white. For Austin and Annie, it was crystal clear: When you're making $130,000 and you're struggling with the price of groceries, you cannot afford to spend tens of thousands of dollars on tools.

Invisible Spending

When I look at couples' Conscious Spending Plans, the major categories where I see overspending are housing and cars. But it doesn't end there. There's plenty of invisible spending that people are shocked by.

Invisible spending is the spending we subconsciously don't want to confront. We play psychological tricks on ourselves to stay in the dark. Here are the most common ways that people miss their invisible spending:

Spending that is part of your identity. To me—a guy who doesn't own a hammer—it was obvious that Austin was spending too much on tools. But it didn't even occur to Austin that $100,000 worth of tools might be a problem. He'd concocted a very logical reason: "I need them for work." Austin needs $100,000 of tools in the same way that I need a spaceship to go to the grocery store.

This is a common identity issue—*I need this thing to be the person I think I am.* You'll see the same thing for trucks, fancy handbags, pricey kids' activities, houses, and travel. I want you to work toward the things you love, but before you buy them, you must be able to afford them. My suggestion: When it comes to examining your spending, everything is on the table, even the things that make you who you are. If you want to live a Rich Life, you'll have to change your identity. Don't think of this as a loss. Think of the next chapter of your life.

Mental bucketing. Our minds play tricks on us. When we're thinking of our spending, we count some expenses—but we ignore others. This is "mental bucketing." For example, it's shocking how many people who have hundreds of thousands in student loans don't consider that part of their debt. When I ask them about their finances, they'll often say, "It's fine." When I ask about the $150,000 in student loans, they laugh and say, "Oh, that doesn't count. I'm taking that to the grave." They also ignore one-time expenses like vacations ("I only took that once, last spring") and discretionary expenses like makeup or snacks ("That was just a little treat").

Allow me to be direct: It doesn't matter if you bought something once, or when you were tired, or when it was raining. It all counts!

Interestingly, people also use mental bucketing in reverse when they don't count money that they actually have. For example, around 40 percent of people don't consider their retirement funds when I ask them how much money they have. They'll say, "Well, I don't really think of that money as real. It's locked in my retirement account." It's real! This is why it's so important to write our numbers down and look at them together.

Not accounting for the true cost of one-time expenses. The human brain is really bad at big expenses. First, we fail to factor in Phantom Costs (see the box on the following page), or all the costs that don't show up on the sticker price. For example, I add 50 percent to the price of my hotel to account for taxes, tips, and meals.

Three Letters That Will Change the Way You Look at Money: TCO

My first car payment was $350. But when I added up all the hidden expenses for my car, including Phantom Costs like gas, parking, insurance, parking tickets, and maintenance, I was paying over *$1,000* per month. This is why I'm obsessed with how much something *truly* costs. Not just the sticker price, but the TCO, or total cost of ownership.

Most of us simply look at the sticker price, never factoring in the Phantom Costs, and then get confused about why we can't seem to get on top of things. One of the best money skills you can develop is accounting for *all* Phantom Costs of major purchases. Remember: You do not want to be surprised by your finances.

Total cost of housing: I add 50 percent to the price of a mortgage. This takes into account insurance, upkeep, taxes, and repairs.

Total cost of your car: You have to factor in not only your monthly payment, but insurance, maintenance, repairs, gas, parking, and so on. The three biggest levers you control are (1) your choice of car, (2) the interest rate, and (3) how long you own your car. Purchase wisely, because you'll likely be spending tens of thousands of dollars more than the amount on the sticker.

You can agree or disagree with my numbers—that's not the point. What's more important is that you factor in Phantom Costs, because they will add up to hundreds of thousands of dollars over your lifetime.

But we're even worse at saving for one-time expenses, especially "unexpected" ones. If you plan to take a $2,500 vacation 12 months from now, you should be putting aside about $210 every month. And let's say you're going to need to replace your roof in about 12 years and it will cost about $15,000. That means you should be putting aside about $100/month for it starting today. (Who does this? Almost nobody.)

Planning ahead is what I mean by going on offense. Once you get out of the habit of reacting to financial situations and instead start looking ahead, you'll give yourself the gift of being prepared no matter what comes your way. You'll realize why it makes so much financial sense to buy and hold on to big purchases like a car and house, where the real savings happen *after* the first few years (the difference between keeping a $40,000 car for 4 years versus 12 years will blow your mind). Most of us don't think like this. We simply stumble into expenses for our whole life, always feeling like we're playing "catch-up"—because we are!

Understanding Overspending

One of my favorite concepts in social psychology is cognitive dissonance, which describes how people handle two conflicting, contradictory ideas. For example, everyone knows that smoking is bad for you. And almost everyone believes that health is important. So how do smokers justify smoking? *"We're all going to die at some point. Might as well enjoy my time here."*

We all know that credit card debt is bad, so why do some people keep spending when they can't afford it? *"At least I'm not like Gerry, who has $50,000 in credit card debt!"* (This, by the way, is why reality TV is so popular.)

People are masterful at justifying behavior that makes no sense. Remember the Money Types I talked about in Chapter 2? Dreamers (page 43) are the most adept at rationalizing unreasonable spending—and most prone to it. Without understanding how the human mind talks its way around certain behavior, there's little chance of changing it.

Here's what overspenders tell themselves:

"It's fine!" Most overspenders don't actually realize they're overspending because they've never truly looked at their numbers. Sure, they've glanced at individual purchases. Maybe they've even peeked at their credit card bill and winced. But they've never fully assessed their entire financial picture, including their net worth, savings rate, investment rate, and everything else included in the Conscious Spending Plan. Shockingly, I routinely speak to couples who are spending more than they make every month *and have no idea.*

"I deserve this." Overspenders have a certain vision of how their life is supposed to be, and that vision is often disconnected from the reality of their finances. If you dig into *why* they overspend, you'll often get an answer like this: "I work hard and I deserve to be able to eat a nice meal." Maybe so, but if I ask, "How do you know what you can afford?" they never have an answer.

"It's not like I do this every day." Overspenders use a clever technique where they tell themselves every cost is just a one-off expense. "I don't take a vacation *every week*. That was a special occasion. It was my fortieth birthday!" If they were honest about how much they spend on these discretionary items—cars, trips, dinners out, clothes—they would have to reckon with the consequences of their actions. Over time, their spending choices become their identity: "I'm the kind of person who stays at the Ritz-Carlton." They avoid an honest accounting because, deep down, they do know they're overspending.

"I want my kids to have more than I had." This is a deeply American invisible script, the unassailable justification we use for overspending and overindulging. After all, who can ever criticize you for wanting to give your kids a wonderful life? The answer is, Ramit

Sethi can. If you really wanted your kids to have more than you had, you would start by modeling a healthy relationship with money. You would teach them the word *no* and explain why. You would know that love is not simply giving kids everything they want, but rather teaching them how to get good at the skill of money—which starts with you.

Overspending can feel overwhelming, but in almost every case I've encountered, overspenders lacked the basic fundamentals: They didn't have a bird's-eye view of their finances, they didn't have a vision of where they wanted their money to go, and they didn't have automatic savings and investing set up. All of this can be fixed! You already know your vision and your numbers. We'll handle the automation soon.

If you've been overspending, it's time to rewrite your identity. Together with your partner, start by answering these questions:

- How would we describe our relationship with money today?

- What do we want our relationship with money to be tomorrow? (Be specific.)

- What changes are we both willing to make to get there?

CAN OVERSPENDERS CHANGE?

Yes, absolutely—if there's a reason to change. Unfortunately, your wanting to make a change is rarely enough. If it were, it would have already worked.

A powerful motivator is a crisp, vivid vision of a Rich Life. Once you and your partner can see the exact place you want to visit, or the joy in your kids' faces as they explore a national park for the first time, then buying random items suddenly becomes less appealing than the rewards of your powerful joint vision. (Revisit Chapter 3 to build or refine your vision.)

For parents, the best motivator is the realization that your kids are watching—and absorbing—your relationship with money. If you have a scarcity mentality, they will probably have a scarcity mentality, too. If Mom is the one who manages money while Dad ignores it, your daughter will probably absorb the lesson that women are supposed to be the ones who manage money, while men can lean back.

Use this motivation! Ask each other, "If we had to be brutally honest, how do we think our kids would describe the way we handle money today? Do we want them to see us fighting about our finances? If we don't change anything, how will they treat money in their future relationships?"

If you don't have kids, look inside: What are the stakes for you to change? What vision would be powerful enough to get you to make a lifestyle change with your money?

"Can We Afford It?"

The way we think about whether we can afford something is usually based on our feelings that day, the amount in our checking account, or how the wind is blowing. How often have you asked yourselves questions like these?

» Can we afford $50 for dinner?

» Can we afford that $1,000 phone?

» Can we afford a $5,000 family vacation?

Those are the wrong things to ask. When you're deciding if you can afford something, here's the right way to think about it:

» Are we automatically contributing 5–10 percent of our take-home pay to our savings accounts every month?

» Are we automatically contributing 5–10 percent (ideally more) to our investment accounts each month?

» Can we pay for this item or experience without going into debt?

When Your Partner Is an Overspender

You already know whether your partner is an overspender. If they are, it can be frustrating and upsetting to watch them derail your shared Rich Life plans again and again. Your job is to understand them deeply and come up with a plan to reach them. (I wish you didn't have to take on this role, but if you want to make a real change together, you'll need to be the one to take the first step.)

When you begin this series of conversations, remember that you've already created a vision and gone through your numbers

If the answer to all these questions is yes, congratulations! You can probably afford it (see page 243 for more specific guidance).

Don't purchase things with your credit card that you can't pay for by the end of the month. I don't want you going into debt for anything, except a house and a car. You're not going into debt to buy a grill. You're not going into debt for clothes. You're not going into debt for a vacation. Either the purchase is covered by the guilt-free money that you've specifically saved for it—or you don't buy it.

When I give people this black-and-white guidance, they are often shocked. *Well, how are we supposed to buy things?* The answer is, you're not! You save and *then* you can buy it. If things are not working out the way you want, it's time to ask, "What specifically can we cut back on so we can redirect funds to this future purchase?"

Knowing if you can afford something starts with numbers, not how you feel. I know this isn't popular to say, but sometimes your feelings are *not that important*. Affordability is primarily about the numbers. Look at the financial answer— *then* you can consider if an item is valuable enough and fits your Rich Life enough to spend money on.

together. Take a second to remind your partner how far you've come, then come in with a positive attitude and genuine curiosity.

First approach

The goal is simply to get them to say yes to having a conversation about their spending.

Try: "I want to have a conversation where we can talk about how we can both feel good about our money. What's a good time to talk?" *(Notice you're not having the conversation, just looking for a micro-agreement by asking for a time. This allows them to mentally prepare and not feel ambushed.)*

Avoid: "We need to talk about your spending."

Creating the plan

The key here is *specifics*. When I first help couples with overspending, invariably I hear the t-word—*try*—as in, "I guess I just have to try harder."

No. I don't "try" to shower every day, nor am I going to "try" to stop overspending. If something is a priority to me, I'm going to make a plan, I'm going to identify areas where I might fail, and then I'm going to attack the problem with overwhelming force.

For instance, if your partner spends too much eating out, ask them how much money they can spend on eating out according to the Conscious Spending Plan (be sure to ask, not tell, so they have skin in the game). Then ask them what their plan is. A bad plan would be "I'll try harder." A good plan would be "I realize I eat out whenever I'm tired. I'm going to plan ahead—like meal prepping on Sundays—so I can take a lunch to work with me. I still want to eat out, but I'll limit it to twice per week." Now, that's a real plan.

Other suggestions for overspenders:

- The overspender is responsible for knowing their numbers and finding a way to manage their spending. The responsibility is theirs, not their partner's.

- Overspenders almost always surround themselves with temptation. If they overspend at Target, they're on the Target mailing list. If they spend too much at Starbucks, they intentionally drive past it every day. Focus on changing your environment if you want to make real spending changes.

- Use the Monthly Money Meeting to share how you're doing with spending. Be patient with your partner: Building a new skill will likely have some bumps along the way. What's important is that they're open and willing to make a change.

- If absolutely necessary, you can use the "envelope" technique, where one person takes a specific amount of cash for the month and once they run out, that's it. I don't love this because it disrupts the account structure I'll outline in Chapter 9. But it is an option for severe cases of overspending.

Following up if there's been even slight improvement

Try: "I noticed that we hit our guilt-free spending number this month! I just wanted to say, I really appreciate it. It means a lot to me." *(Compliments can be given without prescriptive next steps. Let the moment feel good! You can always talk about next steps another day.)* *Avoid:* "That's great. Now let's talk about . . ."

Following up if there's been no improvement or things are worse

Try: "I know we talked about making a change with our finances. How do you think it's going?" *(This should be brought up at a Monthly Money Meeting—not out of the blue. Random critiques about money never produce positive changes. They evoke defensiveness. If things don't change after you've talked several times, it may be time to escalate.)* *Next, try:* "I feel nervous to have this conversation, but I know it's something I have to do. A couple of weeks ago, you and I agreed we would monitor our spending on eating out and drinks. You said you'd be in charge, but I've noticed we've spent more than our plan again. Can you tell me what happened?" *(Let them answer. They'll likely digress into some unrelated topic or turn the conversation back on you. Refocus them.)* "Can you tell me what you're going to do about this?" *(The key is letting them come up with the solution. Do not entangle yourself in the fix when you didn't cause the problem.)*

Finally: "How are you going to make sure this sticks?"

Wrap it up by redirecting to the North Star: "It's really important that you get this under control, because we both have to work together to spend our money like a team."

Avoid: "I knew it. You always say you'll change and then nothing happens."

Whether the issue is overspending or another money affliction, you need buy-in for things to improve. You can set up the perfect meeting structure and say the exact right things, and it's still possible nothing will change. This is reality. That said, I usually find that when people say they've "tried everything," they haven't really tried much. I believe there's almost always a way to improve the way you think about, talk about, and behave with money. But sometimes, your partner just isn't on board.

You'll know because you can feel yourself dragging them along. They'll rarely contribute. Instead, they'll wait for you to suggest something, then begrudgingly agree. If you were to never bring up the topic of money, they'd be perfectly happy to never speak of it again. And if I asked you this question, you'd get a sinking feeling: "Is your partner helping or hurting your journey toward a Rich Life?"

And then, the graver question, the one that's really difficult to ask: "Is this the best partner you could have for your financial life for the next 20, 30, 40 years?"

Ultimately, meetings and scripts can work only if your partner genuinely wants to create a Rich Life together. That's why they're called your partner. If their words and actions reveal to you that they're not a true partner, then you'll know that it's time to ask yourself even more difficult questions.

Low-Value Tasks vs. High-Value Tasks

Low-value tasks

» Comparison shopping to save $2 on blueberries

» Logging in to your credit card app every day to make sure everything's okay

» Feeling guilty that you didn't enter all of your spending into some app

High-value tasks

» Figuring out how to make your spending fit into the four categories of the Conscious Spending Plan

» Creating a big, powerful vision of a Rich Life and using your monthly spending to get there—even if it takes time to save and invest for it

» Talking about money positively and proactively every month—together

Where Almost All of Us Can Cut Back

For 90 percent of the people I talk to, food—whether eating out or ordering in—is the biggest category where there's money to free up and redirect into something that matters more. It's not a mystery. This is an area where most of us are overspending. How do I know? Because you tell me so. In my entire life, I've never heard one person say, "My Rich Life is ordering lukewarm delivery from Chipotle."

There are lots of reasons that restaurant spending seems to slip through our fingers. Food is emotional—buying dinner is about a lot more than just hunger. It's about convenience, impulsivity, reward, and more (see Jennifer and Andrew on page 140).

Tracking restaurant and take-out spending as a couple can be fairly complicated: One of you might buy lunch at work. The other might have a monthly dinner with friends. You pick up a pizza for the kids and pay with the twenty in your coat pocket. You grab something on your way home and don't have the right credit card with you. Maybe you've got bigger kids, and you're Venmo-ing money to

How to Recover When You Overspend

My wife and I recently discovered in our Monthly Money Meeting that we spent *way* more than we thought on a trip to New York. We looked at each other with big eyes, then started digging to learn what had happened. After we figured it out—we spent more on lodging and food than we planned—we fixed it: We adjusted the amount we're putting aside for our next NYC trip, and we cut takeout and a couple of other items that, over time, will balance our finances.

You're going to run into problems—that's a guarantee! But when you plan for it, these problems aren't existential. They become something for you to examine together, like scientists with a microscope.

Did we forget to factor in all the Phantom Costs?

Did we stop tracking our key numbers?

How can we make this better so it doesn't happen next time?

Failure happens in any system. What's important is tackling it as a team—and putting in a fix so that the problem doesn't happen again.

them so they can get food with friends. It's a mishmash, and it can easily get away from you.

I understand. Now let's talk about how to change it.

For tracking, be vigilant about using the same shared credit card for anything that counts as eating out. That will help. Second, be kind and supportive of each other—changing habits around food can be tricky.

I asked my community to share their experiences on slashing funds on eating out/ordering in—and redirecting that money:

"During the pandemic we found a butcher that started delivering to homes, and we've continued to place a monthly order. We freeze it, so we always have delicious cuts of meat ready to cook every weeknight. Because we now do weeknights at home, we don't worry about eating out on weekends."

—*Mary*

"I think the hardest part of not eating out is missing out on the vibe. I'm still figuring out how to get the energy of being in a crowded restaurant—that's what I love most about dining out. One of my Rich Life goals is to start a themed potluck dinner party with friends where everyone brings something— still economically efficient, food is fresher, and get all the social vibes!"

—*Lauren*

"We were eating out at least five to six days a week; the only meal we were making at home was breakfast! Now, we cook every Wednesday and Sunday and we eat leftovers at least one night, which saves us tons of money. I allocate my part to credit card debt. It's hard after a long day to cook and clean up afterward, but watching that debt go down is our reward."

—*Rosana*

Target Is Not Your Rich Life

I'm begging you. Please, please stop with those I'm-overspending-at-Target memes on social media. What will it take for me to stop seeing them whenever I open Instagram? Do I need to close my accounts? My entire business? Just tell me. I'll do anything to make it stop. You know the ones I'm talking about:

"LOL! I went into Target for Saran Wrap and left with $300 worth of stuff. I don't even know what I bought! Anyone else do this??"

I say this with a lot of love: You're too good for this. Your Rich Life cannot be shopping for commodities at a retail store and then boasting how you don't even know what you bought.

I hear too many people half joke about how much they mindlessly spend at Target, walking out of the store with $300, $400, $500 worth of purchases they never meant to make. And there's usually a second joke about not telling their spouse—mischievous look with hand over our mouth! So naughty!—or a major fight when the shopping spree comes to light.

A Rich Life is not wandering into a store, buying a bunch of stuff that makes you feel good for an hour, then going home and forgetting about it. There's no meaning to that. I know this because when I ask people to describe their Rich Life, they never, ever mention Target. Not even the people who spend hundreds of dollars there every month!

Listen, I understand the convenience and sheer appeal. I grew up in suburbia. I know every aisle of Target. They've sold my book! But I find something darkly depressing about these jokes—which are shared almost exclusively by women—because they minimize their dreams, which are so much bigger than a shopping trip.

Lindsey, who was on episode #31 of my podcast, was getting into fights with her husband about her spending at Target. She described stepping into Target like walking into a casino: "I lose track of everything. I just could go and drop $300 if I see a good deal. . . . My scarcity stress goes right out the window. Poof!"

It turned out that she saw Target as a place of joy because that's how she experienced it as a child. She's now trying to replicate that experience—and it's causing financial problems in her marriage.

I asked her, "Do you want to be going to Target as your leisure activity 10 years from now?"

"No!" she replied. "I've got to break that pattern."

Your Rich Life cannot be impulsive spending at a random retail store. A Rich Life is much bigger and more meaningful than that.

Agree on a Worry-Free Spending Number

A young woman messaged me on social media, angry that her husband bought an iced tea every day. She wanted my help to convince him he was wrong. "That's $5 a day!" she said. "It's a waste of money." As we exchanged messages, I asked how much they made. Our rapid back-and-forth suddenly went quiet. Finally, she said, "I'm not comfortable sharing that."

I had to know. I mean, this is why I love my job. I asked again—"ballpark is fine!"—and this time, she gave me their approximate household income: $600,000.

Fascinating. She was messaging me about $5 tea when they make hundreds of thousands of dollars every year. Why? Because money isn't simply about numbers; it's about values. To her, an immigrant who was raised never buying drinks, this was a complete waste of money. To him, the money was inconsequential. It was just a nice treat during lunch.

Couples fight about issues like this all the time, with one partner disapproving of the other's spending habits. This is where a worry-free spending number can solve a lot of problems. For purchases under, say, $20 (or whatever figure you agree on), there's no discussion needed—and no argument. As long as both partners honor the rules, that ends these petty fights once and for all. Pick a number and move on with your life. You have a bigger vision to pursue.

Buying Back Your Time: A Lesson in Underspending

People love the concept of buying back their time. But I've learned that they love the *idea* a lot more than actually doing it.

Think about it: What are some of the things you don't like doing? The most common answers are laundry, cleaning, and grocery shopping. But when I ask people why they haven't spent money to outsource these tasks, they give me a litany of reasons:

- *They can't do it as well as I can.* (Yes . . . that's why you try multiple people and document exactly what you want done.)

- *I can just do it myself.* (I can change the oil in my car, too, but I don't want to.)

- *I'd feel weird.* (At least this is honest—most of us didn't grow up seeing our family pay for help, so by following the American ideal of "not getting too big for our britches," we tell ourselves that paying to have our groceries delivered or our house cleaned monthly would be a "waste of money.")

As the saying goes, if you have a problem that your money can solve, you don't have a problem. That's why in my Rich Life, I cut costs mercilessly on things I don't care about, like a fancy car, but I spend extravagantly on conveniences like bookkeeping, pickup and delivery, and housekeeping. I like to free up time to spend with my family, my friends, and my work.

And frankly, I also like to free up time to do absolutely nothing. I like to watch TV or have a slow morning. More important, that free time isn't simply being lazy: Even though it seems like I'm doing nothing, when I'm relaxing, I'm recovering. I know that when life calls for me to work intensely, I'm going to be rested and ready to perform.

A lot of people frame this kind of relaxation as "being bad." I don't think there's a moral valence to leisure. I'm buying back my time, and I'm going to enjoy myself! Here's a path to buying back yours:

1. *Make a list of everything you do on a weekly basis.* I like weekly because it forces you to get specific with your weekdays and weekends. Laundry, grocery shopping, cooking, vacuuming, mowing the lawn, picking up the kids from school, dropping off returns at UPS, cleaning the car, watering the plants, cleaning the gutters, filling up the gas tank . . . all of it. It's especially revealing to do this exercise with your partner, because they'll point out things you do that you've never considered—and vice versa. On the list of items, circle anything that's not part of your shared Rich Life.

   With your partner, rank your top three items and, finances permitting, start creating a plan to pay for help. (Begin by choosing one area. This doesn't mean you have to hire someone today, but I want you to practice the skill of *making a plan*.) Get creative! For example, if you live in Austin, Texas, search for "Austin at-home car wash." Remember this motto: *My money is good money*, which means that there are people who are happy to help you solve problems if you pay them well.

2. *Accept that "paying the problem away" is a skill.* Most people never hire someone, so when they try to use money to solve a household problem, they fail miserably and conclude that this doesn't work for them. No! It takes time. If you try to hire someone for household help, your first four hires quite possibly could fail. That's normal! Each time, talk through your expectations and document results. Remember, you and your partner are on the same team here. You're probably going to learn that paying more gets you much better results. Finally, the goal is not perfection—it's for the job to get done at least 80 percent as well as you could do it.

3. *If your Rich Life involves freeing up time, make a plan for how you're going to use that time.* I've realized that, unlike me, some people don't like lying horizontally on the couch for nine hours at a time, chasing down increasingly obscure corners of the internet for some meaningless drama on social media. Apparently most people become very anxious sitting around

doing nothing. Weird, but if this is you, I recommend being deliberate about what you're going to do with your new free time. Turn to your shared Rich Life list and talk with your partner: *If we get our groceries delivered, that will save us three hours every Sunday. What should we do with that time? We could go to the park with the kids, see a friend for lunch, or even sleep in.* It's the same as making a plan for what you're going to do with your extra money once you finish paying off debt—you want to take advantage of all the work you're doing!

Chapter 8 Checklist

☐ Get honest about your invisible spending and overspending. Start by having a candid conversation with your partner: What are you spending too much on? Where can you cut back?

☐ Figure out the psychology of your spending. Do you spend because you're tired? Bored? Because you don't feel in control? Spend time acknowledging this and then create a plan to stick to the CSP and keep each other on track. Have regular check-ins to recognize progress and correct mistakes when they happen.

☐ Create a joint worry-free number below which any spending is okay. Like a pack of gum, this number is now inconsequential to you. If you're not sure what this number should be, I recommend starting at $20.

☐ If you're on track with your CSP, consider areas where you might buy back your time. Are there tasks you dislike that you could outsource? If you can't afford it now, make a plan to save for it in the future.

HOW TO SET UP YOUR ACCOUNTS

Build a system so your money flows automatically

M y most vivid fantasies begin as I'm standing in the airport security line.

That's right. Some people fantasize about a torrid one-night encounter or how they'd spend a million dollars. I daydream about how I'd improve the efficiency of an airport terminal. It begins when I'm almost at the front of the security line, where the guy in front of me is on his phone, completely oblivious to all the people he's holding up. I start repeating things to myself. *You have one job at this very second, and you can't do it?* My blood pressure rises. When he finally looks up and lurches toward the agent, he fumbles for his ID. Of course he didn't have his wallet ready.

Then I get to the gate, where the worst behaviors of humanity emerge. I sit down and begin planning how I would run the boarding process of a plane. Delta would wonder why their turnaround time plummeted by 40 percent at this one particular gate at LAX. They would spend $250,000 on a research study, which would lead them back to one person.

Gate Agent Sethi.

A lot of my fantasies involve systems. My wife and I have systems for which credit card to use, who holds our passports when we travel internationally, and who loads and empties the dishwasher.

These systems mean that I always know we have blueberries in the fridge, which drawer the scissors are in, and where our money is flowing. We decided once, then we built a system, and now that system frees us up to think about everything else that matters to us.

This is why I love systems—they mean you don't have to revisit the same issue over and over. You don't have to fight about it. You don't even have to *think* about it. Life is smoother and calmer, and you can focus on the things that bring you joy.

Just as it's a huge relief to never wonder if the dishwasher is dirty or clean, there's great comfort in knowing how much money you have and what you can afford. But it can go beyond just a sense of relief.

With a few tweaks from Gate Agent Sethi, your finances will be calm, predictable, and even magical.

How to Set Up Bank Accounts as a Couple

When I look at the finances of couples, I often see extremely confusing account setups. Money moves haphazardly. One partner spends on the joint card, another uses their personal card. Sometimes they pull money from savings.

No!

I understand the confusion, since most people simply bring their existing accounts into a relationship, then try to retrofit them together. But that doesn't work. It would be like me trying to combine my playlist of Boyz II Men, Celine Dion, and Jon Secada with your music. What a mess.

Couples need to talk about bank accounts just like they need to talk about finances in general—gently, openly, and with a spirit of teamwork. Your bank accounts and credit cards are the foundation of your entire financial system. Let's get them right.

RAMIT'S SIMPLE ACCOUNT SETUP FOR COUPLES

What you need

- *One joint checking account:* Consider this your "money inbox." All paychecks are directly deposited here and then "processed" according to your rules, flowing to your savings accounts, investments, and bill payments—even allowing you both individual guilt-free spending.

- *Three to five joint savings accounts:* Each savings account corresponds to a major goal. For example, your three accounts might be . . .

  - "Emergency fund"

  - "Down payment"

  - "Vacation"

  Money is automatically deposited into each of these accounts from your joint checking every month and rarely comes out. I recommend no more than five savings accounts.

- *Individual checking accounts:* You'll each have your own checking account, giving you the ability to calibrate your personal spending more carefully. This is also helpful if one of you tends to overspend: Now you can limit yourself using your individual money.

- *Individual savings accounts:* These are accounts where you can save for larger individual items, such as a trip with friends or to pay for premium versions of your joint expenses. For example, this is how I pay for higher-end hotels on our joint trips (page 182). Individual savings accounts are automatically funded from your individual checking accounts.

- *Three credit cards:* One for joint expenses, one for your personal expenses, and one for your partner's. The joint card is used for shared expenses like groceries, household costs, and subscriptions. The individual cards give each of you a credit card for guilt-free spending—having separate cards makes it easy to track this spending.

- **_Retirement investment accounts:_** This is where real wealth is created! These include 401(k)s, IRAs, and so on. If your employer doesn't already do this, set up automatic transfers so money is deposited into these accounts every month and almost never comes out until later in life.

- **_Joint personal investment account (optional):_** This is appropriate for high-income couples who have already maxed out their individual tax-advantaged investing options like 401(k)s and still want to continue investing in a taxable account. It's funded from your joint checking account.

How the money flows

Your salaries are deposited directly into your joint checking account (if you contribute to a pre-tax retirement account, like a 401(k), that money will already be taken out of your paycheck). After this, your joint savings and individual checking accounts (and possibly

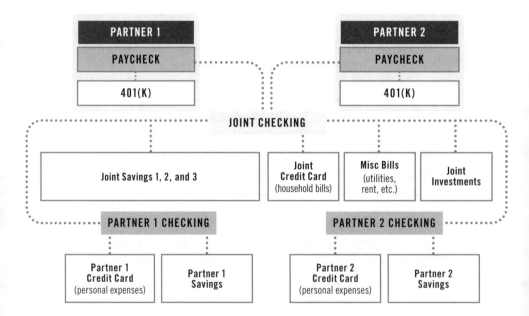

additional investment account) will automatically "pull in" predetermined amounts of money every month. You can set up the timing so if you get paid on the first of the month, your accounts will draw in on the fifth, ensuring you always have money available. It's intentional that the money first flows into your joint checking, then into other checking and savings: You're a couple first, individuals second.

Your individual savings accounts are automatically funded from your individual checking.

For joint expenses, use the joint credit card. That card is paid off in full each month by your joint checking. For your personal guilt-free spending, you each use your personal card and pay it in full from your individual checking account.

That's it! This gets you 85 percent of the way there. If you have this set up, you can take your vision of a Rich Life and make it happen—automatically. No more fights over $10 grocery store expenses. No more wondering why you and your partner aren't on the same page. Just a simple system that applies whether you're earning $50,000 or $500,000 per year.

Set this up now!

I want you to create your system right now, while you're excited about it—so that in three months when your focus is elsewhere, your automated system is taking care of you, flowing beautifully, and supporting your Rich Life. That's the whole point of fixing your accounts and automating the flow of your money: Think about it once, and it takes care of you forever.

You can log in to your accounts and connect them to one another (look for the words *Transfer* or *Add Money*), which will take a few days. Once the accounts are connected, you can set up automatic transfers on any date. For example, you'll want to log in to your joint credit card and set up automatic payments from your joint checking account.

Here's another example, this time with your individual accounts: You might automatically transfer $200 from your joint checking to your individual checking account. You might then set up an automatic transfer of $50 from your individual checking account to your

Which Account Pays for What

Your joint checking account and joint credit card pays for:

» Rent or mortgage

» Groceries

» Household bills

» Kid costs

» Family meals and drinks

» Shared subscriptions and cellphone plan

» Shared entertainment and travel

» *Add your own.*

Your individual accounts pay for:

» Individual entertainment (going out with friends)

» Individual travel (trips with friends)

» Clothes

» Makeup, haircuts, and other personal products and services

» Hobbies

» Personal fitness

» Gifts

» *Add your own.*

individual savings account, plus an automatic payoff of your individual credit card each month.

Working as a team means your finances will improve even faster. Imagine: If you set up your accounts to automatically save $500 per month, in six months, you'll have already saved $3,000. If it's pulled directly from your checking account, you won't miss this money—but you will be building serious wealth.

That's why I'm in a big rush for you to do this now!

HOW YOUR ACCOUNT SETUP WORKS WITH YOUR CSP

I want you to see the relationship between your Conscious Spending Plan and your financial system. When you follow my plan, your accounts will bring the four categories in your CSP—fixed costs, savings, investments, and guilt-free spending—to life.

Fixed costs are paid from your joint credit card, which is paid off from your joint checking account every month. As a reminder, I recommend you pay as many bills as possible on a credit card for the consumer protection, perks such as cash back or travel points, and simplicity in tracking. Always pay the full credit card bill ("statement balance") every month. Pay for expenses that can't be put on the credit card (mortgage, rent, utilities) out of your joint checking.

Savings are automatically transferred from your joint checking account to three to five joint savings accounts, which correspond to your goals, such as a down payment or vacation fund. One of your joint savings accounts should be an emergency fund. You also have individual savings accounts (funded by your individual checking) for personal savings goals.

Investments are handled in a couple of ways. If you're salaried, your retirement account—likely a 401(k)—will be funded before you even see your paycheck with "pre-tax" money. In other cases, like a "post-tax" Roth IRA, the money comes from your checking account and is automatically transferred to the Roth IRA, where the money is then invested. Important note: Remember that *within* each investment account, you still have to invest your money (e.g., in index funds).

Guilt-free spending is simple. For joint guilt-free spending like dates or eating out, use your joint credit card. For individual guilt-free spending, use your individual credit cards, which will help centralize your individual spending and make it easy to track. The joint credit card is automatically paid off with the joint checking account.

Individual credit cards are paid off by their respective individual checking account.

WHY YOU SHOULD HAVE MULTIPLE SAVINGS ACCOUNTS

For most people, savings are an afterthought. Literally, people get to the end of the month and say, "I should probably save something." Or when I ask why their savings rate is zero percent, they say, "I try to save, but . . ."

Just as you don't "try" to brush your teeth every morning, you shouldn't "try" to save. In fact, it's easier than brushing your teeth, because you can set up automatic savings!

Here's where having three to five savings accounts comes in handy. Without those, you'll just put all your savings in one place— essentially a junk drawer—and then forget what the money is for. In my experience, this money then gets tapped and eventually absorbed into the random expenses of life. On the other hand, if you create too many savings accounts—more than five—things become unwieldy and it's difficult to save enough to fulfill 10 different goals.

To set up multiple accounts, check with your bank to see if they offer multiple savings accounts under one account. As of writing this book, the best banks that allow multiple savings accounts are Ally and Capital One. (Find the latest recommendations on my website and social media.)

The key is choosing the right level to save for. Think big items that require one to five years of saving. Add a savings account for a five-year anniversary trip, but not for a meal at your neighborhood Italian restaurant. Or one for a home renovation or a car or special seats at a concert, but not for a four-pack of new coffee mugs.

Choose vivid names for your savings accounts. The more specific you get, the more inspired you'll be. Instead of "Vacation," you might go with "Tuscany in July." Instead of "Special Occasions," maybe it's "10th Anniversary Blowout." Even "Emergency Fund" can be called "The Uh-Oh Fund." Make these accounts *uniquely yours* so every time you both look at them, you get excited.

WHAT IF ONE OF YOU WANTS NICER THINGS THAN THE OTHER?

Here's a common enough scenario: You're shopping for a family car. One of you is fine with a reasonable, no-frills sedan. The other wants a higher-end SUV. What do you do?

The first answer is to decide what you can afford, because if you can't afford the more expensive model, well, there's your answer. In this case, you look to your Conscious Spending Plan and see if both cars' total payments—including gas, insurance, maintenance, everything!—will let you keep your fixed costs under 60 percent of take-home pay.

But let's say affordability isn't the question. Your CSP shows you can afford both models, but one of you wants the higher-end car and the other would rather spend money on nice restaurants.

This is a common issue across all levels of purchases, but I'm going to focus on larger ones like cars and travel, because that's where conflict can really emerge. Here's one solution that I use: *The person who wants the higher-end purchase pays the difference.*

It works like this:

- You jointly decide on a "reasonable" amount for a car in your household. This number would likely be a middle-of-the-road car—could be new or used—that would easily allow you to keep your fixed costs lower than 60 percent. For example, you might choose a Honda Accord with total monthly costs of $650. (As another example, when my wife and I did this for hotels, our "reasonable" choice was a Marriott.)

- Your joint account pays $650 per month toward the car payment.

- However, you actually buy the nicer car, which has total monthly costs of $950. How?

- The partner who wants the nicer car pays the difference— $300 extra per month—out of their personal money.

This might seem overly transactional to some. If so, don't use it, and keep in mind that if you start using this approach too often, you'll develop an unfortunate separation of finances. But for occasional large purchases where one partner genuinely wants a more expensive version—and is willing to spend their personal money to pay for it—this can be an excellent solution.

Ramit and Cassandra's Money System

In a moment, I'll show you how we manage our finances. But I have to start with a confession: When I started writing this book, our system was messier than the setup outlined above. I'm sharing this because I want you to know that all couples have imperfect financial lives. This is normal!

There is no life where we wake up, sip steaming jasmine tea in a minimalist hinoki wood–lined room, then calmly journal and take a three-hour bath, concluding with a perfectly healthy breakfast and 30 minutes of work. That's only in the movies!

Real life is having a 401(k) from an old job that you haven't logged in to in years, a random credit card you never use at the bottom of a drawer, and a $31.20 charge that nobody can figure out. Your finances are not a Swiss watch, but part of a real life where you also have other priorities.

Now, for our financial system. Until recently we were using a cobbled-together version of the setup outlined above. We have specific needs as two business owners, we have a prenup with rules around commingling funds, and we hadn't gotten around to fully simplifying our system yet. Here's how it worked: Our monthly paychecks were directly deposited into our personal checking accounts. At the same time, part of our income was sent to our individual retirement accounts. Then we automatically flowed a preset amount from our personal checking account to two places: our personal savings accounts and our joint checking account, which was used to pay bills and also fund our joint savings accounts. Oh, and it was proportional, which was based on our business income, which changes every quarter, meaning we had to recalculate everything every three months.

As you can see, all of this was way, way too complicated. Good news! It just took me writing an entire book with editors, designers, and deadlines to finally simplify our system. Now all our W2 income flows to our joint checking account, and the rest flows like the simple setup described earlier. God, it feels good to write that.

For spending, we use our joint card for expenses like dinners out, travel, and household items, all of which are automatically paid from our joint checking each month. For individual guilt-free spending, we each use our own credit cards, which our individual checking accounts automatically pay every month.

Here are the tools we use:

Credit cards: As of writing this book, we use a Chase Sapphire Reserve card for our joint spending, which earns us travel points. On the personal side, I have a 2 percent cash-back card from Fidelity.

Apps: None. No need to check accounts daily.

Online banking accounts: We use Capital One for savings and Schwab for checking. (There are plenty of great high-interest savings accounts. You can find my favorites on my website.)

Investments: We use Vanguard, which includes individual and joint investment accounts, plus our individual 401(k)s.

Overall, it's pretty straightforward now! Please keep in mind that Cassandra and I both run businesses with variable revenues that can swing wildly every month. Our situation is fairly complex. But if we can make our account setup this simple, then I know you can do it, too.

Merging Finances When There's a Big Disparity in Income

When we met, Cassandra and I had very different incomes and net worths. On the surface, this doesn't seem like much of an issue—you're getting married, so you just combine everything, right? But if your incomes are vastly different, you're likely to encounter some challenges. Here's how we decided to handle it.

When we got married, Cassandra and I were both renting apartments. She moved into my apartment, which had a higher rent than hers. When we sat down to discuss finances, we realized that if we split things 50/50, her 50 percent split for rent would *still* be higher than what she was previously paying. That wasn't fair to her.

This same principle came up when we traveled. One of my Yes Money Dials is luxury hotels, so when we went away, I wanted to stay in high-end accommodations. But if we split the hotel costs 50/50, that would have completely overwhelmed her expenses. Again, this was not fair to her (also, hotels aren't one of her Money Dials like they are mine).

Because of my income, I'd gotten used to spending a certain amount on travel and housing. Sure, we could have moved into a cheaper apartment—and Cassandra was willing to—but I didn't want that. I liked our place!

The easiest option, of course, is to combine incomes and share expenses equally, as I outline in my simple account setup. But if there are certain constraints, like one or both partners owning a business, premarital assets under a prenuptial agreement, vastly different incomes, or premarital obligations like child support or large student loans, a "combine everything and split expenses 50/50" may not work.

That's when you might want to think about the concept of proportionality. Here's how it initially worked for us: Cassandra and I contributed proportionally to our joint expenses, meaning if she earned $5,000 per month and I earned $10,000 per month, I contributed double. That's obviously much fairer than a 50/50 split. It means if I want to stay at a luxury hotel, I'm paying more—which I should, because I earn more.

Honestly, for most people, this is overkill. If your incomes are relatively similar, you don't need to split things proportionally: If one of you earns $65,000 and the other earns $75,000, just split it.

In our case, though, the disparity was larger, so we went proportional. First, we calculated how much we make. (For business owners with variable income, this can be difficult. The trick is to pick a number that you can confidently pay yourself. For example, if you know your business might make between $60,000 and $100,000 per year, pick $70,000 to be safe. We used that as a baseline.)

Next, we calculated proportionality by adding our incomes together, then dividing each income by the total. Like these sample numbers:

- Cassandra's sample income: $5,000/month (33 percent)

- Ramit's sample income: $10,000/month (67 percent)

- Total income: $15,000/month

We contributed proportionally to our shared accounts (joint checking, joint savings goals), and our system took care of the rest. We revisited the split every quarter, then reevaluated the entire system once a year, during our annual Rich Life Review (see Chapter 10) and adjusted if needed. Truthfully, in the first few years, it always needed adjustment. Remember, incomes change and situations change, and what was once "fair" may not be anymore.

Guess what? We eventually set aside the proportional system. We now contribute our full paychecks to our joint checking account. Even though a proportional system worked, it was too complicated and, more importantly, it created a "me versus you" feeling instead of the money being "ours."

If you're married, you want to structure your finances so they're simple and they drive the right behaviors—feeling connected, working toward joint goals, and both having skin in the game.

We had to work through our own psychological challenges when it came to combining our money. Cassandra did a lot of personal work on her own. I did, too. And we worked with a therapist so we could improve our communication.

I'll share something that surprised me. When we dropped the proportional system and simply combined our income, it brought us

Your Future Is Together

In most couples, one person is more numbers oriented than the other. They're the person who loves to play around with compound interest calculators, recalculate their debt-payoff date, and tweak the Conscious Spending Plan. This can be good—to a point. As someone who is an Optimizer, I know that my own tendencies can become too numbers focused.

It helps to have a phrase to remind you of the point of creating your Rich Life together. Say it with me: "Our future is together."

If your life has a North Star headline—"We want to live a Rich Life"—your life also has a subtitle right beneath it: "Our future is together." This is home base when challenges crop up.

There are going to be times when you don't see eye to eye. Sometimes your partner will want to dedicate more money to certain goals. You might resent this—it can feel like they're taking away money you use for yourself. *Why should we save more for retirement? I want to use that money to travel now.* If you're focusing just on that individual financial decision, it's easy to feel that way. But when you use the lens of a future together, you can see that your decisions are guiding where the two of you are headed as a team.

"Our future is together." Say it out loud. Put it on your fridge, your desk, and at the top of your monthly check-in document (see page 196). You're going to talk about money regularly, proactively, and positively, because your future is together.

closer together *that same month*. It was amazing to see how changing the setup changed the way we felt. Research shows that combining finances produces better outcomes for married couples. This is why I have so much compassion for couples with messy finances. Because I've been there, too. From personal experience, I can tell you it's worth making the change together.

WHAT IF ONE PARTNER MAKES NO INCOME?

You can adapt my simple couples setup if one partner doesn't make an income. Maybe they're a stay-at-home parent, or a student, or suffering from an illness. Or maybe they simply don't work because they don't want to!

First, please know that if you're married—even if you're not working—both partners share the household income. In general, if one partner is saving or investing during a marriage, that money is considered marital property. For retirement you may want to search for the specifics on a "Spousal IRA," which could allow an earning partner to contribute to a nonearning partner's IRA for tax benefits. All pretty straightforward.

But in relationships where one partner doesn't work, I often encounter heated exchanges that go far beyond the account setup. The lower-earning partner routinely becomes obsessed with the word *contributing*, as in:

- "I want to contribute."

- "I want my partner to know I'm contributing."

- "I feel uncomfortable that for all the work I do, it doesn't show up on a spreadsheet, so it's not taken as seriously."

Remember, contributions come in many forms, and nonfinancial contributions are extremely important. Without someone managing the mental load of running the household, handling logistics, and taking care of kids, no relationship would last. *Some of the most important things in life will never appear on a spreadsheet.*

The conversation about contributions is real and worth spending time on. In my opinion, the higher-earning partner has the responsibility of bringing up this topic and acknowledging how important nonfinancial contributions are to a Rich Life. If you have these conversations bearing in mind that you're better together, you'll come to see yourselves as a team. Sometimes on a team, one partner is better at a certain position. Other times, someone gets injured. Roles shift, but if you identify as a team and you talk about it regularly, you'll both feel valued and heard.

Exceptions to My System

My simple account setup for couples will simplify your life and let you automatically save, invest, and spend on the things you love. But candidly, it can't account for the millions of unique cases and unusual circumstances that couples face. That's why I want to be honest about the special exceptions to my system—and even where I might be wrong—so you know what to look out for. Here are specific scenarios in which you may have to adapt the setup.

You're both self-employed.
Your business(es) should run independently with a separate business checking account, business savings account, and business credit card. Money should be sent from the business to personal and—unless it's an emergency—*never* from personal to business. You should pay yourself a stable salary every month. If your business income is variable, pick a number that you can confidently pay and set that as your paycheck to "simulate" a stable salary each month. On a quarterly or annual basis, you can pay yourself more if the business allows. Keep a business savings account where you set aside money for taxes (I recommend 40 percent). Finally, be sure to speak to an accountant about maxing out all tax-advantaged accounts such as a SEP-IRA or Solo 401(k).

You're super-tight on money.

My system works best when you have a buffer for minor unexpected expenses and can afford to estimate your spending, then review and correct your projections over time. But not everyone has this luxury. If your spending is extremely tight, you won't be able to trust that things will automatically work out by the end of each month. Instead, you'll have to carefully monitor expenses until you build a buffer. If this is the case, adapt my system: Track your spending closely as you focus on making as many changes as possible to your income and expenses to build up a healthy financial cushion.

One of you has child-support payments.

One of the reasons I encourage couples to combine finances is that those who don't combine tend to get into more trouble. This isn't simply *because* of the separate finances; it's that these couples are less likely to talk about money in general, so by default they keep their finances separate, creating a culture of "my money versus your money." Because they never proactively talked about their finances, they have no practice when something goes wrong and they *need* to talk about it. But in cases of a significant ongoing individual financial obligation like child support (or, say, the costs of caring for an ailing relative), I can see the utility of keeping accounts separate. Larry, a member of my community, sent this message:

> "My wife and I have been together for six years, living together for four. We've kept our finances separate. We share rent, proportional to income, and go 50/50 on groceries and eating out. She often comes on vacation with me and my child, where I pay for everything, including her flights. When she and I go on vacation together, it's usually proportional to income. We're each able to hit our general savings goals and our retirement savings goals. Combining our finances seems like more work than is necessary—just seems like a bunch of extra paperwork. Any reasons you can think of to combine?"

It sounds like Larry and his wife discuss money and make conscious choices. If they have a joint vision of having separate accounts, and they both understand the ramifications, they can stick with what's working—as long as they meet monthly to discuss money and prioritize their annual Rich Life Review (coming up in Chapter 10).

You're moving in together but not married.

I recommend a "junior" version of my couples system: Open a joint checking account for shared expenses like rent, dinners out, and trips, and—assuming your incomes aren't wildly dissimilar—then contribute equally to that joint account. (If they are dissimilar—say, 60/40 or more—contribute proportionally.) Get a joint credit card for shared expenses and pay the balance from the shared account. Keep your savings and investments separate for now.

"How Do We Track Our Spending Under This System?"

I have no financial apps on my phone. I don't log in to my credit card every day. And neither should you. When you set your system up right, you'll have to track only two or three items in your Conscious Spending Plan.

It's pure chaos to track every expense! And it's also pointless, because in a smooth-running financial system, most days are mostly the same and most months are mostly the same.

Let's start with groceries, which most people think is variable but typically is predictable. If your monthly groceries tend to range from $600 to $700, put $700 in your CSP (always use the high estimate). Since most weeks are mostly the same, with minor exceptions, try to keep your spending to the same amount. And if you have people over for dinner and spend a bit more, cut back a little next month. Done! We don't need to talk about groceries anymore.

I'm not trying to be flippant here. I understand how your grocery spend can fluctuate. But most of us have never actually tried to average out our monthly food expenditure, then gone shopping with that specific amount in mind. Plant a flag, commit to a number, and don't get hung up on $50 here or there (which won't change your financial life anyway).

Now let's talk about the expenses you really *do* need to track. Think of variable expenses that are meaningful to your Conscious Spending Plan, such as . . .

- Eating out
- Travel
- Kids' activities
- Self-care
- Clothes

When we get specific, we realize that only a few key expenses are both variable *and* meaningful (as in, significant enough to make a financial difference). Remember, you don't have to track all of these yourself. You have a partner in this—when you divvy up the work, it's much more manageable.

Identify those variable expenses, pick a number—giving yourself a healthy buffer—and decide who will track which category. If you're in charge of ordering takeout for your family, take on that tracking. From now on, you're responsible for it. And once a month, when you have your Monthly Money Meeting, you can report on how you're tracking to your goal. Your partner will do the same for the areas they own. Over time, you can simplify and even shift to quarterly or annual tracking.

Keep in mind, the point of this book is not to track expenses. It's to live a Rich Life together!

My recommendations to make tracking easier:

- You should both be tracking at least one number so you both have skin in the game. If the tracking feels overwhelming, ask each other for help.

- Treat this process as building a new skill. At first, tracking can be annoying. But give yourself a few weeks and be patient with yourself. It will become much easier—I promise.

- At the beginning, set yourselves up to win by creating a healthy buffer in your Conscious Spending Plan. For example, if your average grocery spending is $600–$700, I recommend giving yourself $800 for the first two months. If using the higher number means that your CSP doesn't work, then you need to cut back in another area. (The CSP is very good at making your decisions crystal clear.)

- If you find that your month-to-month numbers are wildly different—for example, a $300 grocery bill versus $1,300, or months of $0 for travel versus $5,000 in another month—what's usually happening is that your spending is spiky. Maybe you're buying in bulk. Maybe your travel is concentrated around the holidays. The solution is to average the numbers out over a longer period of time. Start with a monthly average, then quarterly, and eventually work your way up to tracking on an annual basis.

- The simplest way to do this is to download your transactions from your joint credit card, then import them into a spreadsheet. This gives you a lot of control, it's relatively simple, and it's free.

- If you want to use a tool to help, I recommend You Need a Budget (YNAB.com). Yeah, I know it's ironic that I literally say "You don't need a budget" and then recommend YNAB, but for people who feel out of control with their expenses, this software has a good approach where "every dollar has a job." If you need a helping hand at first, you can use it for three to four months to build your intuition, then decide if you want to continue with it.

- Remember that this book is not about obsessing over every expense. Track a couple of key numbers, but do not fixate.

- At the advanced level, you won't have to track with a daily or even weekly granularity. My wife and I track on a quarterly basis and, for some large items, even an annual basis. This takes time, skill, and a healthy buffer—but just know that if your Rich Life is more than tracking expenses, there is a future where you don't have to do this often!

No Secret Bank Accounts!

When I speak to couples, I often hear how a mother or aunt once whispered a tiny warning: "Always keep your own money just in case." I want to acknowledge the history behind this, which I hear exclusively from women.

Many of our grandmothers were not legally allowed to open their own bank accounts or even work outside the home without a man's permission. Many of our mothers were not allowed to, either. It wasn't until the 1960s and '70s that women could open their own bank accounts and credit cards.

That leaves lasting effects on the way we handle money. Even today, more women are financially dependent on men than vice versa, so if you've ever heard a cautionary tale about a partner who suddenly runs off or who passes away without warning, you can understand the urge to keep a little money aside.

While I agree with the concept of always having enough in case something goes wrong (see page 145 for my thoughts on an emergency fund), I have to disagree on keeping a secret account. Yes, you should protect yourself—not only from the concern of a partner leaving or passing away, but also the very real possibility of financial or physical abuse. This is why, in my couples account setup, I recommend opening an individual checking account and individual savings account that only you have access to. But these are accounts that your partner is fully aware of.

When you develop a shared Rich Life vision, you need to get it all out on the table: everything you want, everything you fear, and, yes, all of your accounts. If you want your own money, you should have it—but be open about it. If you aren't comfortable being honest about a separate account that only you have access to, that's a larger, more serious issue that I genuinely urge you to explore.

So: Yes to having an individual account in your own name. But no to keeping it secret.

"Can We Just Keep Our Finances Separate If We Both Agree on This?"

Sure, you can set up your accounts in any way you want. It's your money! But if you're asking me, unless you have a special situation (e.g., this is a second marriage), I would strongly recommend combining accounts.

Your future is together, and when you align your money, you get powerful benefits: Merging your finances gives you more purchasing power (you can easily split the costs of everything from toothpaste to housing) and more simplicity (no more focusing on $3 questions like who spent what and transferring funds back and forth). And shared accounts mean you've structurally set yourselves up to think about your life *together*.

There's also great research showing that joint accounts are good for the relationship. In a 2023 study, university researchers Jenny Olson, Scott Rick, Deborah Small, and Eli Finkel tested what would happen if they assigned certain newlyweds to keep accounts separate and others to combine finances. They found that couples who combined accounts were more satisfied with money in their relationships. They also found that couples with joint finances were more aligned toward goals and more transparent with their finances, and they talked about money frequently.

In my experience, couples tend to keep separate finances because they already have their own bank accounts when they get married, and there's no pressing reason to change now. They never have a "formal" series of conversations about money. In other words, many of us simply "slide" into maintaining separate accounts without making a conscious decision. (In fact, in that 2023 study, the researchers included a control group, who received no instruction about whether to combine finances. The result: *72 percent of them did not combine their finances!* You can see how easy it is to never do it.)

Unfortunately, these couples have no practice when, inevitably, something goes wrong and they *need* to talk about money. What happens if one of you loses a job? What happens if someone gets sick? What if there's an unexpected inheritance? When couples sit down and discuss their finances, it's common for them to end up combining their money, which makes their accounts simpler to set up and easier to manage, and ultimately increases their feelings of working together as a team.

Chapter 9 Checklist

❑ Get your checking and savings accounts right by using my simple couples' setup. Opening checking and savings accounts may sound like a hassle, but banks make it easy.

❑ Slim down to three or four credit cards, including a joint card for household expenses. Close the others. Decide with your partner about what cards you will use for what expenses.

❑ Automate transfers into your savings and investment accounts. Make sure to have three to five joint savings accounts (one of which is a dedicated emergency fund) each with a specific goal.

❑ Decide with your partner which categories of expenses you want to track (groceries, eating out, kids' activities . . .) and who will be responsible for each category.

❑ After you do all this, see how it feels. The goal is not just to simplify and automate your financial system, but to have you feel more connected, more like a team.

LIVING YOUR RICH LIFE TOGETHER

*Establish joyful money routines
that actually stick*

For our first wedding anniversary, my wife and I went to a special sushi dinner in New York City. We made reservations months ahead, we got dressed up, and we sat down to a multicourse omakase meal. Everything was delicious, but what I really remember was the experience. At one point, the chef finished with his knife and just handed it behind him without looking, just *knowing* that someone would be right there to take it. Think about the lengthy training, the deep trust, and the sheer attention to detail that went into making that single action happen. As a guy who loves systems, my jaw was on the floor.

I'm drawn to flawless teamwork like this. Some people look for it in football. Some see it in a concert. All I know is, ever since I was a kid, I get a chill running down my back when I see excellence happening in front of my eyes.

Imagine having that kind of relationship with your partner. Imagine the comfort of knowing you have their back and they have yours, so if something comes up in life, you don't even have to look to know that they'll be there to help.

To me, this is one of the most beautiful parts of a loving relationship. I bet you already have this kind of magic with your partner in certain aspects of life. And now that you've set up your Rich Life system together, let's do the final polish to build that beautiful trust when it comes to money.

By the end of this chapter, you'll know how to talk about money every month, how to update your Rich Life vision once a year, and how to handle the minor disagreements that inevitably come up. Let's start now with the Monthly Money Meeting.

The One-Hour Monthly Money Meeting

I promised that when you got your system up and running, you'd be able to maintain your finances in 60 minutes per month. This is where your Monthly Money Meeting comes in.

This session—which is on the calendar and sacrosanct—gives you the time and space to talk about your finances. Throughout the month, if you have little things you want to touch on, drop them into your agenda, knowing there's already a set time to discuss them calmly. My wife and I use a simple Google Doc.

I've noticed that when I use words like *meeting* and *agenda*, some couples think it's weirdly formal. Is it? Maybe. Do I care? No. I'd rather you follow my structured system than keep it "relaxed" (that is, nonexistent) for the next 40 years while you fight over the price of beef jerky.

Sample agenda for your Monthly Money Meeting

1. *Appreciations for each other*

   - "Awesome job tracking down that $50 expense last month!"

   - "I loved the place you picked for date night last Thursday!"

2. *Partner 1 updates*

- Grocery goal: $800. Actual results: $789! "WOO-HOO!"

- "Do you know what this $45.26 charge from February 20 was?"

- Savings update: $6,500!

3. *Partner 2 updates*

- "I need to call Vanguard with you to check that our account setup is right. Free this Friday at lunch?"

- Investment update: $22,700!

4. *Joint updates*

- "We closed the Wells Fargo account" (because they are one of the worst predatory banks in the world)

- "How long until we need to get a new dishwasher? Do we need to save for it?"

5. *Review our numbers*

- CSP review

- Savings account review

6. *Open issues*

- Partner 1: "I'll find out if we have the right amount of insurance coverage."

- Partner 2: "Do we need to use a different target-date fund in different retirement accounts? I'm going to read Ramit's *I Will Teach You to Be Rich* to find out." (Note from Ramit: No, you don't need two.)

- Rich Life planning: "Who's organizing date night this month? Next month, let's start planning our holiday travel."

7. *Wrap up*

- Why I love you

Resources

- Keep a list of easy-to-access links in this part of the agenda, including your Rich Life vision doc.

The tone of the meeting should be lighthearted, even fun. This may take time: When I first ask couples, "When was the last time you had fun talking about money?" 90 percent of them stare at me, and then one of them says, "Never." Don't worry. Soon you'll be jumping for joy when you see how much you're automatically saving and investing each month. More seriously, you'll notice how money becomes so much easier to talk about when your plan is in motion.

You make the meeting fun by structuring it the right way. Just as kids' birthday parties have games, then pizza, then cake, then you get the hell out of there before they all break down, your Monthly Money Meeting is structured so you can connect in a positive way and end on a high note. You'll start by thanking each other for something you've noticed (I'll give you word-for-word scripts below). Then you can tweak what's not working, tackle any open questions, and declare victory and go home.

THE MEETING IS IMPORTANT. TREAT IT THAT WAY.

I have another confession to make: While I was writing this book, my wife and I missed our Monthly Money Meeting a few times. When we finally sat down to talk, I was embarrassed at how I'd let this slip. I'm the "owner" of the meeting—the person we agreed would organize the agenda—and I hadn't kept up my end, so I started off by acknowledging that. Then I told her how I was going to fix it:

- I'd already blocked off time on my calendar the day after each meeting to follow up on any to-dos.

- I'd also blocked off 30 minutes two days before the next meeting to finalize any remaining to-dos from my end. I always send an email with a link to the agenda to make it easy for Cassandra. (Our agenda is a running Google Doc with

A Helpful Acronym

I like the acronym CARE for money meetings because it helps you remember the parts you're most likely to forget.

Compliment: Praise your partner and talk about what's going well.

Accountability: Look at your spending for the month against your CSP and discuss any upcoming expenses and money decisions that need attention.

Rich Life moment: Make a reservation or a plan, or just Google a place you want to visit.

End: Finish the meeting with "I love you."

items for the latest meeting at the top, which allows us to search past agendas if we need to find an old topic.) The link should get sent out at least 24 hours before the meeting, so by sending it two days ahead I was giving myself some buffer here in case something went wrong.

- I added a third 15-minute block the day before the meeting in case anything slipped through the cracks. This is basically me acknowledging that I don't always get to everything on my calendar but creating a workaround to make sure I'm ready.

More importantly, I was honest about not being on top of this. I apologized and I shared my plan. Then we moved on. (I'm thankful to Cassandra for accepting my apology and moving on, too.) Mistakes are going to happen! Own them and keep moving forward, knowing you have a lifetime of chances to talk about your Rich Life together.

One of the things I love about the Monthly Money Meeting is that it gives you time to acknowledge the progress you're making. Like a video game where you rack up points, you can see your automatic savings and your automatic investing increasing, and even what you're going to spend money on in the upcoming month. Do it like this: *Okay, in January, we decided to take the kids on a vacation to California. Let's look at our savings. . . . Yes! [High five.] We're already 20 percent of the way there, and we're right on track to go this summer!*

This helps connect money to joy as you watch all the work you've done together—designing a beautiful Rich Life vision, setting up your accounts, automating your finances—and realize it's beginning to fall into place. Now you can start sharing articles about the place you're going and get excited about the goal. *(We should take the kids to this water park! We should visit this garden! Check out the view at this restaurant. . . .)* By the time you actually get to the destination, you've already experienced huge amounts of joy. This is a powerful way to live your Rich Life outside the spreadsheet.

HOW TO STRUCTURE YOUR MONEY MEETING

Let's expand on the sample agenda from "Our First Amazing Money Meeting" (page 8). Choose a tranquil environment, and minimize distractions. Set a timer—keep the meeting to no more than 60 minutes. And then get into it. Here's a framework for a great Monthly Money Meeting, with sample scripts.

Start with a compliment.
"I really appreciate that you . . .
. . . made that amazing dinner last week for my birthday."
. . . make me feel safe when we talk about finances."
. . . took care of the back-to-school shopping."
. . . got me up to go running with you this morning."

Next, follow up on any open items from last month.
"I was going to set up the transfers from our joint checking account to our joint savings. That's done."
"Remember I said I would look into which kind of mattress we should get? Here's what I found."
"I know I was going to try to cut our grocery bill by $100, but I didn't do it. Here's what I'm going to do next month. . . ."

Then, review your CSP. *(Remember, you're tracking only a few key numbers. See page 125 for details.)*

"How are we doing?"

"Do we need to tweak anything?"

"Are we sticking with the plan?"

"I know I went over on guilt-free spending this month. It was that Nike sale. . . ."

Look at your named savings accounts.

"Wow—we're 30 percent of the way to our goal already!"

"I wonder if we can save more in our New Kitchen fund. What do you think?"

"Just heard that camp tuition is going up. We need to increase our contribution to that account."

Talk over anything else in your shared agenda.

"The mechanic said the car needs a $1,200 repair sometime within the next three months. . . . Let's look at the CSP and figure out how to handle it."

"What was this $200 transferred to checking? I can't figure it out."

"Hey, we'll be done paying off our credit card debt in six months. How should we reallocate that monthly payment?"

"Are we getting a cabin for the reunion?"

Assign tasks by name—divide and conquer. *(Be specific: Who owns it, what's the next step, and what's the deadline?)*

"I'll look into the cabin. Can you take the car in for the repair by next Saturday?"

"Sure. I'll also find a restaurant for your dad's birthday dinner by Wednesday."

"We should link our joint and individual accounts together. Can you do it tomorrow night after work?"

Finally, give yourselves a Rich Life moment to look forward to.

"Hey, should we go to that new seafood place Friday with Cam and Nikki? I'll book it now."

"What's something you'd love to do on our vacation that you've never done before?"

"Did you see that tree house hotel I sent you? Maybe we can go next year!"

And always end with a compliment. *(A good compliment is specific about the meeting and can include how your partner made you feel, something you noticed, even the fact that they were present during the meeting. End with "I love you.")*

"Thanks for making this so easy, even when I got nervous looking at our investments."

"That was tough, but we did it. Next month is going to be even better."

"I'm so glad we're doing this together. It feels good knowing we're a team."

If things get challenging, these are your go-tos:

"Let's look at the plan...."

"If we were to address this using our Rich Life vision, what would we do?"

"What would [pick a loved one—sibling or parent] do in a situation like this?"

"Let's put a pin in this and revisit it next time."

"Can we zoom out for a second? I love you and I know we both want to make a plan that feels good. Can we take a five-minute break, then come back together?"

You can find a template for your Monthly Money Meeting by searching "Ramit money meeting template."

TIPS ON SUCCEEDING WITH YOUR MONTHLY MONEY MEETING

Each partner should bring at least one topic to every meeting.
This is a team effort, so you both should add questions and updates to the agenda. I recommend agreeing that all updates will be dropped

into the document by 9:00 p.m. the night before the meeting. This will eliminate the frustration of one partner waiting to see any updates (which inevitably come in right before the meeting starts). This also gives you both time to prepare so you're not blindsided by any topics.

Not everything has to be perfect!

As a business owner, I've had to learn that parts of my business are messy—broken links, typos, and so on—and I can't fix everything. Because I'm a perfectionist, this drives me crazy. But I also have to accept that *not every problem deserves my attention.* I have to stay focused on the big levers.

Start thinking like this for your money. Certain things are going to be messed up in your financial system, but if they aren't critical, they're probably worth skipping until later—or even accepting as something that may never get fixed. For example, maybe you have an old account with $75 in it, but to get the money, you have to make a two-hour phone call that you dread. Honestly, just let it go.

In our Money Meeting agenda, we have a category called Open Issues, which are things that aren't quickly resolved or we can't get to. Add these types of issues to your agenda. It might take you six months to get to them, or you might never tackle them. But at least they're on a list. In your meeting, if things are going well, go to Open Issues and pick the most important one. You may have to break down large issues ("Figure out retirement accounts") into smaller sub-issues to make progress.

Develop your own style.

Adapt my framework to create your own unique meeting. You may want to rotate who runs the meeting every other month (I encourage this so both of you can put skin in the game). You may want to adapt the agenda, too. For example, my wife and I are constantly trying out different questions to kick off our meeting. Here are a few we're loving right now:

- "What's one thing you'd love to eventually do with our money?"

- "How can we be more generous?"

- "What's a memory about money you have from childhood? Good or bad."

Spend time talking about your wins!

One of my CEO friends once gave me some unforgettable advice when I was preparing for a performance review of an employee. He asked, "How is this person doing?" I said they were doing well, like 90 percent positive. He said, "Okay, in your review, how much time will you spend talking about the good stuff and how much time on the bad stuff?" That stopped me cold. *Even though the person was*

Small Thinking vs. Big Thinking

You can change your money mindset anytime.

Small thinking

» "Managing money" means paying the bills on time.

» "The amount of money we have is the amount in our checking account."

» "We weren't expecting the car repair to cost so much."

» Trying to save "when you can"

» Thinking about your spending on a monthly basis

» Worrying about the cost of a restaurant meal

» Feeling good about seeing a high balance in checking

» Thinking in terms of dollars

» Stressing over the price of lattes

Big thinking

» "Managing money" means focusing on high-impact areas like designing your Rich Life, your savings rate, your asset allocation, and a smoothly running system.

doing great, I was planning to spend 90 percent of my time talking about the things they needed to improve. The new solution: If they're doing 90 percent great, spend 90 percent of the time talking about the positive. Same thing for your money meeting. Beforehand, think about the proportion of positive exchanges you intend to have.

At some point, you have to dive into the numbers.

In many couples, one person wants to focus on the numbers while the other wants to talk about feelings. Yes, it's absolutely critical to discuss your vision and check in with how you're feeling. But this meeting is not just about feelings. *You're running the business of*

» "We understand the difference between what's in checking, savings, and investment accounts, and we know exactly what we can afford."

» "We plan for unexpected expenses by setting aside money *before* we need it."

» Having a specific savings rate (for example, 10 percent of net income) and creating a rule to increase that number by 1 percent every year

» Planning your finances on an annual basis, at a minimum: "How much will we make? How much do we spend on housing? What trips might we want to go on?"

» Understanding Phantom Costs, from the real cost of eating out to the real cost of home ownership

» Understanding how your investments compound and exactly when you'll have $50,000 more and $500,000 more

» Thinking in terms of percentages

» Spending *extravagantly* on the things you love—and having the confidence to know you can afford it, because you've cut mercilessly on the things you don't care about.

your household. That means taking an honest look at the numbers and talking about them in detail. You should feel safe to discuss your concerns, but ultimately you've got to get down to business—goals, numbers, and responsibilities. If you need to take a five-minute break, feel free to. Then come back and work through the numbers.

"What Will People Think?"

When you and your partner first mention a "Rich Life," your friends might be mildly amused. But a year from now, when you've made noticeable changes in your life, don't be surprised if the people around you are saying, "Why are you so obsessed with money? Can't you at least have a little fun?"

We all operate on invisible scripts of what "success" looks like. For most of us, success means a certain kind of house, a certain car, and a certain lifestyle.

So when a couple confidently chooses a different path, people around them notice and often think, *Wait—am I doing it wrong?* That feels bad, so they shift to *No . . . THEY must be doing it wrong.*

I'm sharing this because I don't want you to get caught off guard by reactions questioning your Rich Life decisions. These questions are normal and expected.

They'll start with friendly teasing: "When are you going to get a new car? Are you going to drive that thing into the grave?" (Translation: *I think people should* always *have a new car. Can't you afford something nicer? Why wouldn't you want a car like mine?*)

Then they'll escalate to concern: "Are you sure everything's okay?" *(Do you want people to think you're struggling? Because that's what I think when I see your car.)*

And finally, anger: "Why would you live like this? Who does that?"

Interestingly, people don't care much about your financial choices if they can't see them. For example, you'll never hear someone critiquing your asset allocation unless they're a huge finance dork. But they become extremely bothered by any visible choices you make, especially involving your house, car, food, or children—which are coincidentally the traditional markers of "success" in America.

You might get odd reactions if you . . .

- downsize from a house to an apartment.

- switch your kids' school from private to public.

- move from a big city to a small one.

- stop shopping for clothes for a year.

- buy a wildly expensive bike or designer bag.

- travel two months of the year.

- take flying lessons.

As I'm writing this list, I'm salivating at the drama. (Just for my amusement, please try one of these. Email me and tell me the reactions you get. I live for this.)

Over time, you'll learn to focus more on your own vision than on what others say. At this point in my life, I have a lot of practice laughing off people's remarks about my choices. As I write this, there's a hilarious thread online about my choice to rent instead of buy a house. Multiple people have accused me of being a secret landlord, because why else would I possibly say renting is okay?!

Trust me, America: I have absolutely no interest in spending 15 hours per week replacing light bulbs as the landlord of a single-family house that generates $125/month of cash flow. I know where these wild accusations come from. They come from people who have been told that buying is always a better decision than renting. Now those people see someone who obviously knows about money and is making a different choice. For a split second, this makes them question their belief system: *Did I make a mistake in buying?*

But questioning our deeply held beliefs is painful, so they quickly—and unconsciously—conclude that I must be secretly profiting as a plunger-wielding landlord. When you're confident in your choices, you don't have to argue about or defend them. You'll

Paying for Quality

I think when you reach a certain level financially, you have an obligation to buy well-made things. I recently read that the Persian rug market is suffering because so many people are buying cheap rugs online. Consider the artisanal skills painstakingly learned over generations to create a jaw-dropping rug. That's what my money can support—and I'm thankful I can pay.

Rich people should be delighted to be able to pay full price for experiences, too, because it means that others can experience the same thing more affordably. When you pay full price to go to a museum, you're allowing low-income families to get admission for free. When you buy a first-class ticket, you're subsidizing the economy seats. And when you pay your taxes, you're allowing people to drive on safe roads to national parks while breathing clean air and drinking clean water.

On my social media, I posted some behind-the-scenes shots of me getting clothes made for my Netflix show. People are curious, so some of them poked around and looked up how much the clothes cost. Then I started getting comments about how "obscene" the prices were. But they weren't obscene to me: I paid that much because I love great service and great design, I can afford it, and I want the people working at that company to be treated well. (In fact, I visited the factory in Italy!) I'm grateful that I'm able to spend more on artisanal goods, because they sustain the practice for generations to come.

Wherever you are in your financial journey, you can practice your own version of being abundant and generous. It could mean setting up an automatic monthly donation to a local cause you support, or creating a family rule that you always tip 30 percent, or even indulging in single-origin coffee that's a little more expensive but tastes amazing. It's just another way to enjoy spending your money—starting right now.

be able to brush off the funny accusations that will eventually come your way.

I want you and your partner to be so secure in your vision and your choices that you both can just smile at any reactions you encounter. You'll have a vision and you'll stay focused on your Rich Life, together. That's what matters.

How Much Money Is *Enough* Money?

You really want a number? Okay, here it is: $1.8 million. That's how much you and your partner need to comfortably retire.

Let me explain.

Retirement age: Let's say you retire at 65.
How long you'll live: As of writing this book, American women will live, on average, 14 years beyond 65 and men will live 8 years beyond 65—to ages 79 and 73, respectively. (Now you see why I want you to live your Rich Life *now.*)
Income: Assume you make the median household income of $70,784 and want to continue your lifestyle in retirement.
You need: $1.8 million ($1,770,100, to be exact)

That number isn't random. It's based on financial advisor Bill Bengen's "4 percent rule," which says that you can safely withdraw 4 percent of your portfolio every year of retirement—including increasing your withdrawals based on inflation—and not run out of money within 30 years. (To simplify the actuarial science, we use 30 years because you want to protect yourself from running out of money before you die.) Some bozos claim you can safely withdraw 8 percent per year (and "easily" make 12 percent in the market), but 4 percent is much more realistic. I cover this in more depth in *I Will Teach You to Be Rich.*

If you have $1.8 million in your portfolio, you can safely withdraw $72,000 per year—which, in this example, is exactly the current income you're living on. You wanted to know the number, so there you go.

For a lot of people, that's completely terrifying. So I want to add a bit more nuance. That number assumes you keep spending the same amount in retirement, which won't necessarily be the case. You might spend far less, for instance, because you're no longer commuting or you've downsized.

Do you plan to travel a lot? You might spend more! What if one of you gets sick? Suddenly, you might not travel at all (but have enormous medical bills).

If you've paid off your house, you won't need to spend nearly as much. If you've invested in tax-advantaged accounts, you'll pay less in taxes.

The Life-Changing Magic of Failure Expectation

When I was 21, I asked my perfectly healthy parents if they had an executor for their wills. The table got very quiet. What? Not every 21-year-old kid confirms their parents' financial affairs are in order in case they die?

I have a weird voice in my head that looks at all the ways things can go wrong. If you're a normal person, this sounds horrifying. If, however, you're a lawyer or actuary, you're nodding, saying, "This guy gets it."

I know we spend a lot of time thinking about all the things that can go great—new house, new car, new kids—but we instinctively avoid thinking about bad things like death, illness, and layoffs. I call planning for these things Failure Expectation. Here's my approach: While I hope things will work out, I *expect* them to fail, and I devise very specific steps for that scenario. It's like an airline pilot's checklist for how to handle an engine malfunctioning.

When it comes to money, Failure Expectation gives you a real edge. Let's say you're planning to buy a $600,000 house in three years. You know you want to put down 10 percent

And there are even more factors we didn't consider. We haven't accounted for your social security benefits, any pensions you may have, your asset allocation, or the more technical aspects of "spending flexibility" (such as cutting spending if the stock market performs poorly).

What I really want you to understand is that "How much is enough?" is the wrong question. The right question is "What does a retirement income calculator tell you about *your specific situation*?"

If I had my wish, you and your partner would go to my calculator (search "Ramit Sethi calculator") and use the number you come up with as a starting point to discuss your Rich Life today and an even richer life tomorrow.

($60,000). Taking into account your 7 percent savings rate and your plan to keep the total cost of housing below 28 percent of your income, your careful calculations have you hitting your three-year goal with room to spare.

Now comes the Failure Expectation: Ask yourselves, *What if real estate prices spike? What if mortgage interest rates shoot up? What if one of us loses our job?*

Nobody does this! We simply say, "We want to buy a house." Because you're talking about it now—using the Failure Expectation technique before the failure happens—you can be calm and dispassionate in coming up with a plan for how to respond.

Talk through the options: You might continue renting for an extra year. You might compromise on your 28 percent housing-cost limit and stretch it to 30 percent. Whatever you decide, *write it down*. Now you have a Plan B ready, just in case.

This is advanced stuff. Most people don't even make a Plan A. Creating a culture of thinking about what can go right *and* what can go wrong is great for couples. It bonds you as a team—you two versus the problem—and preempts the tension and blame that can happen when you feel blindsided by a bad situation.

Ask each other these questions:

- What kind of life do we want to live now? In the next 10 years?

- What kind of life do we want to live when we retire? (It's okay if you don't know every detail, but try to get some broad strokes down: Do you want to travel 300 days per year, or move to a farm, or live near your grandchildren?)

- How much would we need for that kind of lifestyle?

- Are we on track? Can we live more of that vision sooner?

- If we're not on track, what changes can we make? We still have time to adjust, but we'll have to do it together.

You're ahead of the game simply by virtue of the fact that you opened up this book.

Changing Your Old Money Story

Executive coach Marshall Goldsmith works with smart people who plateau at some point in their careers. One of his specialties is identifying certain behaviors that worked for clients in their twenties and thirties but don't work anymore. One of his clients learned that they're too rude when giving feedback. And they said, "But I have to be honest. That's just who I am."

Goldsmith calls this "the excessive need to be me." That refers to replaying a story of identity over and over, even when it no longer serves you. Many of us still follow the same stories we grew up with, even when our financial realities have changed. For instance:

"We're not the kind of people who . . .
. . . go to nice restaurants
. . . or stay at expensive hotels
. . . or wear fancy clothes
. . . or have nice furniture."

I saw this in action with critical-care nurses Jenee and Dan (from episode #75), who during the pandemic moved to where they were needed most, working deep in the belly of the Covid crisis. Because demand for travel nurses was high, both Jenee and Dan earned up to four times their typical salary. They took that extra income and paid off their cars, put away $50,000 in savings, and even paid off the mortgage on their house!

Despite having worked hard under difficult conditions for her earnings, Jenee experienced tremendous stress around their new wealth. When Dan broached the subject of purchasing something from his Rich Life list—an expensive car he'd dreamed about since he was a nursing student working nights at Walmart—Jenee simply shut down.

"I just lost it," she said. "We had to stop the conversation because I couldn't handle going any further. . . . We've been so focused on saving that the thought of spending $150,000 on a car is just borderline nauseating. It's just really hard for me to ever understand wanting to spend that much on a car." I asked if there was a number that would be okay for her. She said, "Probably not."

A $150,000 car *is* expensive, no doubt. But what if you can comfortably afford it? What if it's something your partner values, and they save enough to buy it? These questions get to the heart of money and psychology. I recommend you periodically review the stories you tell yourself, such as during your year-end Rich Life Review in the next section.

Do you worry that if you let go of your perception of yourself as frugal that you'll lose the essence of who you are? Do you find yourself not doing or buying things you can afford or demonizing others for spending money on certain things like business-class airfare or front-row concert tickets?

Wouldn't it be interesting to find out *why* some people spend money on nice concert tickets, rather than scorning them? Wouldn't it be nice to get curious about *why* someone would pay more for an airline ticket or a sweater or a mattress? I call this the D-to-C Principle: disparagement to curiosity. It's a lot more fun to get curious than to stay stuck in an old story.

Telling yourself you're "not the kind of person who eats at fancy restaurants" puts a wet blanket on *all* restaurants for you and for your loved ones—and keeps a cloud over potential memory-making occasions like birthdays, anniversaries, and graduations. Worst of all, your stories can become a vise to your partner, limiting them from exploring new areas. Maybe you don't especially love a three-course meal at a nice restaurant, but maybe they do. If your story limits you, it also limits the people around you.

Old stories come with a sense of pride, often because our frugality is what helped us arrive at this level in life. There's also the guilt of changing: "What will people think if we indulge like that?" But you deserve to turn the page and write the next amazing chapter of your Rich Life.

"I Don't Want to Be a Rich Asshole"

Rachel and Jack (from episode #40) are in their mid-fifties. Rachel grew up working class and has always been frugal. Now, through dedicated saving and investing, she and Jack have a net worth of about $5 million. But Rachel nearly canceled a trip because Jack booked a nice hotel room that cost $200 more than she wanted to spend. She won't admit to being rich, even to herself. Here's part of our conversation:

Ramit: Rachel, do you acknowledge that you're a multimillionaire?
Rachel: No. I don't like people who brag about having a lot of money or who have a very ostentatious lifestyle, so when I see that number, it freaks me out a little bit. I don't want to be that.
Ramit: Tell me if this sounds accurate. Did you grow up not liking "the rich"?
Rachel: Yeah.
Ramit: And now that you have *become the rich*, what does it mean?
Rachel: I don't want to be an asshole.

Instead of staying in love with an outdated money story, fall in love with what really matters: your Rich Life vision, the one you create with your partner.

It rarely takes much to make a change. Spending money on something you never would have imagined before? Buying a beautiful pair of pants, or fresh fruit from the farmers market, or even a car that costs twice as much as what you think is reasonable? As long as you can afford it, what's the worst that can happen? You improve your life and make your partner happy? You start to find yourself being drawn to other nice things? Good! Your story should constantly evolve.

In America, we love rich people, but we love to hate them, too. We follow them on Instagram but see them as greedy and evil. Buying a Tesla and posting about it? That's okay. Buying a Ferrari? What an asshole. I hate some of these rich jerks myself. Watching multimillionaires and billionaires say the most heinous, entitled things makes me realize one simple fact: Beyond having terrible morals, they might actually be kind of stupid.

But if you've been successful, there's no honor in pretending not to be rich. It does not make you more virtuous. In fact, it's a tragedy to live a smaller life than you have to. And it's disingenuous, too. I've seen countless people posting on investment forums, saying things like, "It's not like we're rich; we're comfortable. We make $290,000 a year and we have a small portfolio of $2.3 million." Hey. I have news for you: You're rich!

Two problems here. First, you're playing small by refusing to acknowledge the truth. And second, it's incredibly insulting to people who don't have anywhere near what you have. If you're rich, own it, acknowledge it. I'm rich. I worked hard, and I had a lot of help and a lot of luck. And I always said, once I make it, I'm bringing everyone with me. Now I get to do that.

Your Annual Rich Life Review

Years before our honeymoon, Cassandra and I talked about the trip we wanted to take. We worked hard and saved automatically in a savings account earmarked for it, adding a healthy buffer so once we were abroad, we didn't have to worry about an extra meal or an extra excursion. During the trip, we could completely relax because we'd planned ahead. This is what we'd saved for—the ability to not even *think* about money during a once-in-a-lifetime experience. That is what I want for you.

What makes a trip like that possible is designing a Rich Life vision together, tying it to your financial goals, and meeting monthly to stay on track. If you can do these three things, I promise you can live a richer life together than you ever thought possible.

The last piece of the puzzle—your annual Rich Life Review—is the final element in this system. This is a monumentally important event for big-picture thinking and long-term planning. It's a celebration of your successes, a time to strategize about what went right and wrong, and a chance to look ahead, with concrete plans for the next year and beyond. Of course, over time, incomes change, needs change, and circumstances change, so when you do this annual review, you have the opportunity to update your overall financial system and plan one year, five years, even ten years out.

Your Rich Life Review should take place in a different physical location—not at home. I personally prefer somewhere special that helps you think bigger, but do what's comfortable.

My wife and I tend to do our review while we're traveling abroad each year. Some of this is just intuitive—we find ourselves talking about the year ahead as we're out walking or having a great meal. We ask, "What are our dreams for the next year?" Then at some point we sit down together and, over several days, gradually go through the list below. There's no rush. We give ourselves the gift of a leisurely pace.

Whether you travel for your Rich Life Review or just sit down for lattes in a beautiful coffee shop, I want you to remove yourself from daily life and give this conversation the respect it deserves. This is important. It's on your calendar, and it's something you never miss.

I want this to be something you look forward to and enjoy. For most people, money is an obligation, because it's reactive—one more thing you *have* to do. But when you take control, play offense together, and get ahead of it, it's actually fun. Your Rich Life Review is a chance every year to fire up that feeling.

YOUR RICH LIFE REVIEW AGENDA

Here's a quick overview of what to cover and how to talk about it.

Prepare: Look through your spending from the last 12 months and break down what worked, what didn't, and what you think needs to change. For example...

- Did you hit your four key numbers (fixed costs, savings, investments, and guilt-free spending)?

- How well did you do on projecting your expenses? Get granular to the level of groceries, travel, childcare, and so on. Then update your Conscious Spending Plan for next year.

- Review your Money Dials and any Money Rules you created (see page 284). Discard or change any that no longer feel apt; add new ones if you have any.

- Think about what's coming up next year: Any changes in income? Additional expenses? Scenarios you want to start planning for now?

Appreciation: You and your partner can start the meeting by sharing a couple of specific moments from the past 12 months when you really appreciated each other. Prompt memories by looking back through your calendar. You might even want to pull up a few photos of favorite memories. Points here can be small and large. Examples:

- "When our son had a meltdown at Disneyland, you were prepared with juice and his toy. I love knowing that you're my partner and that you're always looking out for us."

- "You pushed us to set up automatic savings in March and I resisted. You were right. I can't believe we already have $3,000 in there! I realize I was holding on to control, but I need to be willing to share more of our planning together."

- "You suggested we take my parents out for a special dinner the day after they moved, and it was just what they needed. I was too overwhelmed to think of it, but you had my back."

What went well: Discuss shared victories, birthday celebrations, potty training, whatever! Include at least one financial win. Examples:

- "We paid off that Visa bill, which feels so freeing."

- "We figured out where the leak was coming from in the basement."

- "We have two kids who love their teachers."

- "We're talking about money every month."

What you would change: Keep it positive, but be honest. Examples:

- "We overdid it on eating out. I need to pack lunch in the mornings."

- "I want us to have a weekend away every few months."

- "That cruise was not so magical after all. We can turn that dial down."

- "I know this caught you by surprise, but the hotel you booked for us was way over budget. I want to talk about how we can avoid that."

- "Our car conked out on us."

- "I want to be able to play golf every so often with my friends."

What would make next year magical? Talk about how you'll live your Rich Life in the next 12 months. What would make it amazing? Examples:

- "Let's sign up for those salsa classes."

- "We can plan a great family trip around my cousin's wedding in Florida."

- "Well, we've always talked about starting a vegetable garden. Let's do it!"

- "Let's have a regular date night every two weeks."

Where do we want to go?

- "I want to take an overnight trip, just the two of us."

- "I want all of us to spend the holidays with my family. And let's stay for a few extra days."

- "What about Greece? I've always wanted to see Santorini."

What do we want to do <u>more</u> of, and how do we want to do it?

What: See our local friends
How: Plan a monthly game night

What: Find a way for kids to spend more time with grandparents
How: Put aside money to fly grandparents in or send older kids to them

What: Travel with less stress
How: Pay a little more for a hotel with kids' activities; pack three days ahead

What do we want to do <u>less</u> of, and how do we want to do it?

What: Eating out
How: Meal prepping on Sunday afternoons and Wednesday evenings

What: Getting surprised by car repairs
How: Look at last year's costs and put aside money for anticipated repairs

What: Overspending on nights out with friends
How: Take the initiative to suggest a restaurant or activity

Where are we today?

- What's our net worth? Celebrate/analyze.

- How did our CSP compare with our actual spending?

- What did we spend too much on? Too little? How should we correct that? (This is usually where people find out they grossly under/overestimated on certain things. That's fine! As long as you do this Rich Life Review, you'll tighten up your CSP every year. For now, just adjust the category numbers for the upcoming year. For example, if you agreed you'd spend $500/month on groceries and you spent an average of $700, change it to $700. Or get honest about why you overspent and specifically what you'll do to get down to $500.)

What's coming up? You might talk about pregnancy, a promotion, a side business starting to take off, a rent increase, childcare changes, the car needing to be replaced, kids starting camp this year, or something else. (Remember, you don't have to solve every single issue you bring up. The idea is to begin conversations that you'll continue throughout the year.)

- How do we want to tackle/think about each one?

- Take your best guess and adjust your CSP accordingly.

Next steps. You want to carefully document what the next steps are, because soon, the glow of the Rich Life Review will wear off and you'll be back to the daily grind. That's when your system helps.

- "In six months, let's check in on our takeout spending. We're aiming to cut it down by 40 percent by then. I'll set a calendar reminder and add it to the top of our monthly meeting."

- "You mentioned you'll know about the promotion at work by March. Can you add that to the March agenda? If you get the promotion, it will change how much we can save and spend."

What If You Were Going to Die Soon?

When I met Julie and Tom, both frugal optimizers approaching 50, Julie had recently recovered from a double-lung transplant. She was healthy, but her prognosis was dire: She was not likely to live more than 5 or 10 years. Julie and Tom were multimillionaires through simple low-cost, long-term investing. Their daughters, 12 and 9 when we spoke, were learning remotely because of the pandemic. The family could literally go anywhere on Earth, sharing experiences and making memories, and still have plenty of interest income on their investments to last a lifetime.

But the Optimizer mindset is difficult to break—even when death is on the horizon. Julie had a hard time spending, and she struggled with the concept of leaving her job to travel. "I'm behaving like when I thought I might live to 90, and there's virtually no chance I'll live till 90," she said. Tom's fear: "At some point, we're going to be looking back saying, 'Why didn't we do the stuff we could do when we could?'—which is now."

Ultimately, Julie and Tom took the leap. Julie quit her job and planned an extended stay for the family in Arizona, escaping the midwestern winter. She and Tom used money to bring them happiness, comfort, joy, and quality time with their daughters in a beautiful environment. However, if you listen to episode #60 of my podcast, you'll hear how difficult it was—even with a ticking clock.

We all have the same clock, but none of us know when it will stop. I wish I could reach out of this book and give every Optimizer and Worrier a good shake: Yes, save, and yes, invest—but remember that a Rich Life is lived outside the spreadsheet.

- "Honestly, I have no idea what's going on with my old 401(k). I'm swamped in January, but I'll figure it out in February and update us. Adding to the agenda now."

Beautiful work! You've looked back on your year, analyzed your numbers, and plotted a vision for the next 12 months. This is a great way to start the new year.

Ramit's Clipboard Test: What Would I See in Your Household?

Way back in the introduction of this book, I talked about coming into your home as an anthropologist and taking notes on what I saw. Now that you've reached Chapter 10, what would I see if I was walking around your kitchen in a lab coat with a clipboard?

Go down this list and note which behaviors I might observe. Check all that apply. Then become an anthropologist yourself and analyze the results!

During our most recent money conversation, we . . .

- ❏ started with a compliment
- ❏ smiled
- ❏ laughed
- ❏ touched
- ❏ high-fived
- ❏ both participated
- ❏ raised our voices
- ❏ shamed each other
- ❏ got angry and stayed the course
- ❏ got angry and stormed off
- ❏ accused each other
- ❏ celebrated a win

Which of the following best describes your approach to money as a couple?

❑ nonexistent

❑ unbalanced (one person takes on the whole load)

❑ chaotic

❑ calm

❑ surgical

❑ tense

❑ in the weeds

❑ improving

We always/sometimes/never . . .

- talk proactively about money   *always*   *sometimes*   *never*

- ignore money issues until they blow up   *always*   *sometimes*   *never*

- actively teach our kids about money   *always*   *sometimes*   *never*

- discuss whom we can look to as financial role models   *always*   *sometimes*   *never*

- associate money with stress   *always*   *sometimes*   *never*

- review our monthly spending   *always*   *sometimes*   *never*

- let our childhood experiences dominate the way we feel about money   *always*   *sometimes*   *never*

- make short- and long-term plans for our money   *always*   *sometimes*   *never*

- automate our finances   *always*   *sometimes*   *never*

Three money-related things I'm grateful to my partner for:

1. _____

2. _____

3. _____

Three money-related concerns that keep me awake at night:

1. _____

2. _____

3. _____

Which of the following apply to your money conversations?

- ❑ indifference
- ❑ unity
- ❑ avoidance
- ❑ awkwardness
- ❑ anger
- ❑ frustration
- ❑ joy
- ❑ teamwork
- ❑ enthusiasm
- ❑ fear
- ❑ excitement
- ❑ decision-making
- ❑ never coming to a decision
- ❑ spinning, talking about random stuff
- ❑ interruptions (for example, one of us is texting or dealing with the kids)
- ❑ gratitude
- ❑ accomplishment
- ❑ confusion
- ❑ relief
- ❑ tension

Three wishes for future money communication:

I hope I can do better at _____.

I hope my partner can do better at _____.

I hope we both can do better at _____.

From reading my answers above, this is what I notice: _____

_____

_____.

How to Stick to the Plan

In movies, I love a good crying scene with swelling music and a complete turnaround for the characters, but that's not how real life works. Here's the truth: Change is hard, and the agreements you've made with one another are what determines your success—that and cold, hard automation.

Yes, it takes discipline! But discipline is fleeting; the most common reason that people go off track is that "life gets in the way." I'm as guilty as anyone. My wife and I have a ritual of daily appreciations that our therapist taught us. Each night, we say one thing we appreciate about the other. But we've found that when we travel, we often forget to keep up the practice. Worst of all, we don't realize it until days—sometimes weeks—later!

If we humans relied solely on discipline, we wouldn't get very far. That's why, over the course of this book, you've spent so much time developing a Rich Life vision and a plan to align your money. The plan isn't just a piece of paper.

Allow me to reframe: This plan *is* life. This plan is what allows you to live the life you want to lead together, to be the people you want to be, to eat the food you want, to visit the places you want, and to raise your children the way you want.

Everything you will need, you now have.

When things get tough, that's when you go back to your vivid, specific Rich Life vision. Because when your shared dreams are crisp and clear—*We want to be holding hands, sipping Aperol spritzes, watching an Italian sunset on a balmy night in September*—you remember why you're tracking variable costs in your Conscious Spending Plan. The "why" keeps you motivated, strong, and rowing in the same direction.

If your partner is doing only, say, 70 percent of what you'd hoped, take that as a start. You don't need to go from zero to 100 all at once. The important thing is that you're stepping into this plan together. Connection is your secret weapon.

You'll notice changes quickly. I promise, as soon as you see $500 appear in that savings account—automatically—you'll both realize, *Wow, this actually works!* Take the win together and double down on that momentum.

You've got the tools.

You've built your Conscious Spending Plan.

You know how to talk about money every month.

And best of all, you're doing it together.

You're living a Rich Life today—and you're on your way to an even richer life tomorrow.

●　●　●

Chapter 10 Checklist

❑ Schedule your first Monthly Money Meeting. Prepare a shared agenda in advance; make sure that you each add at least one item to it. Carve out an hour of uninterrupted time in a calm place and go over how you're doing with your CSP. Remember to begin and end with a compliment!

❑ Talk with your partner about how you'll handle pushback from your friends and family about your new attitudes toward money. What will you say if someone gives you grief?

❑ Discuss the broad strokes of how you'd like to live when you retire, then use my retirement calculator (search "Ramit Sethi calculator") and get some numbers on what you need to save. If the numbers seem impossible, don't freak out! You have time to make adjustments to your CSP *together*.

❑ Looking ahead to your annual Rich Life Review, set yourself up so it's easy to grab the numbers you need. (This will likely happen naturally if you have regular Monthly Money Meetings.)

PART 2

Instant Money Answers If You're . . .

DIGGING OUT FROM UNDER A MOUNTAIN OF DEBT

*Make a plan! There's light
at the end of the tunnel*

Debt can feel like a stifling weight on your chest. People in debt often tell me it's the first thing they think about in the morning and the last thing they ponder at night. Most people try to make payments, but at a certain point, many simply accept that they'll live with this debt forever.

Good news: There's almost always a way to get out of debt—often a lot faster than you think.

Even better news: You can live a Rich Life even with debt. You can set up a debt-payoff plan, automate it, and *still* enjoy things now.

But it's going to take getting honest with your numbers and making some decisions right now. I've found that 90 percent of people in debt don't even know how much they truly owe. And 95 percent have never run a simple debt-payoff calculation. We're going to change that and create a plan to eliminate that debt.

3 Steps to Paying Off Your Debt

1. ***Collect all your debt and interest rates.*** For example, if you owe $13,500 on credit cards, $27,000 on a car loan, and $42,000 on student loans, write that down. Include the interest rates, too. Like this:

	BALANCE	INTEREST RATE
Credit card	$13,500	26%
Car loan	$27,000	6.3%
Student loan	$42,000	5%
Mortgage	$425,000	5%

2. ***Plug each of your numbers into a debt-payoff calculator*** (search online for "Ramit Sethi calculators"). Let's just start with the credit card debt as an example:

   Balance: $13,500

   Interest rate: 26 percent

   Minimum monthly payment: $405 (Find this on your credit card statement.)

   Plug this into the debt-payoff calculator and you'll see that it will take you five years to pay off the $13,500 balance. You'll also have paid over $10,000 in interest. But what if you increase your payment from $405 per month to $505? Suddenly, you cut your payments from 5 years to about 3.5 years! You'll also save about $3,000 in interest.

   Let's look at another example, this time with a mortgage:

   Balance: $425,000

   Interest rate: 5 percent

   Monthly payment: $2,281

   If you pay that for 30 years, you'll have paid over $821,000, including interest. But if you pay an extra $100 per month, you'll shave nearly three years off your payments—and save

$42,000 in interest! And if you add $250 per month, you'll save almost $90,000 and save nearly six years of payments.

This is staggering!

By plugging in your numbers, you can finally take control. You'll know the exact month and year your debt will be paid off. And now you can actually see that by paying more or less toward your debt, you can affect it in a big way.

Now your conversations can be focused around whether to buy that random trinket—or to increase the amount going to your automatic debt payoff.

(Note: If you do decide to pay more toward your student debt or mortgage, call your lender and ask if your extra payments can be applied to the principal, which will pay off your debt faster. And be sure to calculate whether it's better to pay off debt or invest, which I'll cover in the next section.)

3. ***Set up automatic debt payoff.*** This is the most important step of all: Treat your debt like any other expense that you've automated, using the system in Chapter 9. Debt shouldn't be something you "try" to pay off. You run the numbers, make a plan, automate it—by choosing the amount you're going to pay, then setting up auto-payment via your lender—and review it once each year.

One word of caution: Some people—especially Dreamers—tend to play games with debt. These are the people who open yet another credit card to save 10 percent on a purchase at Gap or Home Depot, who get excited at a zero percent balance transfer for 12 months, and who plan to win the lottery or close some massive "deal" to pay off their debt. *They'll do anything except make an automatic debt-payoff plan.* Skip the gimmicks. Set up your system, then move on.

Your Feelings Matter— but So Do the Numbers

Some people just really, really hate debt. These are the folks who agonize over what they owe and want to pay it off as quickly as possible. I understand not wanting debt looming over your head, but when someone tells me their number-one financial goal is to be debt-free, I get suspicious. (That's it? Just to have zero debt? Surely there's more to your Rich Life than simply being at zero.)

In my experience, I find that people who truly hate debt rarely run the numbers. They simply feel "debt = bad" and want the pain to stop. Unfortunately, they often make decisions that cost them hundreds of thousands of dollars, such as shoveling everything they can into debt without doing the calculations to determine what makes the most financial sense.

Worse, they feel bad about having debt, they continue to feel bad while paying off debt, and they still feel bad even after the debt is gone! This fanatical obsession with paying off debt can also put tremendous strain on a relationship.

If you truly hate debt, I respect your feelings. However, you must run the numbers and compare interest rates before making a debt-payoff plan. That's because mathematically, it sometimes doesn't make sense to pay off debt early. We need to at least acknowledge and separate the two components: the emotions and the math. *Okay, this is how I feel, and this is what the numbers say. Now, what do we want to do?*

Here are the basics: If I have a low-interest loan—let's say, a student loan or mortgage at 4 percent—then paying off the debt early is the worse move. That's because I know I can conservatively get an average of 7 percent per year by investing in diversified, low-cost funds, which means that if I pay the minimum on my debt, I can invest the rest and make about 3 percent per year more (7 percent minus 4 percent). Over several years, that is a *lot* of money. Therefore, if I have low-interest debt—which I define as anything lower than 5 percent—then theoretically, I should pay the minimum on the debt and invest the rest.

(What if your interest is at 6 or 7 percent? The answer is it's a toss-up. Personally, I would take any extra money and put some of it toward the debt and some toward investing.)

Here's an example: You have a $750,000 mortgage at 5 percent interest. If you pay it off over 30 years, it will cost you about $4,000 per month. But you hate debt!

You take a careful look at your spending and realize you can find an extra $200 every month. Since you hate debt, you shovel that money toward your mortgage.

- The good news: You just shaved about three years off your mortgage and saved about $82,000 in interest! Incredible!

- The bad news: If you'd invested that $200 per month instead of paying off low-interest debt faster, you would have instead made $240,000.

This is shocking! Paying off this debt early would have saved you more than $80,000, but investing your extra money would have made you $240,000. That's a life-changing amount of money!

Do you see what happened? Paying off debt felt better, but in the frenzy to simply pay off that mortgage as quickly as possible, you likely ignored the numbers—and it cost you more than all your lifetime coffees and vacations combined.

I understand that some people might run the numbers and decide that they *still* want to pay off debt. If you understand how much it's costing you and you intentionally make that decision, I'm all for it. It's your money, and your Rich Life is yours.

Lots of people ask me what I would do. Personally, if the interest on the debt is low (less than 5 percent), I would pay the minimum and invest the difference. But here's the important part: *I would set up automatic payments and automatic investing.* The problem is that most people don't invest the difference—they just spend it. This is exactly why I insist on using my automatic money system: so that instead of money slipping through your fingers, you ensure that it's going where you want it to go.

Finally, avoid black-or-white thinking. What if instead of paying an extra $200 per month on your low-interest mortgage, you decide to pay an extra $100 and invest an extra $100? Your debt will be paid off faster *and* you'll have more money from years of investing.

The thing I want you to remember: When it comes to paying off debt, be sure to factor in your feelings *and* the numbers to make the best decision for you.

What to Do When You're Almost Debt-Free

Being in debt can feel overwhelming and confusing, very much how I feel when I look through a window of Chili's and see people actually seeming to enjoy their food. But here's the real surprise: When I talk to people who have finally paid off their debt, many of them *still* feel stressed out! Debt has become such a part of their identity that they can't shake the way it makes them feel. I want to show you an approach that will let you mentally "turn the page" on your finances once your debt is gone so you can finally feel good about money.

Six months before your debt is paid off, make a plan for what to do with the extra money you're soon going to have. Ask yourself, *What do we get when we're debt-free? We used to spend all this money each month on our credit card debt, but that's going to be paid in full in June. Then what?* Most of us don't take that bird's-eye view, so once the debt is paid off, the money just gets absorbed by random spending— and we still feel like we don't have enough.

The answer is to have a proactive, exciting vision for those newly freed-up funds.

Let's say you're paying off a car loan at $700 a month. It's part of your Conscious Spending Plan. When that car is paid off, you'll have $700 more per month to use toward your Rich Life! I want you to go on offense by making a plan for that money. Where will it go?

If it were me, this is how I would handle it:

- $490 per month (70 percent) would go to investments. As a personal rule, I always contribute at least 70 percent of unexpected money to investments because that's where real wealth is created. If you're in the enviable scenario of investing an extra $500 per month, take it! (This is one reason that you should hold your paid-off car as long as possible: Lower car payments mean more money you can invest, save, or spend elsewhere.)

- $140 (20 percent) would go to guilt-free spending for a monthly date night.

- $70 (10 percent) per month would go to a savings account named "Next Car" because eventually we're going to need one.

Within three years, I'd have invested more than $17,500 and saved over $2,500 toward a new car, and we would have enjoyed 36 guilt-free date nights. You can use this proactive approach whenever you're about to pay off car loans, credit card debt, student loans, and even temporary costs like preschool tuition. Adapt the numbers for your needs and think ahead.

That is the smart way to think about debt payoff.

Instant Money Answers If You're . . .

GETTING MARRIED AND CONSIDERING A PRENUP

Straight talk about a taboo topic

Most people don't need a prenuptial agreement. But some people do. My wife, Cassandra, and I signed one, and we learned a lot about each other during the process.

Like many people, I didn't really know what a prenup was. In fact, if you ask a random person what they think about prenups, they'll immediately start ranting about how unfair they are, that they're designed for rich assholes to screw their partners over while wearing a top hat and shoving a stack of documents through a limousine window.

Yes, people really base their entire view of prenups on an episode of *Richie Rich*.

It's no surprise that these inaccurate beliefs prevail, because prenup information is usually hidden behind the closed doors of attorneys and financial advisors. My wife and I want to change that! That's why we're so open about shining a light on our prenup journey.

Let's go over what you need to know.

- Most people don't need a prenup, because most people don't come to marriage with substantially different premarital assets (that is, assets acquired before marriage).

- In most states and in most scenarios, what you earn *while married* is "a marital asset" and not subject to the prenup. A prenup is primarily focused on *premarital* assets.

- If you're coming into a marriage with a disproportionate amount of wealth, a house, a business, or other assets like a family inheritance, you should probably get a prenup.

- If you decide to get a prenup, each partner should have an independent lawyer. If one partner can't afford it, the other pays for both lawyers.

- None of this stuff is written about publicly in any amount of detail. In fact, there's a lot of very bad advice on the internet. Avoid 24-year-olds on Reddit pretending to be family law attorneys and go to a professional who does this every day. You're looking for a lawyer who specializes in family law or trusts and estates.

Shedding Light on Some Common Prenup Concerns

Let me answer some questions I've gotten from readers:

Q: *"I don't have much, but I have a feeling my partner does. How do I find out if they want a prenup?"*

A: You can just come right out and ask: "Do you think you'll want to discuss a prenup?" This is so unexpected and refreshing. Of course, it helps if you've had a series of conversations about money beforehand so you have a sense of their situation. But even if you haven't, feel free to ask. This is the person you're going to spend the rest of your life with!

Q: *"When do you ask for a prenup? What's the right timing?"*

A: This is a good question because it's not really spelled out anywhere. Most people bring up a prenup when things are getting serious but before getting engaged. That's what I did. We started to have increasingly serious conversations about things like marriage and children. It was a natural time to talk about a prenup. It takes months to finalize one, so the earlier you can begin discussing it, the better. This is a process that cannot be rushed.

Q: *"How do you bring it up? I've heard people say, 'Blame it on your lawyer,' but my partner would roll their eyes at that."*

A: Don't blame your parents or family lawyer. Take ownership. This is something that's important to you, and it's perfectly fine to articulate your needs. Here's exactly what I said:

"I have something I want to talk to you about. I'm nervous to talk about this, but it's important to me to bring up.

"You know that I started my business 15 years ago. Because of hard work and a lot of luck, it grew bigger than I ever thought. Same with my investments.

"Now that we're talking about getting married, it's important to me that we discuss signing a prenup. We can get into details later, but for now, I just wanted to be honest and bring this up so we can talk about it."

To summarize:

- Tell them how you're feeling.

- Be clear that you want to sign a prenup.

- Leave time for the next step as both of you learn more about it on your own.

Cassandra responded in the best way I could have hoped: "Wow, okay. I wasn't expecting that, but I'd be willing to learn more about prenups."

Q: *"Is the process difficult?"*

A: For us, it started off well. We found lawyers and began negotiating. But then it got really, really hard. We were fighting over numbers that seemed astronomical to me, and I felt resentful. She didn't feel understood and also felt resentful. At a certain point, she said, "We need to see a therapist, because this process isn't working." She was 100 percent right.

Our therapist was fantastic at helping us step out of the you-versus-me dynamic we'd found ourselves in. I still remember one question she asked us: "How do you see money?"

To me, the answer was obvious. "Growth," I said. I could literally see numbers and accounts floating in front of my face: *90/10 portfolio. Rule of 72. Tax-advantaged accounts.*

Then Cassandra answered: "Safety." That was a big breakthrough for us—the beginning of our being able to connect on how differently we viewed money.

The prenup process is always challenging because of the inherently adversarial setup. But every couple I know who's signed one says that they never would have talked about money as deeply had they not gone through the experience. (They also say they never want to go through it again.)

Q: *"My partner is so mad at me for wanting a prenup. They say it's like I'm betting we'll get divorced. What should I say?"*

A: I'd say, "I love you. I hope we never have to use this prenup. But if the worst happens and we do separate one day, we'll know we have a plan that we both agreed to when we were at our best—when we were calm and had time to think."

Q: *"How much will it cost to do a prenup?"*

A: As a ballpark figure, assume $5,000 to $30,000. The actual number depends on a lot, including the lawyers you select and how communicative you both are along the way.

One tip for controlling costs: *You manage your lawyers. They do not manage you.* Most people have never managed anyone, especially not a lawyer. The lawyer's job is to look out for every possible contingency no matter how unlikely. Your job—and your future spouse's job—is to jointly come up with a set of acceptable terms that your lawyers help you to sanity-check, polish, and finalize.

Q: *"Could you write your own contract together, then have it notarized?"*

A: No. Do not do this. Just as you wouldn't try to build your own suspension bridge and then drive your car over it with your spouse in the passenger seat, do not try to do your own prenup. DIY with a prenup just makes no sense. If you have assets worth protecting, then you have money to hire a competent lawyer.

Q: *"I have children from a first marriage and want to make sure they're protected. I'm in my second marriage now and realizing I should have signed a prenup. Now what?"*

A: You can sign a postnuptial agreement ("postnup"). Any attorney experienced with family law or trusts and estates can advise you.

Q: *"My partner and I both have divorced parents. It's hard to think about combining our money without thinking how difficult it would be to uncombine it if we ever need to. Should we have a prenup, even though our finances are pretty simple?"*

A: A prenup is just one tool at your disposal. If your assets aren't sizable, consider premarital counseling. (Actually, everyone should consider premarital counseling!) There are some fantastic therapists who can help you both understand your past and create a new future together. The conversations my wife and I had during our prenup process were invaluable, and we never would have gotten that deep without the necessity of a prenup. Those conversations also showed us how valuable a therapist can be. If you're interested, check out the Gottman Institute's site, where you can find a list of great therapists for your own relationship.

THINKING ABOUT A MAJOR PURCHASE

*How to run the numbers on
vacations, cars, college, and a house*

How do you know if you can afford a $2,000 mattress? This is the question that thrust me into my recent obsession, which began on podcast episode #112 when I met a couple who went into debt to buy a $2,400 mattress. Just a few weeks later, I encountered the exact same situation on episode #124 for a $2,200 mattress.

Suddenly, I was intrigued.

I started asking around. How do you know if you're able to purchase a big-ticket item like a high-end mattress? What about a car? A house? A vacation?

The answers were honestly shocking. When it came to the mattress, most of them went something like this:

- "A good night's sleep is part of my Rich Life."

- "It's worth it to avoid back pain."

- "You spend 33 percent of your life sleeping!"

If you're actually trying to make a good financial decision, none of those are acceptable answers. The more I ask people how they formulate their reasons for making their larger purchases, the more I see that most people simply decide they want to buy something, make up a bunch of reasons to justify it ("my back hurts!"), and then buy it. But to truly know if you can afford something, *your answer must involve numbers.*

Remember, we tend to agonize over $3 questions—like the price of dessert—and dramatically underfocus on $30,000 questions, like cars, vacations, and houses. If you get the 10 biggest financial

The Big Purchase Checklist

You can afford it if you can check off all of these:

- ❏ You're achieving these numbers: fixed costs (you're within 3 percent of the 50–60 percent guideline of take-home pay), investments (5–10 percent), savings (5–10 percent), guilt-free spending (20–35 percent).

- ❏ If you are carrying debt, you know the exact month and year it will be paid off.

- ❏ You have an emergency fund. If it's not fully funded, it will be within four years.

- ❏ You know the total cost of ownership (TCO) of the purchase. You've factored in maintenance, taxes, opportunity costs—such as how much you could make from using this money elsewhere, like investing it—and other Phantom Costs.

decisions in your life right, you'll never have to worry about the price of your morning coffee. *So it really pays to get the big decisions right.*

This is such an important concept that I'm going to cover it in detail for some of the biggest purchasing decisions you'll face.

How to Know If You Can Afford a Vacation

It's simple: If you've already saved up enough money for the price of the entire trip, plus 50 percent more, you can afford it. This extra 50 percent covers all the expenses you might forget about, including transportation, tips, taxes, and so on.

To calculate the costs of your vacation, focus on the key expenses:

- *Travel:* Airfare (including taxes), cabs to and from the airport, food and drinks at the airport bar—all of it.

- *Accommodations:* Nightly hotel rates, taxes, tips, and any incidentals.

- *Food and excursions:* Consider how many meals you'll eat out per day, as well as any tours you'll take or sights you'll see. Be realistic here. You don't want to be on vacation worrying about the price of a shrimp cocktail. Get everything out on the table, and when you're not sure, overestimate.

Now take the total amount you see for your trip and add that 50 percent. Even though you factored in all the key expenses above, you still need to account for other Phantom Costs or unexpected expenses, which the 50 percent will cover with room to spare. (In my own planning, I tend to underestimate travel by 30 percent, and that's after years of tracking. Fifty percent is a much safer number to start with.) To hear an example of how this is done, check out podcast episode #148 with Callie and Travis.

If you have that amount saved, congratulations—you can afford it! If you don't, consider your options: You can delay your trip until you have enough saved. You can reduce the length of your trip (an amazing four-day trip might be just as memorable as a seven-day trip). Or you can cut your expenses by finding cheaper flights and accommodations, or even changing the time of year you travel.

How to Know If You Can Afford a New Vehicle

I know, I know. People *need* an $80,000 SUV "for the kids" and the accompanying $75,000 truck so they can haul their boat twice a year. Then, years later, they ask, "Where's all my money going?"

Too many people wonder why they can't seem to get ahead, and when I take a 15-second glance at their Conscious Spending Plan, my eyes bulge out of their sockets. If it's not housing, it's the car payments, which their friendly neighborhood car salesman assured them they could comfortably afford. Buying your car, truck, or SUV is one of the most expensive purchases you'll make, so I want you to get it right. Here's what you need to do:

Know the TCO (total cost of ownership), not simply the monthly payments. That includes everything added up for the life of the vehicle. For example, a $50,000 vehicle will cost far, far more when you add in all expenses, including gas, insurance, parking, registration, and maintenance.

Plan for twice the monthly payment and make sure your fixed costs are still less than 60 percent of your take-home pay. For example, if your car payment is $400 per month, plug in $800 to your Conscious Spending Plan. (Recall that my car payment used to be $350, but with all expenses factored in, I paid over $1,000 per month.) Once you plug in the numbers, is your fixed-costs number under 60 percent? If not, you're spending too much on your car.

Keep the vehicle for at least seven years. One of the worst things you can do is buy an expensive vehicle, then get rid of it and buy another soon afterward. That's because you really start to see savings after your car payment is complete, which for most people is five years. Consider the years with no car payment as some of the best financial years of your lives—you can save more, invest more, even spend more!

Have total debt within the 28/36 rule. A good guideline for debt is to keep your total housing debt under 28 percent of gross income, and all of your debt (including student loans, vehicle loans, and so on) below 36 percent of gross. For example, if you make $75,000 gross income, or $6,250 per month gross, that means you should ideally pay no more than $1,750 for housing and $500 for your vehicles. *Total.* For your housing, that includes your water bills, furniture, electricity, repairs—all of it!—and for your vehicle, that includes gas, repairs, registration, even parking tickets. You can see how shocking this is, because these numbers are far below what almost everyone spends on their housing and car and, in today's market, are often impossible. No wonder people are so stressed out by money. (This is also why I'm a YIMBY, an advocate for building more housing so everyone can benefit from affordable housing. Money is political, so vote in your local elections!)

In general, once you understand these numbers, you'll find that you can comfortably afford a lot less vehicle than you previously thought. That's correct! It might feel frustrating, but by making good decisions early on, you'll thank yourself later—once you've saved a lot, invested a lot, and are breathing easy about your monthly spending.

By the way, if you find that you're already overspending on your car, your options are limited. You may be able to sell it and get something smaller—which can benefit you if you're saving hundreds of dollars per month—but you have to carefully calculate how much you'd end up with. In most cases, I find that people who overspent on vehicles simply have to continue paying, then commit to not buying another car for years and years. This will give them at least five years of not having a car payment (ideally more), during which they can fund their savings and investments.

How Buying That Truck Today Affects Your Life Forever

Somehow, I've gotten a reputation as a guy who hates trucks. But what I actually hate is the *logic* that people use to buy them when they can't actually afford them. So many truck buyers consistently insist that they "need" a truck to haul heavy loads when they spend 98 percent of their time driving exclusively on pavement carrying four bags of groceries and the rare bag of mulch. Let's get real. Plus, once you factor in gas, maintenance, and interest, trucks are extremely expensive. So yeah, I have a problem with many truck purchases.

I'm going to play this out to show you what you can do now to change your future.

» In the showroom, the truck salesman asks, "How much do you want to pay per month?" You pick an arbitrary number that sounds reasonable.

Never, ever make big decisions based solely on monthly payments! Salespeople love this because they can sell you an even more expensive deal, stretching it out over a longer period of time, and collect even more in interest. Instead of looking at monthly payments alone, focus on the total cost of ownership, including maintenance, gas, interest, and insurance.

» You pay a small down payment and finance the rest through the dealer.

Car salesmen love when you finance through them, because they can often make more from the fees on your car loan than from selling you the car itself. It pays to research all your financing options, including from your bank and local credit unions.

» Six months later, money is tight, but you can't figure out why. You open your car loan bill and—when combined with gas, insurance, and all the other hidden expenses—you realize how much you're actually paying.

When you finally add up the total cost of ownership—which you should have done before even going to the showroom—you discover you're spending twice as much as you anticipated per month. And you have to do this for at least five more years!

» You consider selling, but you can't let go of this truck because you'll lose a huge amount on the deal. Besides, it's become part of who you are.

People find it unfathomable to rid themselves of purchases that are tied to their identity.

Other ways it could go:

Option 1: Before you step into a showroom, you run the numbers carefully and realistically. You decide to keep your current car for two more years and automatically save the thousands you would have spent in an account called "New Truck Fund." This cushion alleviates the pain of the increased monthly charges when you finally make the purchase.

Option 2: After running the numbers, you decide to wait a year, then buy a used truck. This decision saves you $300 per month, of which you decide to invest $200 per month and increase your guilt-free spending by $100 per month.

Option 3: You decide to continue driving your current vehicle indefinitely because it still runs fine. You make a plan to save enough to cover a new truck seven years from now, and once you finish filling up your "New Truck Fund," you switch to investing that money.

Whichever option you choose, when you eventually buy a new truck, you'll be ready.

The big lesson: Slow down and make methodical decisions about any big-ticket item, because once you make a decision, it's very hard to go back. One bad decision can wreak havoc on your finances for a very long time—but one good decision can give you thousands of dollars in extra money to save, invest, and spend.

How to Know If You Can Afford College for Your Kids

Every week, I get messages from parents of young children frantically asking what kind of savings account they should set up for their kids. The parents are usually 38 to 42 years old. I always slow them down and ask, "Before we talk about them, let me ask about your finances. How are you doing?"

Almost always, they say something along the lines of "Not great. I only started paying attention to money a couple of years ago."

I understand wanting to provide for your children. Having children is one of the few pivotal moments when people suddenly spring into action with their finances.

Here's the truth: *Your kids have time—but you and your partner have much less time.* That's why it's so important for you to focus on yourselves first and hit your savings and investments numbers *before* focusing on your children's future.

Best case, you have more than enough to help them financially if they decide to go to college. Second-best case, they take out some student loans and work during college. Not a huge deal. But the true worst case is that you don't save enough for yourself, pay for your child's college education, then end up later in life without enough saved at all. There's no student loan for retirement.

You know you can afford to save for your children's education if you're on track for retirement with room to spare. To start, this means you're investing at least 10 percent of your take-home pay. (If you're doing this starting in your twenties, odds are very good that you'll have far more than you ever thought. But most people don't start seriously investing until much later.)

That's why we have to go further and calculate how much you'll have when you retire, which you can do using a compound interest calculator. Plug in the amount you've already invested, how much you're investing each year, assume a conservative 7 percent return rate (I suggest opting for low-cost index funds), and then plug in how many years until you retire. That will show you approximately how much you'll have. As a simple back-of-the-napkin calculation, you can withdraw 4 percent of that per year and not run out of money in a normal retirement. Will you have enough? (For example, if you have a portfolio of $1,000,000 at age 65, you can safely withdraw around $40,000 per year.)

Of course, we're not calculating your social security benefits, possibly lower lifestyle expenses, higher medical expenses, and much more. But you can get a sense for whether you have enough now or—more likely—whether you should get much more aggressive about investing for yourselves instead of putting tens of thousands of dollars away for your children's education.

Please remember this: Paying for your children's college is a luxury. I genuinely hope you can do it, but prioritizing your own financial situation comes first.

How to Know If You Can Afford to Buy a House

In the vast majority of cases where people feel financially stressed out, I can trace it to one simple thing: how much they're paying for their housing.

Housing is, by far, the biggest purchase most people make. It's also filled with Phantom Costs and wrapped in an almost religious mythology. Many people consider themselves failures if they don't own a home. My key message to you is this: Before you make the biggest purchase of your lives, you must run the numbers. (To find more detailed material on buying versus renting, just go online and search for "Ramit Sethi buy vs. rent.")

Sometimes buying can be a good financial decision. Sometimes renting can be even better. But when it comes to weighing your options, the math is highly counterintuitive and very confusing. That's exactly how the real estate industry wants you to feel, so you feel pressured to buy, which, of course, they make a commission from.

I could write an entire book on making this decision, but I'm going to give you the shorthand here. You might be ready to buy a house if . . .

You will live in the same house for at least 10 years. Most people don't know that in the first 10 years, the bulk of your payments are going straight to interest. For example, let's say you buy a $500,000 house. You put 20 percent down, or $100,000. On that $400,000 mortgage, in your first year, you'll pay about $4,000 toward your principal—and almost $24,000 in interest. In fact, it will be 19 years until you're finally paying more toward your principal than interest. I'm not even mentioning how the huge transaction costs of buying and selling require years and years to "amortize," or spread. This is why a house is truly a long-term purchase. As a simple guideline, I add 50 percent to the mortgage to account for all Phantom Costs, so a $3,000 mortgage would actually cost me $4,500 per month in the Conscious Spending Plan.

Your total housing cost is less than 28 percent of gross income. When I say total, I mean *everything*: interest, transaction costs, taxes, insurance, sprinklers, renovations, maintenance—including the unexpected $15,000 repair seven years from now that you don't even know about yet. Now, it's very difficult to hit that 28 percent number, especially in high-cost-of-living cities. You can stretch that number to 30, 32, even 33 percent. But beyond that, you're incurring a lot of risk: What if you have an emergency medical bill? What if you lose your job? Or what if you simply feel stressed all the time?

You've saved 20 percent for a down payment. There are two reasons for this: First, I'm always conservative in my assumptions, and saving 20 percent gives you a lower monthly payment, plus more stability if housing prices decrease. Second, and even more importantly, saving a substantial down payment proves that you can build the discipline and systems to save a considerable amount of money over time. This will come in incredibly handy once you own a house, which many describe as a "money pit"—or a source of never-ending costs you'll need to carefully prepare for. Note that you don't necessarily have to put 20 percent down—that decision will depend on interest rates and other factors. But you should have been able to save that money—keeping it in a high-yield savings account—until you decide to buy.

You have run a careful buy-versus-rent calculation. Most people think wealth is created by buying a house, paying off your mortgage, and then—presto!—you're wealthy. We have to go deeper than that. Sometimes, buying can be the right financial decision, while other times, renting can be the better choice. Of course, there are also other reasons to consider buying or renting, such as children, stability, location, and so on. To understand the financial part of the decision, you absolutely, positively must run a buy-versus-rent calculation, which might surprise you. In your calculation, you'll find that you can assume rent prices will go up, but you'll also find that the costs of homeownership are staggering—much higher than you first think. When you factor in interest, taxes, maintenance, and even the opportunity cost of investing your down payment, you'll often be shocked at how the calculation turns out.

For example, in New York City I once noticed there was a nearby apartment of the same size, with the same number of bedrooms, same view—basically it was the same place. It would have cost 2.2 times more to own than to rent! With a rent of $3,000, it would have cost $6,600 per month to own the same place. I took the difference between owning and renting—in this example, $3,600—and invested it every month. That made me far more money renting than I ever would have made owning (and with fewer maintenance headaches). Be sure to run this calculation before you buy.

You are excited to buy! You should feel elated about the biggest purchase of your life! If you truly love the idea of owning your own place, decorating it, potentially renovating it, and living in that house for 10-plus years . . . then you might be ready to become a homeowner. If not, you should never feel pressured to buy a house. Your Rich Life is yours, and there are plenty of ways to live a very Rich Life without owning a house.

The Secret Costs of a "Good" Neighborhood

Putting down roots in an upscale neighborhood because of its highly regarded schools, safety, or beauty can be a decision you make with the best of intentions—with unanticipated consequences. You might be able to afford the mortgage and taxes in a given area, but can you afford the lifestyle for the next 20 or more years? This means being honest about the effect of peer pressure, which is very real and—especially if you don't have a clear vision of your Rich Life—very costly.

What does it truly cost to live in your community? Go beyond the obvious expenses. When your car needs replacing, are you going to buy bigger and better because that's the norm where you live? Will you hire a landscaping service for your front yard because all your neighbors do? What other costs might be normalized in the neighborhood you're considering?

Take this seriously. Ask yourselves, *Is this place a match for our values and our finances? Is it realistic to think we won't spend money on landscaping/cars/renovations/ socializing when so many others in this area do? What if we bought an apartment—or rented—instead of a house? Are we going to constantly feel one step behind?*

Where you live is a massive decision that will affect every part of your financial life for decades. Get real and determine how much more this area will cost for gas, insurance, maintenance, childcare, and food.

These numbers will shine a light on the decision you're considering. Depending on what you discover, be flexible. Push yourself to think about what's right for your shared Rich Life, not merely what seems like "the best." Once you make the correct choices for your family, you'll be confident knowing you did so with your eyes wide open.

TEACHING YOUR KIDS ABOUT MONEY

Helping your kids build a healthy relationship with money

By this point in the book, you know how profound an impact our upbringing has on the way we see money, even decades later. Our parents deeply influence how we treat money, and if we don't make an intentional effort to understand and change those messages, we pass the same ones on to our children.

So how do you teach your kids to have a healthy relationship with money?

There's more to it than deciding if you should give them an allowance, or even if you should pay for their college tuition. It's about knowing yourself and your money values *first*, then using every chance to show them how money really works.

The good news is that if you're interested enough to read this book, you have a very good shot at creating a healthy environment around money for your kids.

10 Money Conversations to Have with Your Kids

In business, we say, "What gets measured gets managed." In families, we might say, "What's important gets talked about." The ability to talk about money openly and regularly is essential. When I ask people who are in financial trouble what they remember learning about money as kids, their overwhelming answer is "nothing." Their parents never talked about money, so when they reached adulthood, they were defenseless, left to make sense of the world against companies like Wells Fargo and Ameriprise as well as whole-life insurance scammers writing on their whiteboards on TikTok.

If you watch sports with your kids and debate the Ravens versus the Steelers, you're signaling that your family cares about sports. If you talk about where you want your money to go (toward savings, investments, education, housing, traveling to see grandparents), you're signaling that money is important to your family.

To create a healthy relationship with money in your family, shine a light on it: Talk about what you're doing with your money every month, even acknowledge your mistakes with it. Invite your children to get involved.

Here are 10 casual money conversations you can have with your family. Some are meant to involve little kids; others will get older kids thinking. They're just starters for making money a part of your family culture. Add your own.

1. How do we decide if we can afford to eat out this weekend?

2. How should we spend $100 at the grocery store?

3. What is the right way to use a credit card? What about the wrong way?

4. How much does gas cost?

5. Why don't we buy a new car every year?

6. We have $200 to donate to a good cause. How should we choose?

7. Do you know how we pay for this house?

8. My biggest money mistake was . . .

9. Is this worth it? How do you decide? (Examples: nice jeans, an extra blender, a new TV, a trip to the Grand Canyon)

10. If I could save up for one big thing, it would be . . .

Money Lessons for Kids

Kids give you a million opportunities to teach them about money. They ask questions like this:

- "Can I buy that candy?"

- "Why don't we live in a bigger house?"

- "Can I have this extremely annoying toy that plays a song at 431 decibels and has batteries that last for 11 years?"

If you hear that last question, tell them Ramit Uncle said the answer is no. (Indian people put our name first, not last.)

Most parents respond to money questions as they come in, but that's like playing whack-a-mole. After reading this book, hopefully you'll realize the importance of a cohesive philosophy—a vision! Yet the reason we don't have a vision for kids is that we haven't had a vision for ourselves. That's why, over time, we tend to give increasingly simplistic answers to kids' questions about money:

- "None of your business."

- "Because I said so."

- "Stop asking. We can't afford that."

It's no wonder most kids grow up never understanding how money actually works. But most parents do intuitively understand

What You Can Say Instead of "We Can't Afford It"

» "That's not what we're spending our money on today."

» "That's not part of our Conscious Spending Plan." (Be excited to explain the CSP concept to them when the time feels right!)

» "That's not how we choose to spend our money."

» "We've decided it's more important to spend money on X than on this."

» "No." (I love a good *No*. I'm considering creating a service to help parents who struggle to say no to their kids. It'll be called RSN—"Ramit Says No"—and you just send me a message and cc your kids. I'll reply to everyone with a single word: *No*.)

I know it's easy for me to write this. You're the parent, the one who'll have to endure the tantrums, whining, and sulking. But you have a North Star: teaching your children to develop a healthy relationship with money.

the importance of teaching kids about healthy food and healthy relationships. It's your responsibility to teach them about maintaining a healthy relationship with money. Here are some ways how.

GIVE YOUR KIDS THE CHANCE TO *USE* MONEY.

You wouldn't teach your child how to ride a bike by saying, "We don't talk about bikes in this family." You'd give them a bike with training wheels and help them ride it!

Do the same thing with money. As soon as they're ready, get them involved in using money. Once they have skin in the game, kids will learn fast.

Little kids: Invite them to watch you pay a bill online. Explain what paying that bill gives you: a safe place to live, a TV to watch, the fridge that keeps your food cold. Ask them to click the Pay Now button to make the payment. When it goes through, get excited. Give them a big high five. Every time you do this, you're teaching them to connect money with positive feelings.

School-age kids: Give them a role in small family purchases. Start at the grocery store. If they can't buy everything they want, good! Let them learn about making choices. Then have them plan a family dinner out using a specific dollar amount. (Set them up to succeed by giving them more than enough to cover dinner and tax and tip.) The upside is you're teaching them how to make increasingly large decisions, including factoring in Phantom Costs. The downside is they may choose to eat at Arby's and, unfortunately, you have to go.

Tweens: Ask for their input on a major purchase that impacts them, like the family car or a home improvement. Use the opportunity to talk about Phantom Costs like insurance and maintenance.

Teenagers: Include them in large financial decisions for the family. Start by giving your teen the responsibility of planning a full day of vacation, then ask them to share what went well and what didn't. Eventually, ask them to plan an entire family vacation. Lay out the parameters and amount and watch them thrive.

This is how you equip your children. Watching your kids master money by making sophisticated plans and trade-offs, you realize what a joy money can be.

Less than 1 percent of the people I talk to ever learned about money like this. A member of my money-coaching group, Eliza, gave her 11-year-old daughter a money task. I love her story.

She wrote:

"A few weeks ago, I told our daughter that she would be responsible for planning our next family night out. We gave her a $200 budget and asked her to plan dinner and any activities that she wanted for our family of four. OH MY GOD she took to this like a fish to water.

"She researched different options and came up with snow tubing as the activity and chose a nearby diner with malts for dinner. We had her calculate costs with taxes, tips, and a buffer in case prices were different from what were advertised online. It required her to think hard about what she might be willing to cut back on so she could afford the tubing, which she was out-of-her-mind excited about.

"In the end, the evening came in at $193.68. And while my middle-aged body is still recovering from the shock of sliding down an enormous snow-covered hill and eating a burger/fries/chocolate malt dinner, it was a great night. We all learned a ton from the experience. She was incredibly proud of her work, and we were, too."

TAILOR YOUR STYLE TO YOUR KIDS.

You'll discover clues about your kids' money behaviors early on. Some of them will be meticulous with tracking their savings. Others will spend money as fast as they get it.

When my niece and nephew were 10 and 11, I took them to Disneyland. As we walked into the park, I gave them each $50 and said, "Buy whatever you want!" It was amazing to see their different reactions. My nephew loves money. He couldn't stop smiling at the $50 bill. He put that money right into his pocket and kept it, not spending a penny.

For my niece, though, the money didn't even register. She just handed it back to me to hold for her. At the end of the day, we stopped in a souvenir store, where she selected a toy and started walking toward the register—not even looking at the price. On the way she picked up an additional toy, again ignoring the price tag. My jaw was on the floor as I was mentally calculating the cost, plus tax, and starting to sweat. But I told myself, *Ramit, don't say anything.* She got to the register and asked me for the money. When the cashier rang up the total, it was $56. My niece looked back at me to help. Of course, I shook my head no (it's called boundaries, people).

I was curious what she was going to do. She turned to her brother and said, "Can I borrow $6?"

Just from that experience, I learned that my niece and nephew treat money very differently. If I were teaching them about money, I'd know how to adapt my lessons for each of them. (My nephew generously handed over his money as a loan.)

Teaching kids about money is not an exact science. You need to be nimble, try things out, and fail. That's okay! The point is you're making money part of their upbringing, part of your family culture, like food and movies and exercise—and making money *conversations* a natural, joyful part of life.

BE DELIBERATE ABOUT THE MONEY MESSAGES YOU SEND.

Parents are busy. The last thing they're thinking of is developing a set of money messages. But you're sending signals whether you realize it or not.

Often those messages are communicated without saying a single thing. Many of the parents I speak to, for example, genuinely don't realize that "protecting" kids by never talking about money simply teaches the next generation that money is "bad" and a topic to avoid altogether. They don't see that reflexively telling their young daughter, "We can't afford that"—the same phrase their parents used with them—will cause her to feel the same insecurity that her parents felt growing up.

Kids notice if you avoid discussing money, if you stress out about money, and if you and your partner aren't on the same page. They're like little hound dogs, sniffing out every single discrepancy between what you say and do, then internalizing the hypocrisy and ending up on my podcast 30 years from now, saying, "My parents never taught me about money."

Don't let that happen! Let's get it right.

What money messages do you currently send?

Check all that apply and add your own. Remember, these are the money messages you're currently sending to your children, whether you want to or not.

- ❑ Money is stressful.
- ❑ We're fortunate to be comfortable with our finances.
- ❑ We don't talk about money.
- ❑ We work hard and we deserve to have a little fun.
- ❑ Money is something that only Mom/Dad deals with.
- ❑ Money = fighting.
- ❑ We always find a way to make it work.
- ❑ There's never enough money in our family.
- ❑ There's always money for education.
- ❑ We'd better not ask our parents for anything.
- ❑ Sometimes we don't need to spend a lot to have a great time.
- ❑ People like us will always be in debt.
- ❑ It's our responsibility to be charitable.
- ❑ Money is for grown-ups to talk about, not kids.
- ❑ We're resourceful—we always work it out.
- ❑ We don't have to lead a fancy life to be happy.
- ❑ *Add your own.*

What money messages do you *want* to send?

Check all that apply and add your own.

❑ Money is something we talk about.

❑ We spend extravagantly on the things we love and cut costs mercilessly on the things we don't.

❑ We take the time to control our money so our money doesn't control us.

❑ As kids get older, they get to have more involvement with family money.

❑ We make choices about money early because they pay off in the long term.

❑ Kids can ask questions about money (even if we can't answer them all).

❑ Investing is where real wealth is created.

❑ *Add your own.*

How to change the messages we send

You can change the lessons you impart if you're intentional about your psychology, actions, and words. Think of this as a new skill—one where the benefits show up years from now and are carried through generations. Let me offer a few reframes you can start using today.

Psychology:

- Money is something that allows us to have fun together, to eat food together, and to live in a safe place together. We don't need to "protect" our kids from money—we need to teach them about it.

- To teach our kids about money, we have to learn ourselves.

- It's okay to make mistakes, and it's okay to admit them to our kids.

- Our kids don't have to know everything about our finances, but they should be involved in age-appropriate ways.

Actions:

- We make it a point to talk about money as a family.

- When one of us is doing something with money—paying bills, making a grocery list, even deciding which restaurant to eat at—we invite our kids to watch and (when appropriate) to participate. By doing this, we're connecting money with our day-to-day lives.

Words:

- It's okay to say no. Setting boundaries is love.

- It's also okay to say yes! We should teach our kids how to spend money meaningfully. When we decide to spend our money, we teach our kids why. We even invite them to make their own decisions about what's worth it.

- We should be mindful of which words and phrases we use (for example, "We can't afford it") because when we repeat them over decades, kids internalize them and repeat them.

Instant Money Answers If You're . . .

WORKING WITH A FINANCIAL ADVISOR

The shocking math behind financial advisors—and when it's worth it

I believe that most people can manage their money themselves. That's why I wrote both *I Will Teach You to Be Rich* and this book. Once you learn the basic language of money and build the skills to talk about it, money becomes straightforward, empowering, and even fun.

But once in a while, you might need some help. Maybe you have a complex financial situation, like a blended family or looming retirement. Maybe you have a specific question; I once hired a financial advisor to look over my finances and give me a second set of eyes on my asset allocation.

But you should never, ever pay a percentage of your assets as a fee.

I want to show you how much a financial advisor can cost you. The numbers are so shocking, I created an entire section on it.

If you're paying a 1 percent fee—frequently referred to as "assets under management" (AUM)—that 1 percent will cost you about 28 percent of your lifetime investment returns *in fees alone*. Yes, that tiny 1 percent fee will costs you tens of thousands of dollars, or even hundreds of thousands of dollars . . . all while you're constantly being told to worry about spending an extra $10 at the grocery store.

No amount of cutting back on russet potatoes will ever come close to firing the advisor who is quietly charging you a 1 percent fee. This is why auditing their fees is a big win.

Let me say this again. If you're paying your financial advisor 1 percent in fees, you're literally giving away more than a quarter of your lifetime returns to Chet so he can pay for his next BMW. That 1 percent in fees is worth far more than all the lattes you'll ever buy, combined.

EACH MONTH, YOU INVEST . . . *	AFTER 30 YEARS, YOU HAVE . . .	BUT IF YOU PAY 1 PERCENT, YOU ONLY HAVE . . .	THAT 1 PERCENT FEE COSTS YOU ABOUT . . .
$100	$117,607	$97,926	$20,000
$500	$588,033	$489,628	$98,000
$1,000	$1,176,065	$979,257	$197,000
$5,000	$5,880,324	$4,896,282	$984,000

*Assuming you invest for 30 years with 7 percent real returns.

These numbers are almost unbelievable. You should feel chills up your spine. Search online for an "investment fee calculator" and see for yourself.

I don't want you paying hundreds of thousands of dollars in fees. If you want to pay a great advisor a few thousand dollars for a financial plan, or $250/hour—or even $500/hour—great! (I paid my advisor an hourly rate and I was happy to do it.) But never a percentage. You can find advisors who charge hourly or flat fees at napfa.org or by searching "Ramit Sethi advisor recommendations."

If you already have a financial advisor, email them, find out what they're charging you, and make a plan to take control of your money. If they reply with a confusing set of documents or they invite you to "jump on a call to discuss it," you're probably paying an AUM fee.

How to Switch Away from an AUM Advisor

First, know that your money is your money. Your advisor legally cannot keep it. When you transfer your money to a low-cost brokerage account at Vanguard, Fidelity, Schwab, or wherever you choose, you'll do an "in-kind transfer," which means you'll literally just take your current investments and plop them into your new account.

There are a few things to look out for: As much as possible, beware of selling investments, because you may be liable for taxes. Some firms charge a termination fee, which is sometimes negotiable. If your advisor put you into funds that are proprietary or have sales fees, you may have to pay to get out. I hate this, but it happens. You should carefully review the charges to make your decision, but personally, when I've lost trust in someone or some firm, I'm out—no matter what it costs.

Here are the steps for moving your account away from an advisor:

- To prepare for transferring your money, go to Vanguard, Fidelity, Schwab, or whichever low-cost broker you choose. You can do this online or call them. They'll tell you exactly what to do, including opening an account and filling out a couple of forms.

- Email your financial advisor (you want this in writing): "I've decided to transfer accounts and to manage my own money. I'll send you the paperwork. I appreciate your help." Follow up by sending the transfer forms from your new brokerage.

- Go back to your new brokerage and initiate the transfer. Again, you can do this online or call for help. Once your assets are there, you can leave them as is and invest in new funds, you can sell them and use the money to fund new investments—again, taking into consideration tax implications—or if you had the right funds in the first place, you can simply add more to them each month. In general, I like target-date funds as a simple option within retirement accounts.

Quick Answers to Common Questions

Q: *"We like knowing that someone else is thinking about our money. Isn't the fee worth the peace of mind?"*

A: Is it worth a million dollars over your lifetime? When I present the actual amount you'll pay, most people are shocked. Also, no one needs to be thinking about your money all the time. Just choose low-cost, long-term investments and check on them three or four times a year. Even the best active investors (including advisors) fail to beat the market 80 percent of the time. That means the results you'll get investing in low-cost index funds are likely to be very similar to the results you'll get with a financial advisor—minus the fees. If you believe you need a financial advisor for peace of mind or staying behaviorally focused on the long term—which is where they shine—then hire them for an hourly or flat fee.

Q: *"We're scared we're going to mess things up. Will we?"*

A: Money is scary because it's surrounded by confusing language and complicated concepts. But when you make the decision to take control of your finances, you'll realize that it's not that complicated after all: You design your Rich Life, then have your money flow into your key accounts, then invest properly.

My philosophy: You're going to make a few mistakes at the beginning. That's fine! Better to make them now, when the amounts are small, than later, when the consequences are much larger. Remember, like any skill—riding a bike, cooking, speaking Italian—you can master it.

To learn more about investing, my first book, *I Will Teach You to Be Rich*, will help you go on offense. There are also some helpful quick tips on page 272 of this book. Don't let being scared of money cost you hundreds of thousands of dollars.

Q: *"Won't we have to pay taxes if we mess around with our investments?"*

A: If you transfer your investments from one brokerage to another "in kind," you won't incur taxes. Your advisor may charge you a small transfer fee, which is infuriating, but I recommend you just pay it and move on. However, if you sell at a profit, you will likely have to pay taxes. As much as possible, I try not to sell investments.

Q: *"Our financial advisor already has our money in a bunch of different funds. Can we just fire him and leave the money in the investments he chose?"*

A: You may find that your advisor has put your money in lots of funds—which, you'll discover, is often because they make fees from these funds, too. I shudder when I look at someone's portfolio that contains more than 15 funds. It's totally unnecessary—you can effectively diversify with as few as three low-cost funds, and there's a major cost to complexity. It's like someone leaving your house a total mess. Now you have to clean it up.

This isn't a great situation to be in, but at least you're taking charge of your finances now. If you have a bunch of confusing, expensive funds, here are your options:

- Sell the funds and put the cash into simpler funds, such as a target-date fund or index funds. Remember, if you sell, you may incur taxes.

- Leave those funds as is, but shift your future investments to simpler investments.

- Consult a fiduciary advisor who charges an hourly or flat fee to help you decide.

If it's a relatively small amount like $10,000 in expensive funds—which I define as funds with expense ratios (fees) over 0.5 percent or those with front- or back-end loads—I'd just leave it as is. Remember, your future is bigger than your past, and your investments down the road will likely far eclipse that amount. But if you have a lot in expensive funds, or if you're just not sure, it's worth hiring an advisor for a few hours to help you sort this out.

Q: *"Isn't this going to be awkward? He's been so nice to us, and he's been my dad's financial advisor for years."*

A: Yes, an advisor might make it really uncomfortable. But awkwardness is not a reason for you to stay and not change anything. We're not looking for easy—we're looking for a Rich Life.

Although your advisor may resist by trying to convince you they're irreplaceable or that you can't do this on your own, remember *it's your money.* You don't even need to engage with their arguments. Once you decide and tell an advisor you want your money transferred—in writing—they will transfer the money. If they don't, that's illegal.

Breakup Stories

You know I love a little drama, so I asked my community what happened when they broke up with their financial advisors. Here's what they told me.

> *"I just texted him on a random day and told him I preferred to manage my money on my own. He kept texting and calling me that he had something ready for me, and he needed to talk to me. I just ignored it. Never answered his calls or texts after that."*

> *"It was dramatic and hard! She kept contacting me for a year after I 'broke it off.'"*

"He handled it gracefully and outlined the steps we need to take for me to manage my own portfolio. Emotionally, it was harder than I thought it would be to send the email, but in reality it's going as well as it could."

"It was far less of a big deal than I expected. I did it by email and said I was going to manage it myself until I'm closer to retirement age. She said, 'Okay, let me know if you need any guidance as you go along.' Boom. The end. Super easy. When I asked her for the info to transfer it into my Fidelity account, she had it all readily available. No hard feelings. I had built it up in my head to be a much bigger deal. It was way easier and less contentious than I'd expected."

"Easier than I thought. I gave him a chance to 'counter' and he reduced from 1.5 percent to 1 percent: Bye! I wish I hadn't waited so long to do it, but it took me a year to finally build up the courage."

These never get old! I love seeing people take control and keep more money in their pocket for living their Rich Lives. If you have an AUM advisor and you break up with them, send me the screenshots so I can anonymize it and share with the world. Find me on any social media platform.

RAMIT'S RULES ON EVERYTHING

Travel, tipping, credit cards, home buying, creating your own Money Rules, and more

Here are some of my rules for all things financial. Keep in mind that these are my personal rules—including some of the joint rules that my wife and I use—and yours will almost certainly be different. Over time, I want you to develop your own Money Rules about the things that are important to you, so feel free to borrow and adapt them!

RAMIT'S RULES ON INVESTING

Investing is where real wealth is created. Follow these rules and you will almost certainly end up with more money than you ever imagined.

- Invest at least 10 percent of your take-home pay every single month.

- Automate your investments. You should almost never be manually transferring money to your investments (the only exception is when you encounter a windfall such as a tax refund).

- By default, increase your investment rate by 1 percent each year. For example, in December, log in with your partner and change the investment rate from 10 percent to 11 percent. This single action can add hundreds of thousands of dollars to your net worth over time.

- Uninstall any investing apps on your phone. You don't need them, and they force you to focus on the tactical rather than the system-level approach.

- If you're both contributing to your individual retirement savings, great—keep it up. If you're not, now's the time to reset: Contribute at least as much as your company matches.

- To determine which accounts to put your money in, follow my Ladder of Investing. Here's the order of operations:

  » First, invest to get your 401(k) match.

  » Then, max out your Roth IRA, if you're eligible.

  » Then, max out the rest of your 401(k).

  » Then, max out your health savings account, if you're eligible.

  » Finally, if you're both maxing out your 401(k)s and have more money to invest, open a taxable account (this is a standard nonretirement account, also called a brokerage account) and contribute as much as you want. Be sure to search for "tax-efficient fund placement."

- Check your investments only four times a year. There's no need to review them more than that, and the more you check, the more likely you are to meddle, which costs you dearly. Use the calculator on my website (search for "Ramit Sethi calculators") to see when you'll likely have $50,000, $500,000, $1 million, and beyond.

- Don't save for your one-year-old unless you're maxing out your retirement savings. They have time. You have much less.

- Follow Ramit's Chicken and Rice theory: In most industries, top professionals basically follow the same practices and protocols for a simple reason—because they work. If you can figure out those practices, you can save years of time. For example, professional bodybuilders know that to look amazing, they must become experts at training and nutrition (let's set aside the steroids that many of them take). This leads pro competitors to eat the exact same thing: chicken and rice. Why? Ounce for ounce, chicken and rice provides the best nutritional payoff. And this is true in investing: Once you understand the highly counterintuitive math of compounding and fees and time horizons, all roads lead to consistent, low-cost, long-term investing. You can spend years making mistakes and trying alternative investments and market timing and day trading . . . or you can skip all the pain and get it right immediately. Smart investing is boring, slow, and highly profitable. If you want entertainment, get a dog.

RAMIT'S RULES ON DEBT

- Know your two key numbers: how much you owe and the interest rate for each loan.

- Once you know your two key numbers, plug them into a debt-payoff calculator (search for "Ramit Sethi calculators") and know the exact month and year you'll be debt-free. This is incredibly motivating! Celebrate each milestone as you get closer.

- If you have low-interest debt (an interest rate of 4 percent or below), I recommend calculating the total amount you can put toward that debt, then paying the minimum and investing the rest. That's because you can make far more by simple, low-cost investing in the market. For example, if you can afford to put $300 toward your low-interest debt each month, but the minimum payment is $100, I'd pay $100 and invest $200 each month. If you have high-interest debt (anything above 7 percent), I would pay as much as possible. There's one exception: Some people truly hate debt and will do anything to pay it off early. If that's you, feel free to pay extra toward low-interest debt such as a mortgage. But understand it may cost you hundreds of thousands of dollars in lost investment returns.

- Treat credit card debt as a relationship emergency. If you have credit card debt, do not wait a second. I recommend you immediately cut discretionary spending, ramp up payments by $100 each month, then analyze how much more you can afford to pay. Without dramatic action, credit card debt does not get better. It gets much, much worse. Pay it off as quickly as you can.

- You do not have to wait until you're debt-free to live a Rich Life.

- Six months before you pay off your debt, make a specific plan for where that money will go after you're debt-free. If your payments were $600 per month, where will you now put that $600 every month? Automate this new decision as soon as your debt is paid off—don't miss even a month.

- If your debt feels insurmountable, call your lender and ask what options they can provide. Many of them will help you.

- There is always hope! You are not a bad person because you have debt.

RAMIT'S RULES ON CREDIT CARDS FOR COUPLES

- Most couples need only three credit cards: one shared credit card (for joint expenses like groceries and dinners out together), then one credit card for each of you (covering individual expenses like haircuts and hobbies).

- I recommend cash-back cards as a default, but if you prioritize travel, get a travel card.

- Set your cards to automatically pay off the full amount ("statement balance") every month. Don't carry a balance. If you're carrying credit card debt, treat it as an emergency.

- I recommend simplifying your system by closing additional credit cards. This is controversial advice, because when you close cards, your credit score will likely go down. But that dip will be temporary, and you can counteract it by requesting a credit limit increase on your existing cards. More importantly, you'll have a simple financial system that you can deeply understand with just a few great credit cards. (The only exception is if you're planning a major purchase in the next few months, like a house or car, in which case you should wait.)

- Credit cards from retailers (Sephora, Gap, and so on) are the worst. They offer extremely bad payment terms and add complexity to your system. All for what? Ten percent off your purchase of a pair of jeans? Close these cards—follow my suggestion above—and never open another retailer card.

- If you spend enough to justify a premium card, consider one. Go online and search for the name of the card + calculator, like this: "Chase Sapphire Reserve calculator." I keep an updated list of my favorite credit cards on my website (search "Ramit Sethi credit cards").

RAMIT'S RULES ON SAVING

- Save at least 10 percent of your combined take-home pay and divide it among three to five savings accounts, including an emergency fund. Be specific about what you're saving for; instead of "Vacation Fund," call your account "Alaskan Cruise Fund." Instead of "New House," call it "Gorgeous 3BR Victorian."

- Saving should be automatic, with each savings account automatically receiving money from your joint checking account every month.

- By default, increase your savings rate by 1 percent each year (for example, if you're saving 10 percent of take-home pay now, increase it to 11 percent next year). This single change will mean a lot over time.

- All savings should be in high-yield savings accounts. I keep an updated list of the best high-yield online accounts on my website (search "Ramit Sethi accounts").

- Your goal for your emergency fund is to save six months of minimal expenses. It's okay if it takes time to get there. Save toward other goals simultaneously.

- Save for "the unpredictable." Create a savings account called "Unexpected Expenses." In December, talk through the calendar and estimate major expenses you anticipate—replacing an appliance, birthdays, anniversaries, camp tuition, wedding gifts, car repairs, and so on. Total up the numbers, then add 15 percent for everything you forgot. Divide by 12 and set that amount to be automatically transferred from joint checking to the "Unexpected Expenses" account. Suddenly, the unpredictable is covered.

- Create milestones for your money. It makes saving a lot more fun. For example, "Once we fill up our emergency fund, we're going to schedule a regular date night every single week."

Don't be afraid to dream bigger with each milestone. There's nothing wrong with living a bigger, richer life, and I consider it a tragedy to live a smaller life than you have to.

- It's okay to slow down savings during critical times, like when you have a baby or one of you makes a career pivot. For example, if you have to cut your savings rate from 6 percent to 2 percent so you can spend more on childcare, do it! But do it consciously, keep saving something—even $20 per month— and aim to get your rate of savings back to where it was within three years.

RAMIT'S RULES ON HOME BUYING

- Buying a house is optional. You can live the American Dream as a renter, an owner, or anything you want. There is nothing wrong with renting—and in fact, it can often be a superior financial decision. I've made more money renting (and investing the difference in what it would cost to own) in the last 20 years than I would have owning.

- If you're considering buying, you must run the numbers. You should understand whether renting or buying is a better option, the effect of interest on your mortgage payments, the total cost of ownership (see below), the opportunity cost of your down payment, and how amortization works, especially for the first 10 years, during which you're paying mostly interest. If you do not understand all of these concepts surrounding what is likely the biggest purchase of your life, you're not ready.

- Calculate the total cost of a house, not just the monthly payments. Total housing costs include taxes, interest, insurance, maintenance—yes, even the roof repair eight years from now and the gas to Home Depot twice a month. It includes water for your lawn and furniture and renovations. Total means *everything*.

- The more you plan ahead, the easier it is. For example, if you're thinking about buying a house in a few years, log on to Zillow and check home prices in your area. Apply that info to your plans: If the average house in your neighborhood costs $300,000 and you want to do a traditional 20 percent down payment, you'll need to save up $60,000. So if you want to buy a house in five years, you should be saving at least $1,000 per month for your down payment. This is eye-opening.

- Do not buy a house together unless you're married. It could be financially disastrous if something goes wrong.

- Consider only homes where your total cost of housing is less than 28 percent of your combined gross income—with some exceptions. This is where most couples go wrong. Most people believe they can afford much more house than they actually can. Adjust your expectations according to the math. (In high-cost-of-living cities like New York or Los Angeles, the 28 percent rule is difficult to achieve. You can stretch a little, up to 32 percent or even 34 percent, but each percentage point adds risk, especially if you have other debt.)

- If and when you buy a house, don't buy the biggest one you can. This is advice from my parents, who told me that if you get a big house, everyone goes into their own rooms and they don't spend time together. Consider the nonfinancial aspects of the house you buy, like encouraging your family to spend time together—even if that means less space. I would add to that the fact that most people buy a more expensive house than they can afford, and this is the number-one way I see couples get into financial trouble. That's backup for my parents' rule. Factor in your family and what you'll need in the future, but in general, go smaller than you can afford.

- Don't borrow to renovate. Save up the cost and *then* renovate. Or better yet—don't renovate at all! Americans have watched so much HGTV that they genuinely believe it's normal to borrow $50,000 to renovate a bathroom. In fact, they tell themselves "it's an investment!" The majority of renovations do not pay back what you spent. Research renovations before you make them, treat most of them as pure luxuries, and do not go into debt.

- Before buying a home, ask yourselves these four critical questions:

  1. Have we saved up 20 percent of the price of the house? You don't have to put 20 percent down, but you should have been able to save that much in preparation for the heavy and unexpected costs you'll face as homeowners.

  2. Do we plan to live in this house for at least 10 years? This is a good guideline for amortizing (or spreading out) the high expenses related to buying and selling.

  3. Will we be okay financially if the value of our house goes down?

  4. Are we *excited* about buying this house? Is this part of our Rich Life?

RAMIT'S RULES ON CAR BUYING

- Don't buy a car based on monthly payments. A car might appear to cost only a little more than the sticker price because of a long loan period and obscured fees and interest rates. Instead, calculate total cost of ownership by factoring in gas, insurance, interest, maintenance, and even registration and parking tickets.

- Plug your total cost of ownership into your fixed costs in your Conscious Spending Plan. If your fixed costs are between 50 and 60 percent of your take-home pay even including the new car, you're ready to buy.

- If your fixed costs are higher than 60 percent, your options are to spend less on a car or postpone buying, cut other fixed costs, or reduce your guilt-free spending. Some people cut their savings or investments. Most simply never calculate how much they can afford at all. That's how they get into trouble.

- Plan to keep a car for at least 10 years. You really start to see savings a year after your loan is paid off. Every additional year of no payments brings your total cost of ownership way down. As an example, I'm a multimillionaire, my car is not part of my Rich Life, and as of this writing, I've kept my car in mint condition for 19 years.

- My personal philosophy is to buy a new car and keep it for a long time. But you can save considerable amounts of money by buying used.

- There are three reasons to lease a car: First, if you're a business owner and your accountant advises you that you can run your vehicle through your business. Second, if you're wealthy and you're willing to pay more to have a new car every few years. Third, if cars are part of your Rich Life (and you can afford paying more than owning a car for 10-plus years).

- Honestly, just buy a Honda or Toyota and keep it for at least 10 years.

RAMIT'S RULES ON FINANCIAL ADVISORS

- If you simplify your finances as described in this book and *I Will Teach You to Be Rich*, you most likely do not need a financial advisor.

- There are specific situations when it can make sense to hire a financial advisor: If you have a seven-figure portfolio, if you have a complex financial situation including stepchildren or an inheritance, if you have specific questions about retirement (including social security withdrawals), or if one of you simply wants a second set of eyes on your finances, then you may want to hire one. That's okay! However, you must be selective about whom you choose.

- Never pay an advisor a percent-based fee (usually this occurs when your money is managed by your advisor; another way of putting it is AUM, which refers to "assets under management"). A 1 percent fee means that over the long term, about 28 percent of your returns will go straight into the pocket of the advisor.

- If a financial advisor also sells insurance or annuities, run away—that's a salesperson, not an advisor.

- If you decide to hire an advisor, find one who charges an hourly or per-project fee. You can find one at napfa.org or by searching for "Ramit Sethi advisors."

RAMIT'S RULES ON HAVING HEALTHY MONEY CONVERSATIONS

- Always start with a compliment about each other.

- Remember, you're in no rush. Sometimes, the most valuable thing you can do is simply begin a topic and hear each other out. Then you can follow up in the next meeting, and maybe even the next. My wife and I have had topics we've talked about for *years*. But when we finally agree, it all clicks and it feels amazing because we decided together.

- Rotate who runs your Monthly Money Meeting. One person this month, the other next month. That gives both of you skin in the game.

- Be decisive! Do not talk around things forever without moving the conversation forward. Build the skill of being decisive with small topics, like how much to allocate for grocery spending, which will help you become decisive for bigger topics like investment rates and asset allocation.

- If things get heated, take a break. The person who asks for a break is responsible for coming back together. It might be

5 minutes or 20, but come back together. It's an important signal to both of you that money is something to embrace— not avoid—even when it gets hard.

- Assume the best intentions of your partner, and ask them to do the same. Money is hard to talk about. Nobody taught us what to say. So give your partner a little grace when they're not sure how to word something or they second-guess themselves. You both want to live a Rich Life. These meetings help you get there.

- You're better together. This means one person should not overpower the other, even if they know more about money. Slow it down, connect, and make decisions in tandem. Years from now, you'll be so much better off if you've made and followed your plan together.

RAMIT AND CASSANDRA'S RULES ON TIPPING AND EATING OUT

- Tip at least 30 percent at restaurants. We can afford it and we love being generous.

- When staying at a hotel, leave $20 per night, minimum, for housekeeping.

- Ask: *How can we be more generous?* Consider people who aren't normally tipped but would really benefit from a small gift. To go bigger, make it regular, even automatic.

- If two appetizers or desserts look good, get them both!

- Get the exquisite sushi once a year rather than mediocre sushi once a month.

- If a restaurant is called Harry's, has the word *Ale* in the name, or has dark wood and a flag in front of it, just get up and leave. The food will be horrible.

RAMIT AND CASSANDRA'S TRAVEL RULES

- Four-night minimum stay, so we can slow down. The ultimate luxury is not needing to rush.

- At the beginning of a special trip, we always get a glass of champagne on the plane. It sets the tone for something special.

- For flights over four hours, fly business class. We can afford it and we love the comfort.

- Start with a city, end with a resort, which helps us design an amazing experience.

- Spend at least one day at our hotel doing absolutely nothing.

- When calculating what we need for a trip, add 50 percent to the hotel sticker price to get the true rate (which includes tax, tips, any unplanned hotel meals, and miscellaneous fees). For a $300/night hotel, we plan to spend $450/night.

- Car service from the airport. For the things we do a few times a year, if there's a way to make it easier, let's do it.

Create Your Own Money Rules

Over time, I hope you and your partner will develop your own shared Money Rules that are tailor-made for the two of you. Money Rules are a chance to boil down what's most important to you both, enabling you to more easily make the thousands of decisions you'll face. Once you have them, suddenly, you won't have to agonize over questions like these:

- *Should we buy a new car?*

- *Are we saving enough?*

- *Can we really afford to eat out every week?*

Your Money Rules will help you cut through these decisions and focus on the key things that truly matter. This is incredibly freeing, because you can do the work once and reap the benefits for years. Don't worry about these rules being set in stone: As you change, you can always change your Money Rules.

Your Money Rules reflect your values. If you're foodies, or love visiting a new country every year, or both prioritize fitness, that should show up in your spending. If you love building a cozy home where you adore sitting inside on a rainy day, you should see that, too! The most important thing about your shared Money Rules is that you feel deeply connected to them.

Here are a few more of the shared rules that Cassandra and I have created over the years. Some of our rules are small scale, some larger. And they've evolved, of course. For example, during the pandemic, we started tipping much bigger and then decided to make it something we do forever.

- If we have unexpected income, 70 percent goes to investments and 30 percent to guilt-free spending.

- When we're at a wedding, we're the first ones on the dance floor (after the newlyweds' first dance, of course!).

- Whenever our friends do a fundraiser, we always donate.

- Relationships come first. We use this rule when we're debating whether to switch plane reservations to stay an extra day with family. This rule also helped us prioritize what was important for our wedding.

- Build our businesses so we can live our Rich Lives. We try to show up at every family event, even across the country. We also make time to travel on our own. We're intentional about the businesses we're creating and what they allow us to do.

These are *our* Money Rules, not yours. They make sense for our priorities and place in life.

To create your own Money Rules, start here: Do you have any "unwritten" rules around money? What do you and your partner do with your finances that you don't even think about (for example, spend lavishly on live music, or skip appetizers and get dessert instead)? Start from a place of positivity and create your list of 5–10 rules that are meaningful to the two of you and only you.

Your rules should be encouraging and proactive, and at least one should begin with the phrase "No spending limits on..." Think about what you love and what's meaningful to you. If you and your partner love shopping for food locally, then consider adding "No spending limits on fruit and vegetables from the neighborhood farmers market." (In our case, it's "No spending limits on health.")

One good way to spark ideas for Money Rules is by looking at other couples' Money Rules. Here are some from couples in my community. Note how they vary in size and scope, which is how I'd like you and your partner to think—both big and small, with positivity as well as parameters:

- "Don't worry about spending on food when we travel (because we travel so infrequently)."

- "Never lend money to people. Gift it or don't give it at all. Even if they promise to pay it back, it's a gift."

- "If we can afford to eat out, we can afford to leave a big tip."

- "Pay credit cards in full each month."

- "Prioritize community: Buy a modest home with close neighbors instead of a big house in an exclusive neighborhood."

- "Charity is one of our line items."

- "Don't spend one penny to impress anyone."

- "Set aside money for therapy. We call that spending our 'Relationship Health.'"

- "We take one kid-free vacation every year."

- "If we ever see an object we both are strongly drawn to (as in, we independently each say, 'Oh! I really like that!') and it's under $100, we buy it on the spot."

- "We're going to pay for our kids' colleges. We're already saving for them (after maxing our investments)."

- "Whenever we travel, we always schedule a massage for our arrival."

- "We always eat together, five days a week. If one of us is super busy, we'll order in and never question the cost, because eating together is worth it."

- "Safety matters to us, so we spend more on living in a safe neighborhood. Our car is rated well for safety. We buy extra insurance."

- "We spend money on a relationship coach. It's worth it."

- "We spend whatever we want on hiking gear."

- "The cost of our Valentine's Day gifts can't exceed the last two numbers of the year. For example, our 2025 gifts must be less than $25. We started this tradition in 2003, when we went down separate aisles in Kmart to gift shop, with a budget that suited our financial states at the time."

No two sets of Money Rules are the same. You can start a list of your Money Rules right now and let it develop slowly. If you see anything above that speaks to you, grab that rule for your list and adapt it to fit your lives. Once you're in the mindset of Money Rules—and in conversation with your partner around this topic—you'll find rules popping into your head. Keep the conversation going until you land on at least five rules that feel solid. Revisit them annually during your Rich Life Review (see Chapter 10).

Now go for it and build your Rich Life together.

• • •

Conscious Spending Plan	$
NET WORTH	
Assets (current value of car, home, property, business)	
Investments (include 401(k), nonretirement—all investments)	
Savings	
Debt (student loans, credit card debt, mortgage, car loans)	
TOTAL NET WORTH	
INCOME	
Gross monthly income (all income before taxes added up)	
Net monthly income (how much you take home after taxes)	
MONTHLY FIXED COSTS **(IDEALLY 50–60% OF TAKE HOME)**	
Rent/Mortgage	
Utilities (gas, water, electric, internet, cable, etc.)	
Insurance (medical, auto, home/renters, etc.)	
Car Payment/Transportation	
Debt Payments	
Groceries	
Clothes	
Phone	
Miscellaneous (automatically adds 15 percent for things you forgot)	
FIXED COSTS TOTAL	

CONSCIOUS SPENDING PLAN TEMPLATE

SAVINGS GOALS (IDEALLY 5–10% OF TAKE HOME)	
Vacations	
Gifts	
Long-Term Emergency Fund	
Add your own here.	
SAVINGS TOTAL	
INVESTMENTS (IDEALLY 10% OF TAKE HOME)	
Retirement Savings (401(k), IRAs, 403(b), HSA, etc.)*	
Nonretirement Investments	
Add your own here.	
INVESTMENTS TOTAL	
MONTHLY GUILT-FREE SPENDING (IDEALLY 20–35% OF TAKE HOME)	
Eating Out (takeout, delivery, restaurants)	
Fun (concerts, kids' activities, travel)	
Subscriptions (Netflix, gym membership, meal services, Amazon Prime, etc.)	
Miscellaneous (automatically adds 15 percent for things you forgot)	

* Although I'm including pre-tax and post-tax accounts in the same category—such as 401(k)s, IRAs, and standard taxable accounts—I'm doing so intentionally to keep things simple. Investing in tax-advantaged accounts will give you even better financial results over the long term, but calculating the difference in returns for all your investment accounts is outside the scope of this book.

To download this template, search online for "Ramit Sethi CSP."

Acknowledgments

Every author dreams about writing a book that changes people's lives. But we rarely talk about all the behind-the-scenes work that goes into creating one. What a gift to be able to acknowledge the people who've helped me along the way.

My collaborator, Danielle Claro, spent hours and hours diving into my archives and helped shaped the structure of this book—all while teaching me so many valuable life lessons along the way.

My editors, Margot Herrera and Danny Cooper, helped me refine my thinking through countless revisions. I knew I would write this book with my publisher, Lia Ronnen, and the Workman team, who I've worked with for over 15 years. You're the best in the business.

Special thanks to my agent, Lisa DiMona, who always makes me laugh when we talk. What a journey we've been on together.

To my entire team at I Will Teach You to Be Rich, who remind me that I truly have a dream job. You've changed the lives of millions of people and you've done it with integrity and creativity. Thank you.

To my Netflix team, including the entire crew and especially Bianca, you gave me a fresh perspective on money and people.

I want to recognize the courage of the guests on my podcast, who share some of the most intimate details about their lives on *Money for Couples* so we can learn from their stories.

Finally, my wife, Cassandra, has taught me the importance of connecting with my feelings. She's listened to every podcast, read every draft, and taught me the true meaning of "partner." I love you.

Index

What's Next

GET ALL THE TOOLS and templates mentioned in this book, including the Conscious Spending Plan and calculators: iwt.com/couplestools

LISTEN TO MY PODCAST, *Money for Couples,* and watch my Netflix show, *How to Get Rich.* Learn how other couples handle difficult money conversations.

EARN MORE MONEY by using my digital programs at iwt.com/products. An extra $1,000/month can make a substantial difference in your Rich Life.

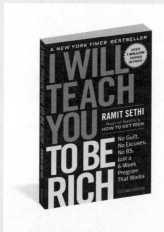

Master your money using my first book,
I Will Teach You to Be Rich.

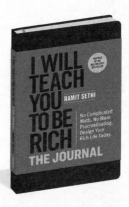

Design your Rich Life using my no-numbers journal,
I Will Teach You to Be Rich: The Journal.